THE

PRICE GUIDE

TO

CLOCKS

1840~1940

Alan and Rita Shenton

ANTIQUE COLLECTORS' CLUB

Front cover: Pottery 'Walt Disney' dwarf clock, made in England, c.1929. See page 301.

Printed in England by
Baron Publishing
Church Street, Woodbridge, Suffolk.

Foreword

The Antique Collectors' Club, formed in 1966, pioneered the provision of information on prices for collectors. The Club's monthly magazine *Antique Collecting* was the first to tackle the complex problems of describing to collectors the various features which can influence prices. In response to the enormous demand for this type of information the *Price Guide Series* was introduced in 1968 with **The Price Guide to Antique Furniture**, a book which broke new ground by illustrating the more common types of antique furniture, the sort that collectors could buy in shops and at auctions, rather than the rare museum pieces which had previously been used (and still to a large extent are used) to make up the limited amount of illustrations in books published by commercial publishers. Many other price guides have followed, all copiously illustrated, and greatly appreciated by collectors for the valuable information they contain, quite apart from prices.

Club membership, which is open to all collectors, costs £8.95 per annum. Members receive free of charge *Antique Collecting,* the Club's monthly magazine, which contains well-illustrated articles dealing with the practical aspects of collecting not normally dealt with by magazines. Prices, features of value, investment potential, fakes and forgeries are all given prominence in the magazine.

In addition members buy and sell among themselves; the Club charges a nominal fee for introductions but takes no commission. Since the Club started many thousands of antiques have been offered for sale privately. No other publication contains anything to match the long list of items for sale privately which appears monthly.

The presentation of useful information and the facility to buy and sell privately would alone have assured the success of the Club, but perhaps the feature most valued by members is the ability to make contact with other collectors living nearby. Not only do members learn about the other branches of collecting but they make interesting friendships. The Club organises weekend seminars and other meetings.

As its motto implies, the club is an amateur organisation designed to help collectors to get the most out of their hobby; it is informal and friendly and gives enormous enjoyment to all concerned.

For Collectors — By Collectors — About Collecting
The Antique Collectors' Club, 5 Church Street, Woodbridge, Suffolk.

Acknowledgements

It would not have been possible to include some of the illustrations and details to be found on the following pages without the generous assistance of many individuals and firms. Although acknowledgement of this help has been given at the appropriate place in the text, it is felt that it is more than justified to repeat our thanks and at the same time to add the following names in this expression of gratitude for the time and trouble taken on our behalf, in what is hoped is a good cause.

Mr. C.D. Belcher
Professor T. Ford
Mr. A. Fox
Mr. A.L. King
Mr. E. Lloyd-Thomas
Mr. C. Osborne
Mr. N.A. Shenton
The Clock Clinic Ltd.

as well as the Staff of the following libraries: Local Studies Department of Central Reference Library, Bradford Area Library, Central Library, Derby.

F.G.A. Shenton
R.K. Shenton

Contents

Price Revision Lists

(1st May Annually — The first will be published in 1978)

As Collectors are well aware the values of Clocks tend to change over a matter of months.

In order to keep the prices in this book fully up to date, the publishers prepare annually a Price Revision List for changes in values up to 1st May each year. This is available by the end of May and costs £1.40 by banker's order which is enclosed with this book or £1.50 cash with order form.

ANTIQUE COLLECTORS' CLUB
5 CHURCH STREET, WOODBRIDGE, SUFFOLK

Introduction

The majority of books written for the horologist have tended to refer to the rare and exotic pieces made by the famous makers of the past. These are invaluable sources of information for connoisseurs with ample means with which to finance their pastime, but of little practical use to the present-day collector. Prior to the Second World War the collecting of clocks and watches together with the study of their principles and technical differences had been the pleasure of an enlightened few. These pioneers had, therefore, been fortunate in having a virtually untrodden hunting ground. Magnificent collections were built up, many of which are now part of the extensive displays in our specialist museums. The fine collection at the British Museum being but one example. The bulk of the items displayed had been acquired by Mr. Courtney Ilbert after a life-long diligent search both in this country and abroad. Through his acumen and insight many unique and rare pieces were recognised, acquired and preserved in his collection. When Mr. Ilbert died in 1957, through funds provided by the Museum, together with monies raised from public subscription, his collection of clocks and watches was acquired by the Museum, Mr. Gilbert Edgar having donated £60,000. Additional material to that already on display in the public gallery can be seen in the Ilbert Room by serious students of horology upon application in writing to The Director, Department of Medieval and Later Antiquities, British Museum, Bloomsbury, London, W.C.1.

After the Second World War interest grew in the collecting of antiques of all kinds and prices began to rise. These prices have so escalated that most of the traditional collectors' items have become impossible to find at attainable prices. Even if the funds are available these pieces are not finding their way onto the open market, remaining in private hands to play the dual role of being a hedge against inflation, but at the same time providing a decorative feature for the home. The natural sequence to this is that those who wish to acquire, research or merely enjoy old timepieces are having to turn to areas that were previously spurned. Fortunately many of the formerly rejected examples have a great deal of merit and are well worth a second or third glance. The Industrial Revolution may have brought with it new factory methods of production to supersede the established handmaking and finishing methods, but this led in turn to the swift introduction of many new ideas and designs. The era of the gimmick and novelty clock had arrived, with quality taking second place. Nothing demonstrates this better than the huge sales in this country of the clocks manufactured by the American factories: cheap reliable and abreast with the latest furnishing trends. The Black Forest clockmakers in Germany swiftly relinquished their older traditional methods and followed on their heels. They also introduced standardisation of parts, the use of machinery for the slow laborious procedures and assembling of workers under one roof to work. These simple lessons were ones that the English clockmakers could not and would not accept. They doggedly kept to their beliefs that the customer wanted above all things a quality clock and that they would pay for it. They refused to accept that there was a different clientele — the working man. Admittedly there was still the rich land or factory owner who wanted the best and could pay for it, but such people were vastly outnumbered and now only formed a small part of the potential market. Several English companies did see the problem and attempted to compete — the British United Clock Company being one of the first, but they went out of business through still attempting to produce too good a movement at a competitive price. As early as 1747 there had been in the English horological trade diversity of labour, with each man specialising in one part of a clock or watch, but this was only a cottage industry with each man working in his own home as an outworker on piece rates. It can readily be seen that this method of working in no way lent itself to an industry where the various components were of standard size or pattern, and while in some circumstances the method is highly desirable it is not conducive to producing any item in quantity at a competitive price. There was the added problem of distributing raw materials and collecting the finished products from these scattered workers.

Slowly realisation dawned, but by this time the market had been taken over by foreign goods and so the trade limped on through the 1900s still producing good quality movements but being undercut as regards price by competitors. The dependency upon foreign goods was highlighted during and at the end of the First World War by the almost total absence in the shops of the simple alarm clock. Although many of the cheaper clocks had been cased in this country to avoid Customs duty as well as complying with the average Englishman's preference for our case designs, the movements had been shipped from Germany. Between the two World Wars endeavours to revitalise the industry were made. Several English factories opened up and appeals were made to 'Buy British' which were emphasised by exhibitions at Wembley. However, the repeal of the various trade tariffs did little to help home industry, with the final blow coming in the form of the Anglo-German Agreement in 1933 when the tariff was lowered from $33\frac{1}{3}$ per cent to 25 per cent. The refusal of some to purchase German clocks because of the maltreatment of the Jews did little to help, and it is now realised that it was part of Hitler's overall plan to dump cheap clocks in this country and thereby kill our industry. Eventually after the Second World War, during which the dire need for clockwork mechanisms on timing devices, shells, etc., had highlighted the plight of our horological trade, large sums of Government money were used to finance expansion and update machinery.

This brief résumé of the background of the trade during the period of 1840 to 1940 explains why so many of the clocks described in this book are not of English manufacture. They are, however, typical of the period and it is hoped that the following pages provide some intimation of the overall picture of the spectrum of clocks on the market during those years. Although many months have been spent in researching and documenting the examples shown and described here, it is appreciated only too well that a great deal has of necessity been omitted. In some instances this has been through lack of space, and in others unavailability of sources of information. It is hoped that this book will be regarded as a pioneer work in its field and that it will stimulate interest and provoke a sufficient volume of new information to assist in the compilation of further editions in even greater depth of detail.

A final word regarding the examples that do not have any indication of their value. In some instances this has been for reasons of courtesy to their owners and in others through the sheer impossibility of such an undertaking in an unsettled market.

Chapter 1

MARBLE-CASED CLOCKS

If asked which clock most typified the Victorian drawing-room with its air of middle class respectability and solidarity, it would not be necessary to look further than the polished black marble mantel clocks that appeared in abundance through the reign of Queen Victoria and well into the Edwardian period. Although marble and onyx had always been popular, especially on the Continent, as a material in the making of decorative clock cases there had not been a widespread vogue for these solid cases until the mid-nineteenth century. There would appear to have been a number of contributory factors. As the quantity of clock movements manufactured was increased by the new factory methods of production, so the need grew for cases in which to house them. Advancements had also been made in the cutting of marble and similar materials. During the eighteenth century the marble had to be rough sawn and it had not been possible to obtain thin sheets. With the coming of the mechanical saw at the beginning of the nineteenth century, it became possible to obtain sheets as thin as 4mm, and it can be noted that many of the later Belgian marble clock cases have only thin facings of marble over a cement framework. Possibly these technical achievements, together with the then prevalent French fashion for ebonised furniture, provided the necessary impetus. The tragic death of Prince Albert and the Queen's subsequent mourning may have played their roles in the prolonged appeal of this style of case in England; more likely the vogue for neo-classical furniture and the prize-winning cabinet by Wright and Mansfield at the Paris Exhibition of 1867 was an influence.

That these clocks were imported in large numbers is indisputable. Smith & Sons Ltd. of The Strand, London, lists them in their 1900 catalogue amongst their 'Foreign Made Clocks' and with few exceptions they have French movements.

The source and nature of the material used to case them is less certain. One writer describing the clocks at the French International Exhibition of 1889 refers to "a show of those cheap black marbles found in Belgian quarries and cut, polished, and finished for the French market on French soil, as the quarries are not far from the frontier." He goes on to say that "the white and grissotte marbles are drawn from Italy, yellow marbles from the Pyrenees, red from Greece, malachite and lapis lazuli from Russia, onyx from Mexico". Strictly speaking the term 'marble' when used in this context is not accurate. Geologically marble is a calcite that has changed its physical appearance due to metamorphosis, but the term is frequently used in the trade in a broader sense. The material referred to as 'Belgian marble' is not a marble at all. The Ardennes district of Belgium possesses large deposits of a hard limestone with a wide range of colours which includes a dark grey/black variety. It is this that is referred to as 'black Belgian marble' but for the sake of clarity this term will continue to be used rather than the more accurate 'black Belgian limestone'.

T.D. Wright when reporting on the French clockmakers in 1889 states "nearly all the marble cases are made in Belgium; sometimes imported complete, but more often all the finished pieces are separate, and are put together by the clockmaker." This only clarifies the *French* sources. The questions that arise are: Did the English importer also import the complete cases? Or the finished pieces from Belgium for our casemakers to assemble? Or did we use local stone? Some of the cases are slate (as were many of the cheap 'marble' chimney-pieces), in which event this would have come from either Caithness or North Wales. Curiously neither area can provide any information as to whether they supplied slate specifically for the clock casemakers. From information generously supplied by Dr. Trevor Ford it appears that there was a source of suitable material in Derbyshire. A dark grey limestone that polished-up black was quarried around Ashford-in-the-Water from the sixteenth until the beginning of the twentieth century. This, as with the Belgian limestone, is usually referred to as 'marble'. It was quarried, sawn and polished locally with much of it being supplied for the making of chimney-pieces, tables, vases, jewellery, etc., and was an extremely thriving industry. Again no specific references can be found of any casemaking on a commercial basis, although the odd case is known to have been made. Although not conclusive, it is felt that sufficient evidence has been assembled to demonstrate that suitable material for making these cases was available in this country, but it is not known if it was a commercially sound proposition to use it. It may have been cheaper to import. A few marble casemakers are listed in trade directories of that period and one patent was taken out in 1855 by Moses Poole for 'Marble Sculpturing' which was a method of embossing clock pillars, but in all probability if cases were made here it would have been by the chimney-piece manufacturers of whom there were a great number.

As can be seen from the illustrations the cases range from monumental edifices embellished with bronze reliefs to simpler cases with coloured marble or brass pillars, or even small severely plain cases. Accompanying side ornaments were common, but few have been preserved. These can be matching vases, figures, candelabra, etc.

The construction ot the cases is not without interest. As can be seen from Figure 1, they were built up from these pre-shaped pieces — some solid marble, others hollow. The base, main structure and side 'pillars' comprising a fine cement carcase veneered with thin sheets of black marble. The very large cases were reinforced with metal rods that were bolted through the top and bottom sections to give added strength. If feeling sufficiently strong to up-end a clock, it is possible to see the retaining washers and nuts. The smaller, lighter cases, Figures 16 to 19, merely had metal rods keyed into the cement across the corners. According to Britten the cement used by the marble casemakers was "composed of Russian tallow, brick dust and resin melted together, and it sets as hard as stone at ordinary temperatures".

To reconstruct one of these cases is no simple matter if the basic carcase is damaged. If it is intact, it should be possible to remove the old adhesive and replace facings or solid shaped pieces of the case. Lime and white of egg were used for adhering closely fitting surfaces, but a modern epoxy or contact adhesive could replace the older recipe. To attempt more than relatively minor repairs can lead to disappointment, so it is as well not to purchase a clock that requires major renovation to the case on the assurance that it just needs a little work carried out on it. Considerable difficulties can be experienced with even the minor task of tightening the threaded rods holding ornamental columns in place as they are frequently rusted. Prevention is better than cure, so never lift a large heavy clock by the top alone; always support the full weight by lifting from the bottom to avoid the sheer weight of the case pulling the segments apart.

Problems can also be experienced when attempting to restore the original polish, which has been dulled through exposure to dust and heat from a coal fire, etc. Originally putty powder (oxide of tin) was used on a felt pad. It is important before attempting to repolish to remove any greasy marks by cleaning with benzine (not petrol). If the colour has faded, a good quality black shoe polish softened by gentle warming is ideal. For the final gloss it is difficult to improve upon a good wax polish, without any silicone, as this removes the organic impurities in the marble and dulls the surface. Proprietory polishes such as Gilbert's and Wilkin's were sold in their day; sometimes concoctions of bullocks' gall, soap lees, turpentine and pipeclay were resorted to! For light coloured marbles a mixture of quicklime and soap lees spread over and left on the case for twenty four hours, cleaned off and polished with fine putty powder and olive oil was said to produce a good result, though it would be necessary to ascertain first that the case was made of true marble and not some other ornamental stone. Donald de Carle in his book *Watch and Clock Encyclopedia* lists some hundred and seven "Marbles and Ornamental Stones suitable for the manufacture of clock cases". A simple test for marble is to place a few drops of acid on a freshly cut surface: if bubbles form the case is made of marble. Spons' *Workshop Receipts for Manufacturing Mechanics and Scientific Amateurs* (any edition) provides a rich source of information for anyone wishing to indulge in pursuing the older recipes for polishes, etc.

Finally, while on the subject of cases, it is necessary to mention the American 'marbleised' cases and those with an 'Adamantine Finish'. The former was achieved by paints and enamels — Edward Ingraham of Bristol, Connecticut, patented a method of 'Japanning Wooden Clock Cases' in 1885, while the latter was a coloured celluloid applied as a veneer. The American manufacturers were obsessed with complying with the latest fashions and furnishings but at the same time needing to keep their overall costs competitive. Although they did import some genuine marble or onyx cases, they usually imitated them with other cheaper materials. They achieved this by making iron or wooden cases in appropriate styles and then copied the veining or colouring of marble by the two methods just mentioned. In a 1906 catalogue of one manufacturer, the comparative prices are eight to eleven dollars for a marbleised wooden case, twelve to twenty dollars for a marbleised iron case and thirty dollars for a genuine marble one. Figures for placing on the top of the case or a pair of side ornaments could then be chosen from another section of the catalogue according to personal taste. Most of the large manufacturers produced these cases between 1867 and 1914 as can be ascertained from contemporary catalogues, including those of W. Gilbert Clock Co., Seth Thomas Clock Co., Terry Clock Company and the Ansonia Clock Company. Some of the cases were so well simulated that it is necessary to touch them in order to determine by texture and temperature that they are not in fact made of marble. A second look reveals a poor quality paper dial, thin pressed hands and an American movement. These movements being very similar in finish and appearance to those made by the German factories. The name of the company making them is usually stamped on the back plate.

The vast majority of the black Belgian marble-cased clocks have French or German movements, although there are some interesting exceptions as shown by the example in Figure 23. The French movements are all of a relatively high standard but those made by Japy Frères being of special note. This family was one of the first in France to tool-up in order to mass produce clocks and parts of clocks as well as an amazing variety of items of hardware. They soon became one of the largest suppliers of *blancs roulants* (just the two plates of the movement, separated by the pillars and with the mainspring barrel in place) for many clocks especially carriage clocks. In the Exhibition of 1855 they were awarded a Grande Medaille d'Honneur for the volume of their output (60,000 *blancs roulants* in a year) while still maintaining a high standard with regards to quality. The five brothers traded under the name of 'Japy Frères' from about 1837 onwards, but after 1854 'Japy Frères et Cie' appeared, followed in 1928 by 'Société Anonyme des Établissements Japy Frères'. Although nominally eight-day movements, many of the French clocks happily carry on for fourteen days before needing to be rewound. Variations occur – prior to 1880 there was a tendency for the strike to be on a locking plate rather than a rack. There is one extremely simple way of ascertaining which method was used, as the mechanism incorporating a locking plate (alternatively referred to as a count wheel) is readily visible on the backplate of the movement, whereas that for a rack is on the front plate and therefore hidden from view unless the clock is dissembled. The alternatives of a gong or bell have no dating significance in this context. It is interesting to note from contemporary advertisements that a gong cost fractionally more than a bell. The opposite would be true today. It is worth remembering that if purchasing a clock minus its bell or gong it is not possible to replace one with the other, and that the best source of supply for either is another clock of the same type! At the risk of stating the obvious, do check if there are two winding apertures to see if the gong or bell is in place and not missing. A friend omitted to note and realise the significance of the two holes and is still searching for a suitable gong.

It is also advisable to check the pendulum. So often they have become separated from the clock in a salesroom and a substitute found. On many of the French movements corresponding numbers are stamped upon the backplate of the movement and the pendulum. The other numbers on the pendulum indicate the length of the required pendulum, i.e. 5 6 meaning 5.6 French inches. One French inch (*Pouce*) equals 1.0657 English inches and so for all practical purposes they are the same. There is usually an adjusting nut on the pendulum for regulating the clock, although many examples also have an adjusting device attributed to Achille Brocot of Paris. Born on the 20th July, 1817, the son of a clockmaker, Louis-Gabriel Brocot, Achille Brocot is reputed to have been an above average pupil. He left school when he was fifteen. His parents were pressed by his tutors to allow him to continue studying at the école polytechnique, but his father refused as he felt that he was already sufficiently well versed in mathematics to join him at the workbench. There is a maze of diverse evidence as to whether it was the father or the son who deserves the credit for the various mechanisms bearing their name. The Brocot suspension in Figure 2a appears in the addition to the patent taken out in 1840 by Louis-Gabriel Brocot for various improvements mainly related to temperature compensation. However, it is claimed by Redier in his obituary of Achille Brocot that Achille devised the suspension one day while conversing with his father's colleagues upon the merits of a good suspension. He goes on to say that his father was delighted with the new mechanism and quickly set about manufacturing them commercially somewhere outside Paris. In fact this was their sole occupation for some time. There is no doubt that they quickly became popular with the trade, and with only minor changes continued to be used on most French clocks until the end of the century. Apart from their effectiveness as a method of regulating the clock, they had the added advantage of removing the need to turn the clock round to adjust the timing, as the adjustment was by means of the small arbor above the number 12 on the dial.

6

The escapements illustrated in Figures 3a and 3b raise further speculation. The father did patent in 1826 an escapement which is in all probability that shown in Figure 3a, but it was most likely to have been the son who perfected it and provided the decorative visible escapement seen on so many French clocks, as illustrated in Figure 3b. Variations do occur, but the principle remains that of Brocot. He was awarded a Medal for this at the 1851 Exhibition and eleven years later at the International Exhibition in 1862 another Medal for his "general manufacture and inventive genius". Another type of visible escapement is shown on the clock in Figure 206b.

The perpetual calendar as illustrated in Figure 4a is attributable to Achille Brocot and it received much praise when shown by him at the 1849 Exposition. Again according to Redier, Achille was responsible for designing simple, less ornate marble cases and four-glass cases for mantel clocks. It is known that he came to England in 1845 to promote sales and examples have been seen of clocks made by this family. One being a marble-cased clock with all parts signed and numbered, with a fourteen-day movement, striking on a bell, with a centre seconds hand and Brocot perpetual calendar. Carriage clocks bearing his trade mark have also been found — this according to Charles Allix in *Carriage Clocks* being the letters A and B within a five-pointed star. Eventually after his father's death, Achille sold the business in Paris and opened one in St. Petersburg, Russia where his work had always been favourably received. This failed to be the anticipated success and he returned chastened but not discouraged to Paris where he returned to work with the successor to his old business until he retired through ill health. He died in January, 1878. Obviously some original research is necessary to clarify firmly the role of each member of the family, but sufficient is known to realise that any clock with a movement (not just utilising one of the Brocot inventions) made by either of them would be a desirable piece.

Any difference in quality between one French maker and another is barely discernible, which is hardly surprising when it is remembered that all the *blancs roulants* originated from a mere handful of factories all using the same methods and were often only finished and cased by the 'makers' — the Japy Frères organisation being by far the largest. Not content with manufacturing the movements they also processed their own brass, iron and steel. Other equally commendable names that appear on the backplates of the movements — those on dials are

7

inevitably those of retailers – are 'S. Marti and Co.', 'F. Marti' and 'A. Mougin'. From the *Dictionnaire des Horlogers Français,* by Tardy, it is possible to obtain the approximate dates between which any manufacturer or retailer was operating. Details will frequently be stamped on the backplate of Awards received by the manufacturer at the various Exhibitions held in Paris, London, etc. This does not always refer to the clock upon which the information is recorded, but frequently is intended to indicate that a particular maker has received an Award for one of his products. However, they do assist in documenting and dating a particular example and this is always gratifying to the owner and adds a few pounds to the value of the item in question.

Some of the movements are German and it is possible to see a marked difference in quality between the French and German movements without having to refer to names on the backplates. Comparison of the French movement in Figure 5 with that of the German in Figure 6 demonstrates some of the major differences. The French movements have a higher machining standard which gives sharper angles which are usually only associated with the appearance of the best hand-finished clocks. The pallets are finished dead hard and brightly polished and have worn well through their years of wear. The German movements have thinner plates, ill-defined angles and edges, soft pallets which have frequently worn with use and most important of all, they have lantern pinions. Their French counterparts have solid pinions. Further subtle differences can also be evaluated by studying the appropriate entries in the clock material section in the Appendix.

The movements are held in place by straps extending from the back bezel to the front as shown in Figure 6. One of the commonest reasons for these clocks stopping is that, as either the front or back has been opened, the whole movement has been inadvertently slightly rotated. It is easily done and equally simply rectified.

Examples of styles of hands, dials, etc., found on these clocks can be noted by studying the illustrations in the pages of the clock material section in the Appendix. It is also informative to note the difference in prices depending upon either the quality of finish or material used for each part as the same principles apply today when assessing a purchase.

Most collectors ask for some guide lines regarding pitfalls to avoid when contemplating a purchase. If the item in question is only a few pounds, possibly there is no better and cheaper teacher in the long run than personal experience. However, for more expensive ventures it is best to be cautious, especially if "the movement only wants cleaning"! Cleaning a French movement is no task for an inexperienced amateur and many professionals are wary of the task. The movement is extremely delicate and it is only too easy to damage the fine pivots. Further complications arise if the movement has a striking train. For those who insist upon proceeding themselves, *Watch and Clockmaking and Repairing* by W.J. Gazeley is one useful source of information.

As well as assessing the timekeeping qualities of the clock, one other point to check is whether the clock is authentic in all details, i.e. original pendulum, dial, hands, etc. Some of these are obviously not vital but, if the price is high, should be correct. At the other end of the scale it is possible to be fobbed off with a 'marriage' of a movement in a different case to that in which it started life. It is sometimes argued that as originally the movements and cases were manufactured separately such an interchange nowadays would be quite legitimate restoration. This opinion is endorsed so long as the replacement is commensurate with the original design and neither the case nor the movement have had to be adapted for this marriage. An example of what should not be done is ably demonstrated by looking at the illustrations in Figures 2a, 2b and 5. The bezel and dial shown in Figure 2b should have a movement with a Brocot suspension adjusting device — the aperture is made for the arbor through the bezel and top of the porcelain dial. However, upon dismantling the movement it was discovered that it was the basic movement as shown in Figure 5 without a Brocot suspension and never had one. Once the movement is cased there is no way of checking for this discrepancy apart from confirming that there actually is an arbor and not just an aperture in the dial.

Some comments regarding the price a collector could expect to pay for one of these clocks is to be found in Chapter XIV.

Further examples of clocks with more exotic marble and ormolu cases will be found in Chapter XI.

Figure 1

An exploded view of a marble clock case. Note that while the shaped pieces are of solid marble, the side 'pillars' are hollow, with only the outer facing being of marble. The carcase is of cement. A zinc tube normally encased the movement to exclude dust falling from the interior of the case. The base is enclosed by a wooden plank which provides support for the gong and also acts as a sounding board.

2a

2b

Figures 2a and 2b

A French movement clearly showing the mechanism invented by
Achille Brocot in 1840 for adjusting the timing of a clock by altering
the length of the pendulum suspension. The small arbor on the right of
Figure 2a protrudes through the dial and/or bezel of the clock (see
Figure 2b) and by means of a watch key or the smaller end of a double
ended key the length of the spring can be adjusted.

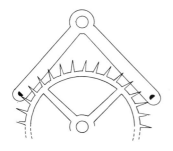

3a

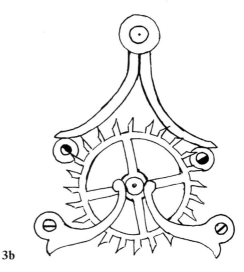

3b

Figures 3a and 3b

The two escapements shown here are both attributed to the Brocot family of Paris. It would appear from studying the information readily available in this country that the example in Figure 3a was patented by the father Louis-Gabriel Brocot and later perfected to become the version seen in Figure 3b by his son Achille Brocot (1817-1878). However, a further reference mentions the grandson Paul Brocot (1846-1882) as having perfected an escapement! It is known that he was in business with his father, Achille, in 1873 with addresses in 6, rue de Parc Royal, Paris and 8 Red Lion Square, London, W.C. It is sufficient to say they were a talented family.

12

4a

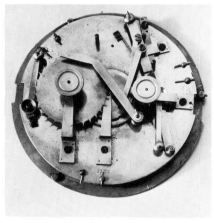

4b

Figures 4a and 4b

Achille Brocot was responsible for introducing a perpetual calendar of
which this is one type. The advantage of a *perpetual* calendar is that the
need to reset the mechanism at the beginning of each month is
removed. This dial shows Month, Day of the Week, Date, Phase of the
Moon and Equation of Time. The latter being the difference between
mean and solar time, which agrees four times a year, as marked by small
sunbursts on the dial, c. 15th April, 14th June, 31st August, a'
25th December.

Figure 5

A typical French movement found in a great variety of cases including those made of black Belgian marble. Note the thick plates with sharp, well finished edges, solid pinions and well crossed out wheels. This example has no provision for a Brocot suspension.

Figure 6

A typical German movement made by the Hamburg American Clock Company (the trade mark of crossed arrows is stamped on the backplate). Note the thin plates, lantern pinions and heavy arbor in contrast to those of the French movement. Further more subtle differences can be seen by studying the replacement parts available for the two types of movements in the clock material section appearing in the Appendix. Any of the clocks in this Chapter with a German movement would command a much lower price than one with a French movement.

Figure 7

An impressive clock, 17½in. high, the case is of black Belgian marble decorated with cast bronze mounts and mouldings. The porcelain chapter ring has a recessed gilt centre with a visible Brocot escapement; an escapement invented by Achille Brocot (1817-1878) of Paris. This particular example has steel pins but it is not unusual to see agate used for this purpose. As well as the adjusting nut on the pendulum, the length of the suspension spring may be altered by means of the small arbor protruding through the dial above the number 12. This particular form of adjustment is also attributed to Brocot. The movement is numbered with matching pendulum and with rack striking on a gong. The size of this example is a possible disadvantage but nevertheless the expected price would be between £100 and £150. Similar examples without visible escapement and poorer quality bronze mounts would be half these prices.

16

Figure 8

The case of this clock, 17in. high, is of black Belgian marble with inlay of green marble and brass pillars and finials. The porcelain chapter ring has a recessed gilt centre inscribed with the name of the Bournemouth retailer. The exceptional feature of this clock is the bevelled glass front that provides a sight of the two-jar mercury pendulum. Access to this is through the back of the case by means of a neatly hinged marble door. Similar clocks have been seen with an Ellicott pendulum. A clock of this quality would realise between £110 and £125. A visible escapement would increase the basic price by £15–£20.

Figure 9

An unusual black Belgian marble case with brass mounts and feet. The porcelain chapter ring has a recessed gilt centre decorated with a brass rosette. The movement is numbered with a matching pendulum and the maker's name – Jules Rolez Limited, Paris – is stamped on the backplate. Jules Rolez is known to have made movements during the nineteenth century at St. Aubin-sur-Scie, Paris. This is a good quality movement with rack striking on a gong. Features that would raise the price of this clock would be the practical size, the unusual shape of the case and an uncommon maker's name recorded on the movement.

£45 – £70

Figure 10

A similar clock to this appears in the 1900 catalogue of S. Smith & Son Limited, 9 Strand, London retailing at £1 10s. with an eight-day movement, and £2 2s. with a fifteen-day movement striking on a bell. The height of the case is 12½in. high and is made of black Belgian marble with a green marble contrasting inlay. The bezel is highly decorative and the chapter ring is of polished black marble with engraved and gilded numerals and a recessed gilt centre. This was obviously a presentation clock and as the small brass plaque is only glued in position it provides interesting historical information while not damaging the case. The fifteen-day movement is numbered with a matching pendulum with the maker's name — Japy Frères et Cie — stamped on the backplate. It is a matter of personal opinion as to whether the additional documentation from the catalogue enhances the price.

£45 – £60

Figure 11

The case of this clock, 13½in. high, is again made of black Belgian marble, with cast bronze feet, ornamental pillars and drop piece. The frieze in the tympanum is in bas relief. The dial has a polished black marble chapter ring in which the numerals have been engraved and then gilded. The recessed gilt centre is engraved with stylised foliage. The movement is numbered with a matching pendulum and bears the maker's name – S. Marti et Cie. Striking is on a rack and gong. This example has all the virtues of being of a reasonable size, of having a highly decorative and exceptionally good quality marble and bronze case as well as having a named movement.

£45 – £60

Figure 12

A black Belgian marble-cased clock, with bronze relief and thin brass columns. The dial is of porcelain with a gilt recessed centre. At some stage the pillars have been lacquered black — a common phenomenon which some attribute to a deep sense of mourning upon the death of Prince Albert, but one suspects is more likely to be due to a desire to avoid the necessary cleaning and polishing.

£30 – £45

Figure 13

Although a similar architectural style case to that in Figure 12, the use of contrasting coloured marble for the pillars instead of brass makes the overall appearance rather heavy. When inspecting this style of case care must always be taken to note that the pillars have not been cracked and are only being held in place by the metal rods through their centres.

£25 – £60

Figure 14

An extremely well finished case in black Belgian marble with a green marble top and inlay. The dial has a black marble chapter ring with green marble centre, and skeletonised brass numerals. The door at the back is glass. This is not an unusual feature in the better quality cases although it is more common to find a metal door with ornamental piercing covered with gauze. The backplate has the stamp of the maker (Vincent et Cie) and the information that he had received a Silver Medal for his clock movements in 1834.

£50 – £95

Figure 15

An interesting and attractively designed case of black Belgian marble with contrasting insets of green marble. The quality of the case is demonstrated by the use of solid marble for the scrolls, etc., and the deeply incised decorative markings. The dial is plain white enamel without protective bushes to the winding apertures. In common with most of these clocks there is a Brocot suspension. Striking is on a locking plate and bell. The movement is numbered with corresponding pendulum and the name 'Japy Frères et Cie' is stamped on the backplate, indicating a date after 1854.

£40 – £80

16 *(see over)*

17 *(see over)*

18

19

Figures 16, 17, 18, 19

The similarity of these four clocks is misleading. Figures 16 and 18 have fifteen-day movements, striking on bells, while the other two have eight-day movements and are timepieces only. Although the clock in Figure 16 has a well shaped solid case the dial is white enamel and very puritanical. It is uncommon to see the letters 'S' and 'F' indicating adjustment for 'Slow' and 'Fast' either side of the adjusting arbor above the numeral 12 in this type of clock. The other striking movement in Figure 18 would have a slightly higher value as the dial is of porcelain and a few pieces of decorative brown veined marble have been added to the case. Although simple both of the timepieces have a good feature. The clock in Figure 17 has a fancy bezel and an undamaged dial. That in Figure 19 while having a plain dial, slightly damaged due to careless use of the key when winding, does have some shaped pieces of veined red marble decorating the case.

£25 – £35

Figure 20

Although solid this case with its classical columns and pediment is well proportioned. The black Belgian marble surfaces are broken up by the red marble columns and plinths, while the incised traceries are gilded. In most instances the original gilt has faded or worn away, although this was by no means a standard feature. Many of the cases relied purely on the effect of plain grooves or markings for decoration. The chapter ring and recessed centre are both of porcelain with protective brass bushes to the winding apertures. The movement in this clock and that shown in Figure 21 were made by F. Marti et Cie. Fritz Marti is known to have been making movements at Vieux-Charmont in 1876 and won medals in 1908 for his work.

£30 – £45

A similar example but only a timepiece could be expected to be
£20 – £40

Figure 21

A well constructed case of black Belgian marble with green marble pillars. The movement is by F. Marti et Cie.

£30 – £50

Figure 22

There is no doubt that the value of this clock lies largely in the aesthetic appeal and quality of the bronze figure surmounting the case. By far the greater proportion of the total value would depend upon this feature rather than the movement or the fact that it still retained its matching side vases. Unfortunately the clock in many of these elegant sets has been cannibalised in order to obtain a desirable bronze. £95—£100 depending on whether the figure is spelter or bronze.

Courtesy of Sotheby's Belgravia

Figure 23

This timepiece, 15½in. high, has been included as an example of a marble-cased clock with an English movement. The architectural styled case was made of solid marble with the figure of a sphynx on top. The engine-turned dial is gilt with the name 'Barraud & Lund, Cornhill, London' engraved between the hour markings. Lund was in partnership with Barraud between 1838 and 1869 but the style 'Barraud & Lund, Cornhill, London' was only in use between 1844 and 1864. It is known that the firm made at least two black marble Egyptian-style clocks c.1858 and shortly after 1864. In his book *Paul Philip Barraud,* the author, Cedric Jagger, feels that the work on the Suez Canal between these dates may have had some influence on the choice of case decoration. Both documented clocks had a circular fusee movement with recoil escapement. These additional facts concerning the makers and the probable circumstances in which the clocks were made should greatly enhance their value.

£140+

Figures 24a and 24b

This fantastic clock stands nearly four feet tall, is twelve inches wide and weighs nearly two hundredweight. It is included to demonstrate that not all marble clocks were small shelf clocks, nor were they plain and dowdy. The identical clock was offered in the 1901 catalogue of Smith & Sons Ltd., of 9 The Strand, London for £30:—

"Beautifully designed in Green Mexican and Algerian Marble, Solid Ormolu Gilt Mounts, inlaid with Cloisonne Enamel of various colours, 15-day Movement of the Finest quality, Striking Hours and Half Hours on Deep Toned Cathedral Gong."

This description adds considerably to the interest of this piece. How many clocks were made to this design is not known, although the existence of two have been noted. The first appeared in a London salesroom in 1975 and realised £1,300 (one would have expected this at least to be doubled now). The second is at present in private hands. Fig. 24b shows the movement which is of good quality and French. The word 'Brevete' and initials 'S.G.D.G.' around the letters 'GLT' are stamped on the backplate. According to the *Dictionnaire des Horlogers Français* by Tardy this was the mark of Thieble of Paris. Thieble took out a patent for an improved pendulum in 1865.

24b

This realised £2,300 at Sotheby's
Belgravia in December 1977.

Chapter II
SKELETON CLOCKS

It was not surprising that in an age which was rapidly becoming industrialised and mechanically minded that there should develop a demand for clocks with visible movements. To the retailer it was an 'eye catcher'; to the family, especially the children, it satisfied the desire 'to see the wheels go round'. Although never acknowledged by the horologists of their day as having any special merit, these clocks admirably blended with the décor of that period and joined the wax fruit, imitation flowers and stuffed birds — also under glass domes — in front of the large overmantel mirrors on the chimney-pieces. They were not cheap clocks as can be ascertained from the prices given in the 1865 catalogue of Smith & Sons of Clerkenwell. The prices quoted — £2 10s. for a simple timepiece and £10 to £12 for 'York Minster, striking half hours on bell and hours on gong' — would not have suited the pocket of the average working man.

While skeletonised iron-framed clocks were common in the sixteenth century, the brass-framed skeleton clock first appeared in France during the 1750s. The names of Le Roy, Lepaute, Berthoud and Lepine being some of the French makers associated with their design and manufacture. The most noticeable difference between the French skeleton clocks and those made later in England was that the French rarely, if ever, used a fusee and the general design was far more ornate with delicate crossing out of the wheels. Even the bases, as can be seen from the example in Figure 25, were far more ornate with many added embellishments.

Although skeleton clocks were conceived on the Continent, the English clockmakers soon followed suit and from 1820 until 1914, when commercial production finally ceased, there was a steady market for these clocks. Naturally examples were on display at the Great Exhibition of 1851, including one superb chiming skeleton clock by Moore and Son of Clerkenwell. The location of this clock is not generally known. It is at present in the possession of the Norwich Union Insurance Group, who have generously supplied the following interesting information concerning the events leading up to their acquiring this desirable piece. The clock remained unsold in the showrooms of Moore and Son from the time of the Exhibition in 1851 until 1863 when it was sold to Mr. Joseph Langhorn for the sum of £215. Mr. Langhorn having been prosperous in business, decided at an advanced age to study medicine. Having qualified as a doctor he eventually took up residence at Ashburton in Devonshire. In 1878 he returned the clock to its makers with instructions to repolish and enamel it, as it had been "somewhat damaged by the humid Devonshire air".

In the meantime he decided to donate it to the Directors of the London and Westminster Bank while still alive sooner than their having to await his death. He had bequeathed the clock to them in his will. The Bank declined to accept this gift as they were unaware at this stage in the developments of its value and felt it was rather a large item to accommodate in their offices. After receiving their refusal he approached the Norwich Union Fire Office, as it was then known, who accepted the gift "with pleasure and gratification". However, Dr. Langhorn died before the clock reached the Norwich Union and, as he had not altered the bequest in his will to the directors of the Bank, legal problems arose. Eventually the Bank directors waived any claim and the clock was set up in 1878 at the entrance to the Boardroom of the offices of the Norwich Union in Norwich where it has remained in splendour to this day (Figure 26). It is thought that two comparable models exist — one in Russia and the other in the United States.

Smith & Sons, J. Moore and Son and other Clerkenwell makers provided fifty per cent of the total output of skeleton clocks. Some provincial towns such as Birmingham, Liverpool, Ashbourne (Derbyshire) also had skeleton clock manufactories. The name on the clock is rarely that of the maker but usually that of the retailer. In fact many of the London business houses objected to the maker's name or trade mark appearing anywhere on the clock — no doubt wishing to pass them off as one of their own products. Exceptions to this rule are the clocks bearing the name of 'James Condliff of Liverpool'. Although later members of the family carried on manufacturing skeleton clocks they all retained the characteristic unique to James Condliff — a horizontal balance and helical hair-spring. His name is prominently displayed — usually on a small name plate fixed to the base of the clock. The example in the Liverpool City Museum has the additional information engraved on the rear of the base that 'This clock was made entirely by

Thomas Condliff for the late James Condliff'. Not all these clocks are in museums and examples do appear on the market from time to time, at a high price!

As can be seen by the examples illustrated the designs for the plates fall into two categories: architectural or ornate scrollwork. The architectural designs were intended to portray in some instances specific buildings, cathedrals or monuments. Lichfield Cathedral with its spires, York Minster, Westminster Abbey, Brighton Pavilion and the Scott Memorial in Edinburgh being a few. The Scott Memorial design was exclusive to W.F. Evans of the Soho Factory, Birmingham. It is readily identifiable, even to those not familiar with the monument, by the two gilt figures of Sir Walter Scott and his reclining dog at the base of the building. The story that only one was ever manufactured is completely fallacious. Admittedly only one was made originally and shown at the Crystal Palace Exhibition in 1851 and this is now in the City Museum and Art Gallery, Birmingham. However, many more were made in the ensuing years as it proved an extremely popular design especially in Scotland. Being identifiable with an interesting history these clocks tend to fetch a good price.

Normally the ornate frames holding the movements were cast and then hand finished, lacquered or frost gilded. The latter being a softer less brilliant finish. Designs to customers' personal specifications would be more likely to be hand pierced from the solid brass. It is impossible to describe how to differentiate between cast and pierced brass as it is a question of varying textures. It is necessary to be shown the two types. By the nineteenth century the brass manufacturers were expert at casting and so it is only rarely that a blow-hole can be seen in a piece of cast brass. It is equally unlikely, although not impossible, to be able to detect sawmarks on the scrollwork of an example that had been hand pierced, as these should have been removed in the finishing.

The bases were of marble (white marble usually), walnut, mahogany or pinewood painted black with a velvet covered centre. The marble bases being stepped to take the glass shade while many of the wooden bases had an incised groove into which the shade neatly fitted. The final touch to exclude dust and pollution was a ring of chenille encircling the base of the dome. Chenille is difficult to obtain now and the more prosaic cording for cushion covers is an admirable modern substitute. To achieve the best results measure the circumference of the base of dome and deduct an inch. Measure off the length of cord required but before cutting encircle the sections of cord where the cuts will be made with a piece of sticky tape. Then cut through the cord and tape at the appropriate places. If the tape has been bound sufficiently firmly this will ensure that the ends of the cord do not unravel. Next butt-joint the two cut ends with epoxy adhesive. The sticky tape can be removed when it is certain that the join is holding and the result should be a virtually invisible join. Crimson is inevitably the best choice of colour for the cord.

The problems of damaged or missing domes are not so easily solved. Repairs can be achieved but they are far from sightly. When it is recorded that W.E. Chance & Co. of Oldbury, offered in their 1856 catalogue some two hundred different sizes the unlikelihood of finding a replacement of the correct dimensions is fully realised. The shades from stuffed birds and dried flowers are usually too narrow from back to front and in any event too tall. It is possible to have domes cut down — this costing about £5 a year or so ago — but few firms will attempt the task. This is always undertaken at your own risk, as old glass is notoriously unpredictable and it is not unknown for it to shatter into a pile of fragments. Added problems are created by the fact that many of the domes are not oval, but shaped at the 'corners'. A price in the region of £25 to £35 could be expected for a dome for a medium to large skeleton clock. Some collectors have resorted to having rectangular glass cases made with brass corner strips but these do not have the same appeal. This case style was fleetingly introduced by Smith & Sons of Clerkenwell which supposedly gives an excuse for the substitution.

The simple timepieces with anchor or deadbeat escapement were by far the most common, but many incorporating a striking train were also made. This ranged from an uncomplicated single blow on the hour with possibly another at the half-hour to those striking on two or more bells or even musical chimes. In English examples striking was always on a rack. Wire gongs appeared on later examples. The duration of time for which the clock ran ranged from one year, three months, one month to the more usual eight days. The dials were either solid chapter rings silvered or gilt with engraved or painted numerals, although there are examples of enamel with painted numerals. The more ornate fretted examples appeared later. Although these are attractive in their own right they do not make for easy reading of the time as can be seen from the examples in Figures 27 and 28.

A few years ago it was jokingly stated that the domes were worth more than the clocks, but this is no longer the case. Apart from the decorative appeal of skeleton clocks, they also embody a large number of interesting escapements and deserve a longer description than space allows here. One of the finest specialist books ever published was written by F.B. Royer-Collard and entitled *Skeleton Clocks.* A great deal of intensive research was carried out by this author and the book deals exhaustively with the many small variations of these clocks. The only information that can be added here are a few comments pertinent to a prospective purchaser of one of these clocks.

The problems surrounding replacement domes have already been discussed. As the ornate frames serve as the back and front plates of the movement, cleaning this is only made possible by completely dismantling the clock. Whether this can be successfully accomplished by an amateur depends to some extent upon the complexity of the example in question. Unless the frames are badly tarnished it is a matter of opinion whether there is any great merit in undertaking the task. If the dome is not tightly fitting and the brass not lacquered it is going to acquire a fresh patina in a relatively short period. As lacquering needs to be carried out under professional conditions to look well, it is not advisable for a home handyman to attempt this. However, a gentle rub with a coat of any silicone polish does delay discoloration.

As with all items that increase in value the point is reached where it is commercially viable to start 'reproducing' examples. This has occurred with the skeleton clock. The motion work of a basic skeleton clock is identical to that in a fusee movement in many a good quality English dial or three train board room clock, so it is not surprising that when the latter were not fetching a good price many felt it made more sense commercially to cannibalise them, have plates cast and reassemble them as skeleton clocks. After all, this is virtually what was happening at the cheaper end of the market at the turn of the century. A small jobbing clockmaker would purchase plates — possibly from Smiths of Clerkenwell — and a fusee movement and finish them to the best of his ability. To detect these 'conversions' can be difficult for the newcomer to the field of horology as it is only by having seen and studied the genuine pieces that the subtle differences in finish are noted. The finish of an old piece would have been achieved arduously by hand methods. Only in this way can the plates be nicely finished off with sharp edges polished along the greater dimension. Modern short cuts using buffing machines tend to blur and round the angles. It is often stated that the number of crossings out of the wheels give some indication of the authenticity of a clock, but this is an over-simplification. While it is true that there is more likelihood of a good quality three train movement having had many hours of work put into it which would include a high number of crossings out, a lower number do appear quite genuinely on the early simple examples. It is the quality of the work not the quantity that is important. As can be seen in Figure 37 a good example has them slightly taper from the centre with all the angles sharp and the corners in no way rounded.

In 1973 a series of articles appeared in the *Horological Journal* entitled 'How to make a Skeleton Clock' by John Wilding. These were later published in book form. This publication led to a great deal of activity among the workshop enthusiasts as could be seen by the fine displays at subsequent Model Engineer Exhibitions. It is doubtful if any of these ever came onto the open market and in any event the total output from this source was minimal. However, several firms did start producing castings of plates for these clocks (see Figure 36 for one example) and if sufficient additional hand finishing was carried out the end result could be deceptive. It must be emphasised that the motivation behind the manufacture of these plates was above reproach. The trouble lies in the motives of some of the people into whose hands they have fallen. Apart from the English sources, some reproduction skeleton clocks have been imported from Spain. Those on the market several years ago having plastic bases, but those manufactured by Marton and Gain, S.A. of Spain are on wooden or onyx bases.

Two further examples of these clocks are to be found in Figures 140 and 255a. One is a French miniature skeleton alarm and the other an electrically rewound skeleton clock.

Courtesy of Keith Banham

Figure 25

An elegant French 'boudoir' skeleton timepiece of the first half of the nineteenth century. The large wheel is typically French, but it is unusual to find a French example with a fusee. This is a highly decorative piece and would demand an exceptionally high price for this reason alone.

Figure 26

A description of the Moore Clock is taken from the house magazine of the Norwich Union Insurance Group. "This clock was made for the Great Exhibition of 1851, and is one of the finest specimens of workmanship in existence. It chimes the quarters upon eight bells and strikes the hours on a ten inch hemispherical bell concealed in the base; it also discharges each hour a very finely constructed machine playing twelve operatic selections; all the pinions are finished in the same manner as the best astronomical regulators, and the greatest accuracy is displayed in the fashion of every other portion. The frames are very massive, and having been polished and lacquered, were afterwards enamelled by a process then only known to the makers of the clock. The escapement is a finely constructed dead beat, and the pendulum has a steel rod and polished steel plates under enamelled and gilt rosettes. The clock is supported upon four pedestals standing upon a polished steel plate, which rests upon a massive carved walnut stand. It was one of the clocks which gained for Messrs John Moore and Sons, a Medal for excellence, and by the most competent Judges was considered the best specimen in the Exhibiton." Details of how this company came to acquire the clock will be found in the main text of this Chapter.

Figure 27

The clock shown in this illustration is a later example with a very ornate frame and fretted dial; it has, however, full striking on a gong. It is an attractive example — having well crossed out wheels, domed collets to the two ratchet arbors, fusee and chain and stands on a pleasing base of white marble and mahogany inlaid with brass.

Two train movement £900+

Figure 28

17in. including base and dome. This example is an eight-day timepiece standing on a white slightly veined marble base with marble bun feet. The design of the frames indicates that it was made by Smith & Sons of Clerkenwell. It is a well proportioned clock with an exuberantly fretted dial, recoil escapement and conventional lenticular bob to the pendulum. This would have possibly been the style of the clock that Smith & Sons were selling in 1865 for £2 10s. This figure would need to be greatly multiplied to reach today's market price.

£400+

Courtesy of Keith Banham

Figure 29

An English year-going skeleton clock with two subsidiary dials. The left hand dial records the weeks of the year, while the right hand dial shows the date. The points to note are the exceptionally thick plates, large barrels and extra sturdy chain all of which are essential to withstand the tremendous torque of the very strong main spring used due to the long duration of the clock's running time. In contrast the wheel work is exceptionally fine and delicate. The rectangular brass base is engraved with the name 'B. Parker, Bury St. Edmunds'. These year clocks are extremely rare and fetch several thousands of pounds on the open market.

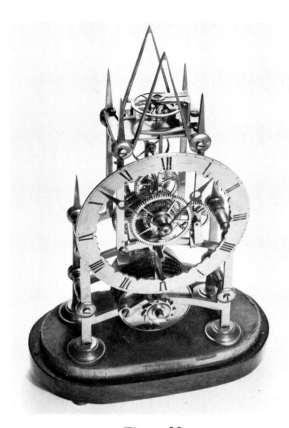

Figure 30

This is an early example of a skeleton clock as is borne out both by the plain silvered dial and the dates of the retailer whose name appears engraved on the dial. Joseph Watson and Son, The Market Place, Cambridge, can be traced in Directories as having been in business between 1823 and 1853. It is an exceptional example in so far as it has a horizontal platform lever escapement. This can clearly be seen in the illustration. These more unusual escapements greatly enhance the price of these clocks and most certainly would not be found on any of the modern reproductions. The base is mahogany. The unusual escapement is the important feature of this clock.

£750+

Figure 31

This small compact skeleton clock is on a gilt gesso and wood base, and has a gilt chapter ring and month dial engraved with the legend 'C. Elisha, Duke Street, Piccadilly, London.' The sunburst effect around the month dial is due to the position chosen for the calendar wheel. There are two unusual features concerning this clock. The first being that it is an English skeleton clock with a going barrel. The omission of a fusee would imply a French origin, but upon studying the movement it can be seen that this had been omitted in order to plant an extra wheel and pinion to obtain a duration of a month. The style of the frame and general finish make it indisputably English. A further feature is the pendulum bob. In order to add to the effective length of the pendulum the bob has been *half* filled with *lead shot*. The alternative would have been a longer pendulum with a conventional fully-filled bob and the movement mounted on pillars to gain the required height.

The name of 'Calib Elisha' is that of a maker of some consequence. It has been possible, with the assistance of Mr. Clive Osborne, to ascertain that he was in business between 1823 and 1850 in the vicinity of Piccadilly, London. The fact that he was engaged in watchmaking prior to this is known from the watch that was hallmarked in 1821 bearing his name and the information that he was Watchmaker to the Duke of York. An Astronomical Regulator shown by him at the Great Exhibition, 1851, had a compensating pendulum ball (spherical bob) of his own invention. Other items displayed by him were a watch 'with a radii compensating apparatus' and a device using extremely sturdy chains and Bramah locks to constitute 'a safety door'. By now his advertisements carried the accolade "Watchmaker to His late Royal Highness, the Duke of York, Her late Majesty the Queen of Hanover and His Royal Highness, the Crown Prince of Hanover etc. etc." Additional details of the clock can be found in an article published in *Antiquarian Horology* for December, 1972, and written by C.K. Aked and Dr. F.G.A. Shenton.

If placed on the market the price of this clock would be greatly enhanced by the unusual technical features and the data that research has uncovered regarding the maker.

Extremely difficult to evaluate as similar clocks do not appear on the market. It is possibly unique with a valuation of £900+.

Figure 32

18in. high including base and dome. This is an eight-day timepiece with 'one at the hour' strike on a brass bell. Closer examination shows several features that make this clock a desirable piece to a collector. Firstly it has a dead beat escapement. Secondly the shape of the brass-covered bob is cylindrical as opposed to the more usual lenticular shape. Thirdly the seconds dial is not a very common feature on a skeleton clock. Lastly it has the curiosity of having the numeral VI incorrectly engraved (this has been reversed). This particular illustration also shows clearly the chain round the barrel. In some instances these clocks originally had a gut or steel line, but many that had chains have had it replaced by the latter as chains are difficult to obtain nowadays. It should be possible to detect by noticing the shape of the groove in the fusee whether a clock was intended to take either a rounded gut or steel line or a flat chain. The chains for these clocks, as well as chronometers and verge watches, were made in Christchurch, Hampshire, partly as a cottage industry and partly in small factories by women and young girls. A nicely proportioned example with some interesting technical aspects.

£600 – £700

Figure 33

17in. including base and dome. The highly commendable feature of this rather severe looking eight-day timepiece is the vertical English lever escapement. This is an extremely unusual escapement. Other worthy points are the fusee with chain, maintaining power, nicely finished wheels and rounded collets on the screws holding the pillars. The plinths are cast brass.

£500 – £800 because of the unusual escapement

Figure 34

9½in. high including base and dome. This is a small neat timepiece in a simple Gothic style, with a recoil escapement and fusee with steel line. As can be seen through the centre of the dial one wheel has not been crossed out. As the provenance of this clock is known it is possible to state that this is not due to any conversion but merely typical of a number of the early examples. Although a pleasing clock it was one of the more basic types without a great deal of embellishment, as can be seen by the fact that there are only four crossings out in the wheels and the lack of collets to the screws holding the pillars around the ratchet arbor.

£250+

Figure 35

English striking skeleton clock in the form of Westminster Abbey. Note the unusual chapter ring; high number of fine crossings out on the wheels, and the shape of the bell and pull repeat cord. A similar ornate example with a three train movement plus an unusual escapement made by an important maker *can* realise £4,000–£5,000.

Figure 36

The castings, dials hands, etc., shown in this illustration are a selection of those manufactured by a firm in Gloucestershire. For a time they supplied the entire kits including a single train fusee movement, base and dome.

Figures 37 and 38

These two clocks are examples of modern reproduction skeleton clocks. They both have eight-day fusee movements, with striking 'one at the hour' on a brass bell. However, comparison between the crossed out wheels on the two clocks exemplifies the desirability of this being light and fine. The example in Figure 37 is of an average standard, while that in Figure 38 is rather heavy with wide crossings. Both examples have a wheel that is not crossed out.

Many reproductions are priced £350+

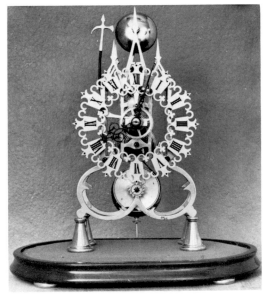

37

Courtesy of Stow Antiques

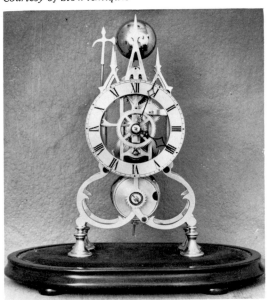

38

39a

Figures 39a and 39b

19in. high including dome and base. The name 'F. Butt — Chester'
appears on the small plate screwed below the barrel. This retailer has
been traced as 'Frans Butt,' a retail jeweller and watchmaker who was
in business between 1880 and 1887 at 32 Eastgate, Chester. The design
of the frames and the fretted, silvered dial is compatible with these
dates. The movement is an eight-day timepiece with recoil escapement
and 'one at the hour' striking on a brass bell. Note the shape of the
hammer — these hammers were often in the image of a halberd, flower,
bell or even human hand.

39b

As can be seen in Figure 39b, the lower half of the pendulum rod is wood; this would have been intended to overcome the expansion and contraction of the more conventional brass rod. The cylindrical zinc bob is unusual — they are usually lenticular.

Complete with original dome, striking movement, and a traceable retailer it would be difficult to find a similar example under £350. Quality of finish would escalate this considerably.

£500+

Chapter III

TORSION CLOCKS

These clocks can be referred to as 'Torsion Clocks', '400 day Clocks' or 'Anniversary Clocks'. The first name alludes to the twisting motion of the pendulum bob, while the second indicates the duration for which some models run, with the last drawing attention to the use to which they are often put — namely presentations upon birthdays or other anniversaries. This last name originated in America but is becoming widespread in the jewellers' advertisements for modern examples.

Mention is made by a watchmaker Robert Leslie 'of Merlin Place in the Parish of Saint James, Clerkenwell in the County of Middlesex' in his patent of 1793 which, among some twelve improvements in 'Clocks, Watches and other Time-keepers used either at sea or on land', mentions a pendulum with 'a horizontal circular . . . motion'. This is possibly the first mention of a torsion pendulum, but it is doubtful if the idea ever left the drawing board. The first torsion pendulum clock produced commercially was that patented in 1841 by Aaron Dodd Crane (1804-1860) of New Jersey, U.S.A. His first patent of 1829 is basically for a clock with only two wheels and the phrasing of the reference to the pendulum, although suggestive of a torsion pendulum, is somewhat ambiguously worded. The 1841 patent, however, definitely was for a torsion pendulum clock — one that was intended to run for a year before needing to be rewound. This was manufactured and marketed by The Year Clock Company of New York, with later models being introduced which ran for eight days or a month. Examples are extant today, but it is doubtful if they would be found outside the United States. The cases were those of typical ogee shelf clocks of the period, and the pendulum 'bob' comprised one or more balls depending upon the model. A very few striking models were also manufactured.

Another type it would be unlikely to find outside the United States but which should be mentioned is the torsion pendulum marine clock patented by Samuel B. Terry of Plymouth, Connecticut in 1852. This appears in a number of cases typical of that period. The term 'marine' is used in America to mean a clock with a balance rather than our definition which infers a chronometer for use at sea. It could be said that the electric clock described and illustrated in Figure 252a, the mystery clock described and illustrated in Figure 173, as well as several others with similar mechanisms, could be referred to as 'torsion clocks'. While this is correct as a technical description, most horologists intend the term to apply to the clocks described in this Chapter.

It was not until 1880 that Aaron Harder of Ramsen, Germany, devised and patented the torsion pendulum clock as we think of it today — a movement with a rotating pendulum, usually on a circular base under a glass dome. The clocks were initially produced by the Willmann Company of Freiburg, Silesia. In 1881 their manufacture was taken over by Gustav Becker also of Freiburg. It would appear that these first models had some minor technical or production problems as production soon ceased. These difficulties were rapidly overcome and Harder took out his first American patent in 1882, although the firm that was now manufacturing them (Jahresuhren-Fabrik founded by August Schatz in 1881) had commenced production prior to that date. Examples of these early models can be seen in Figures 40, 41 and 42. It is interesting to note that striking examples were introduced — whether these proved too costly or difficult to produce is not known but they disappeared from the range offered at a later date. The strike was either on a bell or gong.

Torsion clocks proved to be extremely popular and have continued to be so until the present day. By the turn of the century several other companies were producing them, having adapted the original design slightly to avoid controversy regarding patent rights. These were all German firms, except for one French manufacturer, Claude Grivolas, who in 1907 had taken out patents in this country and his own relating to these clocks. Whereas the weights for adjusting the timing of the clock are normally visible on the top of the pendulum disc, he envisaged containing them within the disc itself. The weights were adjusted by means of a key inserted through a small hole in the rim of the disc. Within the next few years he took out further patents replacing the adjustable weights with tubes of mercury, but it is not known whether these were ever produced commercially. A further patent in 1907, made provision for the ready accessibility through the backplate to the escapement. Examples of his clocks are illustrated in Figure 43a.

The case style adopted by most manufacturers was that of a

movement on a circular brass base covered with a glass dome, although some examples are recorded as having a four-glass case. Later catalogues of this century do depict examples in art nouveau and other cases, but it must be remembered that catalogues can also be listing styles they would be prepared to provide if requested, and not styles that were already in stock. During the 1920s and 1930s competition was extremely fierce and finances stretched and it would have been foolish to have wasted money and resources on making case styles that no one was going to buy. There was always a casemaker who would quickly make one up as and when required. This does not mean that the complete catalogues were an antiquated form of market research — the majority of the models were sitting on the shelves waiting to be purchased.

From the collector's point of view it is the clocks produced before the First World War that are the most desirable. It would be difficult to select any maker as having produced vastly superior clocks to his competitors as they were nearly all of a high standard. Those that were perhaps not quite so solidly constructed or well finished are so much in the minority that they are therefore rare and sought after for this very reason! The example illustrated in Figure 44 demonstrates this point. A further example would be the model with pin pallets and lantern pinions introduced by Kienzle around 1900 for a short period.

Few manufacturers stamped their names on the backplates. It is more likely to find serial numbers, patent numbers or possibly the name of the importer. One helpful book has been written by Charles Terwilliger entitled *The Horolovar Collection,* but it is at present out of print. By studying the patents taken out by the various manufacturers together with contemporary catalogues he has managed to identify many of the makers and their products. The vast majority of the patents taken out were concerned with either the problems arising from the effect on the pendulum spring by changes in temperature or methods of protecting it from damage during transit, etc. Several attempts were made to invent a temperature compensated pendulum (one example by Claude Grivolas has already been described) either mechanically or by altering the composition of the metal used for the spring. In 1904 a Frenchman, Eduard Guillaume, patented an alloy that was eventually marketed under the name of 'Elinvar', but although theoretically the solution some problems arose with its use in torsion clocks and so most of the springs manufactured prior to the First World

War continued to be made of steel. By 1949 all springs were made of phosphor bronze which was later replaced by yet another alloy.

A guard in the form of a metal strip or a slotted tube running the length of the backplate to protect the spring was another innovation. That patented by Gustav Becker can be seen illustrated in Figure 46b. Other attempts to avoid kinking the spring when moving the clock involved changes in the design of the top suspension. Eventually a device using gimbals was introduced.

In the interests of accuracy it is possibly best to confine suggestions as to points to note when attempting to date one of these pre-1914 clocks to the following general observations. The earliest examples had a flat disc with two adjusting discs mounted on the top surface, which was attached to the lower end of the spring by a device with a pin. The base would be of soft wood with a separate spun brass outer cover and inner rim to define the margins of the glass dome. The centre would be covered with velvet. An example of one of these early models is illustrated in Figure 40. Within a few years, but still before the turn of the century the flat disc of the pendulum acquired further ornamentation in the form of a 'crown', and was attached to the suspension spring by means of a hook arrangement. The base now became the conventional circular spun brass base. An example of this type of clock is illustrated in Figures 45a, b and c. Within the first ten years of this century further innovations were adopted, some decorative and others to overcome inherent faults in the suspension spring. The four-ball pendulum of varying designs was introduced, as were various spring guards and it became common to find two circular apertures either side of the spring high up in the backplate in order to facilitate adjusting the pallets. All of these last features can be seen in Figure 46b.

Naturally the First World War halted production and the exportation of these clocks from Germany, with only a relatively small number being manufactured between the Wars. The changes during this period were nearly all concentrated upon additional decorative features rather than any technical advancements. The illustrations in Figures 47 to 50 are from the 1936 catalogue of A. Schatz & Sohne of Triberg, Germany. The plates and bases of many of these later examples were thinner than their predecessors. Not all of the movements ran for a year — some of the cheaper examples only ran for a month. The term 'cheap' here refers to their original cost as they are now rare and sought after as far more of the true 400-day variety were manufactured.

After the Second World War several of the German factories retooled and recommenced production. After a period of tremendous sales, supply and demand settled into the steady pattern held to this day. The features found on these post-1953 models, that would not be seen on earlier more collectable examples, would be levelling screws to the base, a small spirit level on the base and a device to lock the pendulum to prevent it swinging during transit.

Although true of all repair work it is even more important not to commence 'adjusting' these particular clocks before fully understanding their mechanism otherwise a single fault can be rapidly turned into a multiplicity of shifting variables! Again Charles Terwilliger's book *The Horolovar 400-day Clock Repair Guide* is of tremendous assistance. One soon learns that it is vital that they are kept level. The next most common reason for their malfunction is that the spring has been damaged in some way. It is possible to obtain replacement springs — the best source being Southern Watch and Clock Supplies Ltd. of Orpington, Kent. Replacing domes is again a problem, but not such an overwhelming one as in the case of the skeleton clocks. A few of the standard sizes manufactured for the modern torsion clocks also adequately fit the older models. Sadly more and more of these are of plastic rather than glass, but it should still be possible to obtain the latter from firms in Clerkenwell, for instance.

Figure 40

The circular wooden base of this clock has a velvet covered centre, with only a brass trim round the centre and exterior of the base which suggests a date prior to 1900. The dome rests in the deep groove. The dial is white enamel with the words 'R.L. Patent 2182, U.S. Patent 269052, DR Patent 2437' encircling the centre. The U.S. Patent number is for the patent taken out by Aaron Harder in 1882, and so it would be logical to assume that this was made by Jahresuhren-Fabrik. The other points to note are the fact that the bob is 'pinned' to the suspension spring and not hooked, and that the pendulum bob itself is of the earlier design without a crown. Although this model still appeared in the 1893 Jahresuhren-Fabrik catalogue as can be seen in Figure 41, this must have been one of their first products with the patent numbers being prominently displayed to discourage competition. Later examples do not have these numbers displayed.

As an early example this would realise about £200

Jahres-Uhr.

Höhe 300 mm = $^1/_3$ natürlicher Grösse.

Fein poliertes, sichtbares Werk.

1 Jahr Gehwerk.

Miniatur.

Nr. 2.

400 day Clock
with open movement
polished brass.
Height of Clock 8 inches
Height af Shade and Stand
10$^1/_2$ inches Scale $^1/_4$
Timepiece.

Pendule à 400 jours
mouvement visible
laiton poli.
Hauteur 300 mm.

$^1/_4$ de la grandeur naturelle
sans sonnerie.

Figure 41

A page from the 1893 catalogue of August Schatz showing the miniature timepiece manufactured by them at this date.

As an early example £150
A missing or damaged dome would devalue the clock by £20+

64

Jahres-Uhr.

Höhe 400 mm - ¹/₄ natürlicher Grösse.
Fein poliertes, sichtbares Werk.

1 Jahr Geh- und Schlagwerk.

Nr. 2a.

400 day clock
with open movement
polished brass
Height of clock 12 inches
Height of Shade and Stand
16 inches Scale ¹/₄
Striking.

Pendule à 400 jours
mouvement visible
laiton poli
Hauteur 400 mm

¹/₄ de la grandeur naturelle
à sonnerie.

Figure 42

A further page from the same catalogue of 1893 but showing a striking model. Striking examples are very rare and this must double the basic value of a similar non-striking example.

Over £200

Figure 43a

This is an extremely interesting advertisement which appeared in 1924 to promote the torsion clocks manufactured in France by Claude Grivolas. The points to note from the three examples shown are:—

1. The use of his patented pendulum bob with the adjusting discs mounted internally.
2. The four-glass and oval glass case styles although unusual for a German-made torsion clock were common in French examples.
3. The totally unconventional and distinctive style of the third example with matching candelabra.
4. The fact that the movement is 'hung' in the two top cases and not supported in the normal manner by at least two pillars. See Figure 43b on page 68 for more comments on the movement.

It is unusual to find one of these clocks with a French movement and this, together with the fact they are so well documented, would raise the price to between £200 and £300. The final price would be influenced by the case style.

67

Figure 43b

This enlarged view of the movement patented and manufactured by Claude Grivolas of Paris could not be more informative! It confirms that these clocks were entirely of French manufacture, provides the trademark of Grivolas (a linked C and G) at this date, and clearly shows his patented method of easy access to the escapement to avoid having to dismantle the movement completely.

Figure 44

Although the quality of the finish of the brasswork of this clock is thin and poor, it is a rare example made c.1905/6 by Franz Vossler. This manufacturer had ceased production by the beginning of the First World War. The points of interest about the clock are the fact that it has a front wind, only runs for thirty days, and has a silvered dial, in contrast to the more usual white enamel or porcelain dials.

The price in this instance is governed by the name of the manufacturer. £100+

Figures 45a, 45b and 45c

A sturdily constructed and yet decorative example of a torsion clock with a porcelain dial and pie-crust bezel on a circular spun brass base. The date of this example would be early 1900s. The points to note in order to reach this conclusion are:—

1. Lack of spring guard.
2. Lack of viewing aperture.
3. 'Crown' to the pendulum bob.
4. Hook attachment between the suspension spring and the bob.

Good quality example £100+

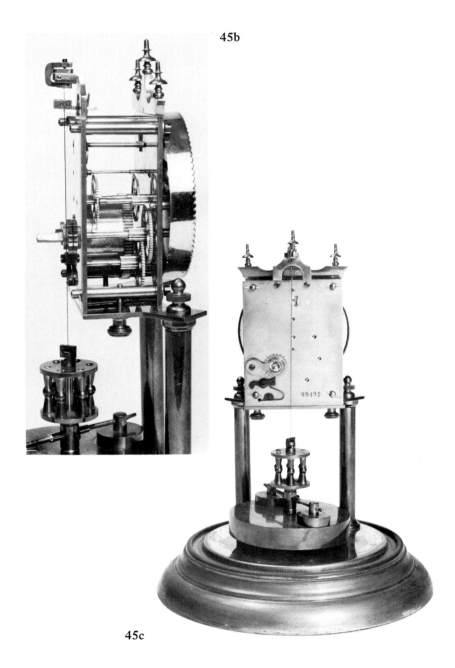

45b

45c

46a

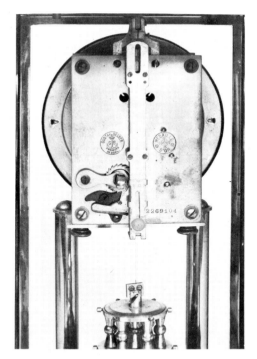

46b

Figures 46a and 46b

This clock was manufactured about 1905 by Gustav Becker of Silesia, Germany. Although he did produce a few clocks between the two Wars, his main period of productivity was prior to the First World War. Some further details concerning this maker will be found on page 249. His trademark of an anchor with G B can be seen on the backplate, together with the stamp referring to the fact that he was awarded a Medaille d'Or at the Schlesien Industrial Exhibition of 1852.

This had no connection with the torsion clock, but was given for his work on regulators.

The suspension guard clearly seen on the rear view of the movement was introduced by this maker about 1905, as were the two small circular apertures either side of the suspension guard that were intended to facilitate adjusting the pallets.

A pleasant example by a documented maker. £150+

Figures 47-50 are taken from the 1936 catalogue of August Schatz of Triberg, Germany. To the modern eye a chrome finish is not so acceptable as gilt, but was a novelty at this date.

£60+

Figure 47

Height including dome 16in. Apparently two finishes were offered, either gilt with an enamel dial or chrome with a silvered dial.

Figure 48

Height including dome 12½in. In a gilt or chrome finish.

Figure 49

Height including shade 12½in.
The base and pendulum were chrome-plated and the dial silvered with raised figures.

Figure 50

Height including dome 12½in.
The base and pendulum were chrome-plated with a silvered dial.

Chapter IV

CARRIAGE CLOCKS

It would be presumptuous to attempt to add any information to that already copiously recorded in the book *Carriage Clocks* by Charles Allix, but for the more general reader a few interesting facts can be recounted here.

The imagination of the general public, rather than that of the horologist, has been caught by these clocks and the prices in many instances have risen out of all proportion to their true worth. Fine and complicated examples by French makers such as Bréguet and Garnier (see Figure 51), or the English makers McCabe or Dent, naturally command and deserve a high price but many of the late 'bread and butter' timepieces made in the early years of this century have no great horological merit. In many instances the intrinsic value lies in the ornate case only.

The origin of these clocks stems from the *pendule de voyage* made by Abraham-Louis Bréguet (1747-1823) in the first decade of the nineteenth century. They were masterpieces of design and craftsmanship with many complicated mechanisms. Later Paul Garnier (1801-1869), with the introduction of a simple basic design using his escapement, made it possible for these clocks to be produced more cheaply. He is generally regarded as 'the creator of the Parisian carriage clock industry' – an industry that existed into the 1900s. Strangely enough few of these clocks were sold in France but thousands were exported to England.

Between approximately 1826 and 1845 the framework of the cases was pinned and brazed, with a sliding rear door, but after this the parts were screwed together thus allowing for a greater degree of variation in the case designs. To facilitate the mass production of these clocks the manufacturers tended to keep to a few standard sizes: 'Mignonnettes' below 4¼in. with the handle raised; 'Full size' between 5½in. and 9in. with the handle raised and 'Giant' over 9in. with the handle raised. Decoration of the cases embodied many arts, with ornate pillars of cast caryatids, or brass with cloisonné or enamel work, etc., while the side panels were frequently finely pierced or given enamelled designs on porcelain. The presence of a pair of fine Limoges panels naturally escalates the price of the clock dramatically. Designs were obviously influenced by prevailing fashions in other fields, and these can be used as a very rough yardstick in dating a particular example. The oriental influence is noticed in the 1905 to 1910 era while designs characteristic of the art nouveau style soon followed.

Although the clocks were finished and cased in Paris, virtually all the movements *(blancs roulants)* came from either Saint Nicolas d'Alierment near Dieppe or the Jura region of Franche Comté. The main source being the factory run by the Japy Frères. The escapements were obtained from specialist manufacturers working along the French-Swiss frontiers, with the mainsprings coming from yet another source. Thus, while using standard parts, a wide diversity of clocks could be produced with variation in type of escapement, with or without strike or complicated calendar work, etc. Several alternative strikes were employed which could be on a bell or gong, the use of a bell pre-dating that of a gong with the changeover period occurring in the mid-nineteenth century. The variations are as follows:—

Plain Strike:	On the hours and half-hours, with or without the repetition of the hour by single blows.
Petite Sonnerie:	This sounds on two bells or gongs usually of differing tones with the result that this is referred to as ting-tang. At the quarter past the hour one ting-tang (two blows) is struck.
	At the half-hour two ting-tangs (four blows) are struck.
	At the three-quarters past the hour three ting-tangs (six blows) are struck.
	The hour is struck normally on single blows.
Grande Sonnerie:	This time the preceding hour is struck at each quarter by single blows as well as the appropriate number of ting-tangs.
Minute Repeater:	The striking is similar to a *Grande Sonnerie* but with the additional feature of having the number of minutes past the last quarter sounded as well. The time of 3.50 would sound thus:

> Three blows (three o'clock)
> Three ting-tangs (three-quarters past)
> Five single blows (five minutes past the three-quarters)

The best makers signed their names and it is needless to point out that these pieces fetch hundreds of pounds in the salesrooms. Some of the earliest makers were Garnier, Lépine, Bolviller and some of the later Jacot, Crocourt and Margaine.

In the event of the erroneous impression having been given that all carriage clocks were made in France, mention must be made of the English carriage clocks. They are, horologically speaking, important clocks made by important makers and often those examples appearing on the market are well documented from workshop records which is always an added advantage. They tended to be larger and heavier than their French counterparts and made use of a fusee and chain. Early examples, by such makers as J.F. Cole or Vulliamy, had lever escapements but later makers of the second half of the nineteenth century, such as Frodsham and Dent, tended to use a chronometer escapement. Although still referred to as 'carriage clocks' this escapement did not readily lend itself to safe transportation. These clocks may have been used more often than not as mantel clocks which perhaps explains the mahogany or rosewood cases that are often found in place of the more usual brass. The English carriage clocks were never intended for other than the extremely wealthy, and although many manufacturers shared a common source for the rough movements, escapements, etc., as did the French makers, each evolved his own style of finishing which was superbly carried out.

The manufacture of French carriage clocks declined after the turn of the century and those that were produced in the first years of the 1900s, before production finally ceased, were of rather poor quality — thin plates, poor crossing out of wheels, very plain mass produced cases, etc.

English carriage clocks of a continuing high standard are produced to this day. One firm so doing being Thomas Mercer Ltd. of St. Albans. Early in the 1970s there began to appear reproductions of carriage clocks in the French style (without fusee) but made in England. Nowadays there are several firms manufacturing them and the only point in mentioning them here is to give a word of caution. They are extremely well-made and desirable clocks, just so long as the purchaser realises their lack of years! Unfortunately a few, a very few, are being 'aged' rapidly. It is obviously financially worth the time and trouble to work on one of the small miniature reproductions now available to make it look a great deal older and then sell it for two or three times the intended price. It is difficult enough for an experienced eye, let alone an inexperienced one, to detect any tell-tale signs. One of the only safeguards is to purchase from a reputable dealer who is jealous of his good name. With the present cost of labour it is fortunately not a practical proposition to reproduce those examples with highly ornate cases or complicated mechanisms. This does, therefore, limit the unscrupulous to certain basic types only on which to work.

Another point to note is whether the escapement has been changed. The majority of the mass produced French carriage clocks utilised a cylinder escapement. Although this escapement appears more complex, it is in fact easier to mass produce than a good quality lever escapement. It does not, however, rival the good timekeeping qualities possessed by a standard lever escapement, reflecting especially changes in main spring tension. For this reason it had been usual to include in cylinder watches stop work to confine the mainspring power to approximately the middle third of the spring. It was not surprising, therefore, that as the cylinder became worn or required servicing, many were replaced by a new platform lever escapement. In assessing any purchase it is important to differentiate between this replacement lever escapement and an original quality lever escapement that may have been original. An original lever escapement would command a higher price than an original cylinder escapement, whereas a replacement lever escapement would be lower. It is usually quite easy to note a replacement as the quality of the conversion work is not up to the standard of the rest of the movement. Many of the original platforms are in fact silvered. Frequently the words 'Swiss' or 'Swiss Made' appear on a replacement. Examples of the two escapements can be seen in the Appendix on Clock Materials.

By virtue of their purchase price carriage clocks are not suitable clocks for an amateur to contemplate repairing. The only exception could be the replacement of a cracked or broken glass panel in a standard case that can be easily dismantled (i.e. screwed, not brazed at the joints). As the thickness of the glass varies it is as well to take the damaged panel when ordering the replacement.

It is hardly necessary to indicate what is a desirable carriage clock — what is more to the point is how much the collector can afford to pay! Naturally a damaged case or cracked dial is a disadvantage, especially as the modern offset litho enamelled dial in no way equates with the old enamel on copper specimen. It should be possible, by studying the evaluation and current price guide at the end of the book, to come to some conclusions as to what affects the price of the various types of carriage clock and in what proportions. It is then up to the purchaser to decide whether he wishes the value of his clock to be in its case decoration or unusual movement.

51a

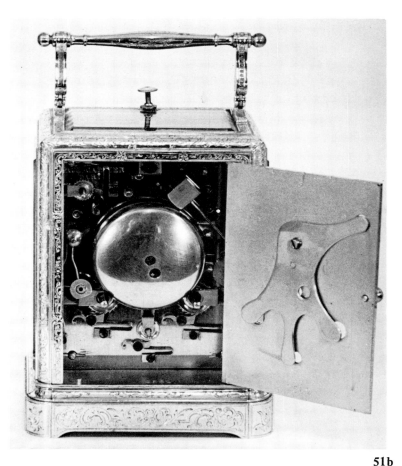

51b

Figures 51a and 51b

6in. high with handle raised. This is a beautiful clock made by an important French maker – Paul Garnier, 1801-1869. Note the one-piece case, the white enamel dial panel with chapter ring, alarm dial and inscription 'Paul Garnier H^{er} Du Roi'. Points to note from the rear view are the shutter on the door to exclude dust from entering the movement through the winding holes, the bell and the matching numbers on the case, movement and door (No. 2562). Striking is on the hour and half-hour. The escapement is the original (chaff-cutter escapement) as invented by Paul Garnier and patented by him in 1830.

£600

Figure 52

Although this superb English striking carriage clock bears the name
'James McCabe, Royal Exchange, London' and the serial number 3180,
it would have been produced by one of his descendants who carried on
the business after his death in 1811. This example would have been
made between 1850 and 1883 when the firm closed. The case is
beautifully engraved with a subsidiary seconds dial and stands 9½in.
high with the handles raised. The movement has a lever escapement and
strikes and repeats the hours. An example like this of an English
carriage clock by a good maker is not only difficult to find but also
very expensive.

53a

53b

Figures 53a and 53b

This is a good example of a typical English carriage clock. The points to
note are the enamel dial, and engraved dial surround. It is doubtful if
the carrying handle is original. The door is opened by means of a small
lever in the base of the case. The side view of the movement in Figure
53b gives a clear view of the fusee and chain.

Timepiece as illustrated, wrong handle, £800
with strike, wrong handle, £1,200
Timepiece, right handle, £1,000
with strike, right handle £1,600

Figure 54

This example has its original carrying case and key. Note the removable slide to the front of the case which may be stored at the rear of the case when the clock is in temporary use. Provision for storing the key has been made in the framework of the case below the hinge to the lid. The double ended key is sized one end to fit the winding arbor and the other for the hand set. The case is exceptionally elegant with decorative pillars, finials and filigree work depicting two dragons and foliage. The dial is of ivory porcelain with a gilt centre trim. The movement is that of a plain timepiece with its original cylinder escapement. An almost identical clock was selling in 1900 for £2 2s.

Timepiece – £200
With strike – £350

Figures 55a, 55b, 55c, 55d and 55e

An excellent set of illustrations of a *grande sonnerie* carriage clock with repeat and alarm made by Drocourt. Figure 55a is a general view.

Figure 55b shows the backplate with winding arbors, going train, strike and alarm, and the setting for the hands and alarm. The two silvered bells are one within the other but it is possible to see the two hammers which strike the ting-tang on the right and the hour striking hammer on the left. The trade mark of Drocourt (the letters D and C with a carriage clock between them) is above the left winding arbor.

Figure 55c shows the base of the clock with the strike, silent and *grande sonnerie* levers. The serial number of the movement (6615) can be seen. The name Darley is that of the retailer.

Figure 55d shows the barrel for the going train with the smaller barrel for the alarm appearing above.

Figure 55e shows the barrel for the strike work — this is nearly always larger than that for the going train. It is just possible to see the fine wheelwork and pinions above.

£1,200

55b

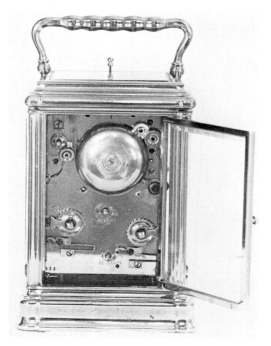

55c

55d

55e

Figure 56

8in. high with handle raised. Although somewhat similar in outward appearance to the clock in Figure 54, this example has a repeater movement (strikes the hour and half-hours and repeats the hour and five minute intervals at will), and an original lever escapement. The pierced panel dial has a motif of birds and strapwork with an enamel hour circle and recessed gilt centre. The movement is numbered 3509 and was made by Gay, Lamaille & Co. who are mentioned as working in Paris and London in 1880.

As illustrated, £800; with ordinary hour repeat, £400.

Figure 57

5in. with handle raised. This is an extremely unusual example and provides a fine debatable point. The carriage clock is frequently defined as a small portable clock with a horizontal platform escapement. In this instance, however, there is in a typical carriage clock case a movement with a vertical balance wheel escapement mounted on the backplate. There is no doubt that it is an identical movement to that of the VAP drum clock depicted in Figure 116b.

While this example cannot, by any stretch of imagination, be regarded as a high quality timepiece it is substantial and well made. Moreover it is of great interest to a collector by virtue of its unusual escapement. Very few other examples have been seen.

£70

Figure 58

This appears to be yet another simple 'bread and butter' carriage clock but upon closer examination some interesting details appear, which enhance its value. Firstly, it is complete with its maroon carrying case and key and the movement has retained its original escapement. Secondly, and most important, it is possible to identify the 'Lion' trade mark stamped on the backplate. Albert Villon opened a factory in Saint Nicolas d'Aliermont in 1867 which later became Duverdrey & Bloquel. From 1910 they produced a wide range of finished carriage clocks which are distinguishable by this trade mark. Today the factory manufactures alarm clocks but does produce a few carriage clocks signing these on the backplate and back door 'Duverdrey & Bloquel, France'. Without this documentation and original case and key this type of late clock would hardly qualify as a collector's piece.

As illustrated, £70; without mark or travelling case, £60.

Figure 59

An English carriage clock made by Jump of London in a 'humpbacked' case style that originated with Bréguet. The silver case is hallmarked and so it is possible to date the clock. Jump of Mount Street was in business from the mid-nineteenth century to early twentieth, the life of the business spanning two generations. This particular example has an aperture showing phases of the moon and subsidiary seconds dial. Other examples have been noted with perpetual calendar mechanism. A choice collector's item.

60a   60b

Figures 60a and 60b

6in. with handles raised. The carriage clock on the left hand side of
the illustration (Figure 60a) is in a one-piece case which indicates a date
prior to 1850. This is commensurate with the fact that striking is on a
bell and not a gong. There are two marks stamped on the backplate;
one of the maker (Japy Frères) and the other the retailer (Henri Marc
of Paris). Apparently Japy Frères not only supplied *blancs roulants* to
the rest of the trade but also sold complete carriage clocks. The
movement is numbered 37703.

The example on the right (Figure 60b) is included to provide an
example striking on a gong instead of a bell.

60a, £400–£450; 60b, £180, if repeating then £220–£250.

60c

Figures 60c and 60d

Rear views of the two carriage clocks in Figures 60a and 60b.

60d

Figure 61

7½in. high with handle raised. It is hardly surprising to note from the inscription at the base of the clock that it was a presentation clock. It is a handsome example. W.J. Walsham, 1847-1904, to whom it was presented, was a surgeon of some note at St. Bartholomew's Hospital — a fact which adds interest to the clock. The gilt brass case is solidly constructed and has two fine hand-painted side panels — both signed. One has a lady stooping to remove her overshoes before entering the house, while the other shows her, still in her outdoor apparel, playing with a pet bird. The backplate carries the stamp GL with the words 'Patent Surety-Roller'. GL indicates that the clock was made by E.G. Lamaille of London and Paris. Mention is made of a Gay, Lamaille & Co. of London and Paris in 1880. The movement is French, has its original lever escapement and striking is on the hours and half-hours with a repeater mechanism.

As illustrated: £800
with porcelain dial £1,000

Chapter V

LONGCASE CLOCKS

The popularity of the longcase clock was at its peak during the eighteenth century, but the demand began to decline from the beginning of the nineteenth century. By the mid-1800s the dominance of the London maker was waning but provincial makers continued to produce these clocks for another twenty to thirty years. It is among these later provincial clocks that the collector will find sensibly priced examples of interest. The cases were made locally and reflected their regional styles, and were therefore of a more individual style than many of their London counterparts. Quality of case varied according to the skill of the craftsman. It would appear that he could be either the local carpenter or cabinet maker as chance had it. The cases of these provincial cases tended to be larger — both taller and wider — than those made in London and were usually of solid oak or pinewood. Mahogany cases in the provinces are far more rare. The example in Figure 62 illustrates the more individual approach often found in these cases.

Examples with brass dials are exceedingly uncommon. By now the white painted dial — often with gaily painted scenes and corners — had made its appearance. Various reasons are given for this change. Some say that it was enforced by the high price of the brass and further skill needed to work it, whereas others say that the white painted dial was easier to read. Opinion varies according to whether the answer is coming from a northern or southern source! Most of these dials were supplied as were the movements from the clockmaking centres that had evolved, e.g. Birmingham. The names on the dial are rarely those of the makers but those of the retailers. It is possible to find stamped on the dial plates, and possibly the movements, the initials or name of the true maker. However, it is necessary to dismantle the clock to find these and this is not always possible before purchasing the clock. Mention is made of these Birmingham makers, together with a great deal of additional information on these clocks in the book *The White Dial Clock* by Brian Loomes. The names on the dial can be checked in *Clock and Watchmakers of the World*, Volumes I and II, but it has not been possible for the compilers to confirm in all instances whether the names are those of makers or retailers.

At the date in question few clockmakers made their own movements. The majority as already indicated came from Birmingham, Coventry, etc., where they were produced on semi-factory lines with a certain amount of standardisation of parts. This is one reason why these clocks have, until recently when the supply of older longcase clocks outstripped the demand, found little favour with the collector. With few exceptions these movements were thirty-hour only, although obviously some more expensive eight-day movements were necessary for the more wealthy customers. Calendar work is found on a fair number, but far more show the phases of the moon either in the dial arch or through a small aperture in the dial. To the countryman it was far more important to be able to foretell how dark the night was going to be before he ventured forth than which day of the week or month. In sea-faring areas times of high tide are commonly found.

Not all the movements were mass produced; as late as 1880 or 1890 there were a few, a very few, genuine clockmakers scattered through the countryside, and in the preceding years there had been several well known clockmaking families whose work is now much sought after. They had frequently originated from clockmakers who had left the big cities through religious or other personal reasons and set up working in areas where these did not apply. Many of these clockmakers had Quaker origins or were refugees from other countries, especially from the Continent following the unrest of the 1848 period. The best sources of information on these makers are to be found in the books devoted to a specific region and its clockmakers. A list of these will be found in the Bibliography.

When contemplating a purchase it is wise to bear in mind the possibility of the movement and case being a 'marriage'. As previously commented this is acceptable so long as the movement and case are contemporary and neither have had to be adapted to accommodate the other. The presence of active woodworm is a further possibility, although there are successful modern methods of controlling this. Some renovation to the cases is to be expected, especially the repair or even replacement of parts of the plinth. Many of these clocks stood on damp stone floors that were frequently washed down and therefore the wood became rotted in parts.

It is possible to find dial restorers who will repaint a dial, and whether it is preferred to keep the old authentic worn dial or have it restored is a matter of individual opinion. Again dealers in clock materials can supply modern replacement weights, finials, keys, etc., that are quite acceptable. It should be possible to undertake the cleaning of the movement from one of these clocks and more than adequate instructions can be obtained from many of the old handbooks or new books stocked by most horological booksellers. *Repairing Antique Clocks* by Eric Smith was written for the relative beginner to workshop horology. Problems will arise if new pinions or wheels are needed to be cut, as few amateurs can undertake this task and many of the restorers send them to the specialist wheel cutter. The problem is not so much the cutting of the wheels but obtaining the correct cutters. Through pressure of work it is not uncommon for wheels to be with the cutter for several weeks or even months.

Although there are London made longcases of this period, the style that continued to be made irrespective of current fads and fashions was the regulator. Here the floor standing longcase style of regulator is being referred to and does not include the Vienna regulator which is quite a different matter. As the primary purpose of a regulator is precision timekeeping all unnecessary motion work or complications such as strike, etc., were avoided. There was little point in losing, through the friction introduced by the operation of the striking train, the advantage gained by the high standard of workmanship put into these clocks. Many of them were made as one-off pieces by skilled clock repairers for their own use, while others were made for the trade by such makers as Dent, Barraud and Lund, J. Smith and Sons of Clerkenwell. Depending upon the source the quality will vary. The Victorian case style for these clocks was a mahogany round topped case, with a fully glazed door at the front and little embellishment, as in the example shown in Figure 66a. Most jewellers and clock retailers kept one on the premises by which to regulate and adjust clocks and watches in for repair and many of them have been retained as part of the shop furnishings. The dials are plain and simple, usually silvered with the minute markings around the circumference and the two smaller subsidiary dials showing seconds and hours. This unusual arrangement is due to the movement being designed to avoid friction caused by the more usual central arbor and concentric hands. Various forms of pendulum compensation were used, with a compromise being made between the theoretical ideal and the aesthetic appeal. As a consequence the mercurial pendulums were with glass jars as opposed to metal; the Harrison gridiron pendulum with its alternating rods of brass and steel proved another favourite. For the purely functional regulator the invar pendulum tended to be chosen. Invar is an alloy of nickel and steel discovered by Dr. Guillaume in 1904. Its expansion at different temperatures is negligible — the name comes from *'invar*iable'.

Whether there is any credence in the story that the sonorous Westminster chime of Big Ben greatly influenced the domestic taste for deep-toned chiming clocks is not certain, but it is certain that there was a great upsurge of popularity for this type of clock during the late Victorian and Edwardian period. Harrington patented his tubular chimes in 1885 and there is no doubt of their success. Fewer longcase clocks were manufactured with bells at this time. The alternative to the tubular chimes being 'cathedral' gongs — gongs with a deep resonant note. Depending upon the chime there were either eight or four tubes with an additional one for striking the hour which was in some instances replaced by a gong. This was possibly to obviate the need for an even wider case to house the ninth tube, as well as providing a contrasting note. Cheaper models only had tape gongs, which in turn were replaced in the 1920s by rods. This last change was both for reasons of economy and the demand for smaller clocks. There is no doubt that the size of the weight-driven clock with tubular chimes became and still is a problem. Although now considered choice collectors' pieces, especially in America and Germany, few modern homes will readily accommodate a clock of this size. It must be admitted, however, that even though it may appear ostentatious to the modern eye, the large heavily carved case with its glass panelled door enabling a view of the polished tubular chimes and pendulum is certainly most arresting!

The most commonly found chimes used were the Westminster (on four tubes), or the Whittington (on eight tubes). The Westminster chime being by far the oldest, as it originated from the fifth bar of Handel's 'I know that my Redeemer liveth' and was expanded into the present chime by Dr. Jowett and Mr. Crotch when this was needed in 1793 at St. Mary's Church, Cambridge. It was then known as the Cambridge chime and only became known by usage as the Westminster chime after being chosen for Big Ben at Westminster. The story regarding the Whittington chime is that it was so named after Dick Whittington who, on hearing the sound of this chime from the Bow Church, Cheapside, retraced his steps to London and ensuing fame and fortune. Sometimes the St. Michael's chime (on eight tubes) is used as a third alternative. There would appear to be some divergence as to its origin. It is usually attributed to St. Michael's Church in Hamburg, but the following interesting comment was seen recently in an issue of the *American Horologist and Jeweler* magazine. A set of bells was cast in London and installed in the steeple of St. Michael's Church in Charleston, South Carolina, in 1764. During the War between England and America the bells were captured and shipped to England, where they were later found by a Charleston merchant and returned to Charleston. However, cracks were found in some of the bells and in 1823 they were sent back to London to be recast. Unfortunately, during the Civil War in America they were destroyed but the fragments were returned to the original London bellfounders and the bells once again recast. Finally, in 1867, the eight bells were yet again installed in the steeple and the tune they rang out was 'Home again, home again, from a foreign land'. Since then they have been left undisturbed.

Many of these clocks were exported to America and the east. Most manufacturers recognised the need for, and adopted, alternative construction techniques to allow these clocks to function well in hot climates with the minimum of skilled attention. It is only necessary to read the extensive list of countries to which one firm, Gillett and Johnston of Croydon, sent their turret clocks as well as a large range of domestic clocks, to realise how sought after were our quality clocks of that period.

This firm also manufactured these weight-driven clocks with tubular chimes and made the clock presented by the Borough of Croydon to HRH the Prince of Wales upon the occasion of his marriage. This had a handsome carved rosewood and ivory case. William Gillett began work as a small clockmaker in Hadlow, Kent, under the patronage of Lord Sackville of Knowle. He later worked in Clerkenwell before establishing his business at Croydon in 1844. He was subsequently joined by Charles Bland and then in 1877 by Mr. A. Johnston. The name of the firm became Gillett and Johnston which it has retained until this day. They are still world famed for their turret clocks, but have ceased to make clocks for the domestic market. This part of their business was transferred to F.W. Elliott Ltd. in 1923. This firm was founded by James Jones Elliott in 1886, who had served his apprenticeship with Bateman of Smithfield in London. Prior to 1901 the firm carried on their business at Percival Street, Clerkenwell,

London, where they manufactured fusee and chain quarter chime bracket clocks. In 1892 he took out a patent for 'Chimes struck on stretched wires by hammers as in a piano forte' which was used with slight modification by clockmakers until well into the 1920s, if not later. The normal striking action, intended for a nest of bells mounted from back to front of the movement, had needed modification for the innovation of the tubular chimes hanging across the back of the clock case. Their weight-driven tubular chime clocks were such a success that larger premises were needed and the firm moved to Rosebery Avenue, Clerkenwell, London.

In 1909 J.J. Elliott Ltd. amalgamated with Grimshaw and Baxter and the factory moved in 1911 to Grays Inn Lane, and in 1917 to St. Anne's Road, Tottenham. The association did not last and the two firms parted company in 1921, when Frank Elliott, James' son, sold the name of J.J. Elliott to Grimshaw and Baxter. Frank joined the firm of turret clock and domestic clock manufacturers, Gillett and Johnston Ltd. in Union Road, Croydon. In 1923 Frank Elliott formed the present company, F.W. Elliott Ltd., and took over the production of the Gillett and Johnston range of domestic clocks. Unlike a number of other firms, which made their own movements but sent out to casemakers for cases, both of these firms manufactured movements and cases. As the production methods and case designs of both firms were somewhat similar, identifying differences are too subtle to be readily noticeable. Neither firm is aware of any numbering sequence being stamped on movements, nor of varying trade marks, although from the advertisement shown in Figure 68 it would appear that Elliotts did at one time possibly use one. Examples of both firms' clocks appear in the illustrations.

From the catalogue published by Smith & Sons Ltd. of 9 Strand, London, c.1900, it is interesting to note that they offered among their range of clocks manufactured by them some twenty one registered longcase designs housing movements striking either on bells, tubular chimes or gongs. One case is in the form of a 'miniature' Big Ben — Westminster Tower and all — which stood some 10ft. 6in. tall. The examples striking on bells could be had for a further £10 striking on 'Nine Tubular Bells', or there were the alternatives of repeating action for a £1 extra, a mercurial pendulum for £5 extra or a moon dial for a £1 extra. Most of the models illustrated had moon dials, similar to that in Figure 71.

Other manufacturers advertising the fact that they made longcase clocks in the years immediately after the First World War were A. & H. Rowley, 4 Theobalds Road, London, W.C.1., who were established in 1808 and W.H. Evans & Sons, Soho Clock Factory, Handsworth, Birmingham. Further details of the former will be found on page 144.

The British Empire Exhibition which opened at Wembley on the 23rd April, 1924, was intended to promote home industries — 'Buy British' was a common slogan at this time. Among the horological exhibitors the following are mentioned as manufacturing longcase clocks:—

F.W. Elliott Ltd., Union Road, Croydon

John Smith and Sons, 42 St. John's Square, London, E.C.1

Pleasance and Harper Ltd., 4 Wine Street, Bristol

The model displayed by Pleasance and Harper Ltd. being an extremely rococo reproduction of a Louis XVI case but housing a movement with tubular chimes, similar to that seen in Figure 72.

Interest in these Edwardian chiming clocks has never completely disappeared. Although F.W. Elliott Ltd. discontinued the model with nine tubular chimes and only retained that with five tubes, they have now reintroduced the former due to the increasing demand for these clocks. One firm in Germany — Joseph Kieninger — has also commenced production. Neither of the firms are contemplating reintroducing the truly massive examples but rather those standing 6ft. to 6ft. 6in. tall.

The majority of the movements found in these large chiming and striking clocks are English, but there are a few that were manufactured by Winterhalter and Hoffmeir of Germany. These are of such good quality that it is often only by the trade mark on the backplate (W. & H. Sch.) that the country of origin is realised.

Inevitably the American factories produced similar clocks but it is doubtful if any found their way onto the English market except through private channels. The only movements that were imported from abroad in any quantity were those used in the cheaper chiming clocks as shown in Figure 77. These were from Germany and chimed and struck on rod gongs, which although surprisingly melodious are considered inferior to either the tubular chimes or tape gongs. Further details concerning the movements with rods will be found on page 129, where their use with regards to shelf clocks of the same period is discussed.

If purchasing an example in need of restoration it is wise to locate a source of supply of suitable replacement tubular chimes. To replace a whole set is simpler than restoring one or two of the initial chimes. If replacing a full set it is possible to choose tubes of the correct material and calibre to provide both visual and aural symmetry. When replacing one tube, however, it is difficult to trace a tube that matches the remaining parts, both in note and size. Care also has to be taken when hanging them to ensure that the tubes are freely suspended by cords passing through the holes in their sides and that they neither touch each other nor their support. The hammers originally had their faces softened by thin pieces of chamois leather. A certain amount of trial and error is needed to adjust the hammers to strike the tubes at the correct point, and at the same time to achieve some equality of tone. If possible it is as well to hear the chimes through to verify that the pin-barrel is not damaged. This can be restored by any of the restorers that undertake work for music boxes, but this again adds to the initial cost of the clock and so needs taking into account when assessing the total outlay.

Figure 62

8ft. 1in. The case of this clock is a typical example of a provincial clock of the mid- to late-nineteenth century. The case is of oak inlaid with fruit-wood and ebony. The dial is signed R. Snow, Padside, with a seconds dial and a revolving day/night dial in the arch. A Snow family of Padside have been mentioned in *Country Clocks and their London Origins* and *The White Dial Clock* both written by Brian Loomes. Apparently they were a farming family (father and three sons) who carried on clockmaking as a secondary winter occupation. This clock style is rather late to have been made by any of these specific Snows, but it is possible that a twentieth century movement was added to an earlier case by a later member of the family. The overall size of this clock would be a deterrent to most collectors. It fetched £480 in the saleroom early in 1977.

Figure 63

This is an attractive example of a provincial mahogany clock with a white painted dial with a subsidiary seconds dial and calendar aperture. The dial arch is painted with a scene depicting a castle, river and bridge, with floral corner pieces. The name John Thomson on the dial could be the maker, but is more likely to be that of the retailer. The price at auction in 1977 was £300.

62

63

Courtesy of Sotheby's Belgravia

Figure 64

This is a good example of a well-proportioned mahogany longcase clock of Scottish origin. The white painted dial has Commerce as the subject for the colourful painting in the dial arch. The maker's name — George Lumsden, Pittenweem — on the dial is not without interest and would, therefore, add to the value of the clock. There were two George Lumsdens — the father known to have been active between 1818 and 1849, and the son known to have been active between 1849 and 1899. The former was apprenticed to John Smith a noted clockmaker, also of Pittenweem, who excelled in complicated movements including an elaborate musical clock with several dials and playing eight tunes.

Figure 65

A further example of a provincial white dial clock, this time in an oak case. The case is well made — a point to note as the quality of the case varies considerably depending upon whether the maker was a carpenter or joiner. The dial has, apart from the gaily painted picture in the dial arch and spandrels, the added features of a seconds dial and an aperture showing the date.

64

65

Courtesy of Kingston Antiques

Figure 66a

6ft. 6in. This is a good example of a Victorian mahogany longcase regulator with a mercurial pendulum. The points to note are the minute markings around the perimeter of the dial, the seconds dial below the 12 position and the twenty four hour dial above the 6 position. It is more usual to find the conventional twelve hour dial.

Figure 66b

Movement of the regulator shown in Figure 66a. The points that denote a high quality movement in this instance are: the substantial plates and pillars, the fine crossing out of the wheels, a high count train and jewelled pallets. Notice too the sharp angular appearance of the dead beat escapement in contrast to the rounded form of the more commonly found anchor escapement and the consequent upright teeth of the escape wheel.

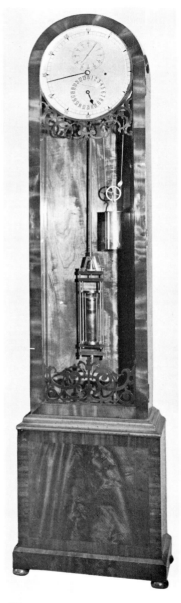

66b

66a

Courtesy of Derek Roberts Antiques

Figures 67a, 67b and 67c

An early weight-driven tubular chime clock by J.J. Elliott Ltd., of
Croydon. Although the clock is large the proportion and classical design
of the case makes this an elegant example. The dial is silvered and has
the typical flowery engraving where the eighteenth century example
would have had a simple matted surface. It has raised skeletonised
Roman numerals, engraved centre with name 'Elliott, London' engraved
below the winding aperture and a sunk seconds dial. The huge
movement is three train striking on a tape gong, with the alternative
chimes of Westminster or Whittington on eight tubes. The points to
note from the interior view of the trunk in Figure 67b, are the three
brass-cased weights for chime, time and strike, together with the eight
tubular chimes suspended in parallel across the back of the case. The
small cord on the left-hand side of the striking weight is to activate the
pull repeat mechanism. As with most chiming/striking clocks of this

67c

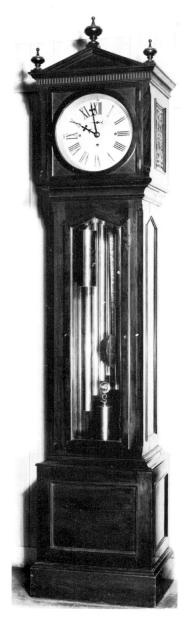

67b

67a   *Courtesy of F.W. Elliott Ltd.*

period provision has sensibly been made for silencing them at will. In this particular example this is by means of small levers through the dial above the number XII and to the left of the number IX. The third lever to the right of III is for selecting the chime. As can be seen from Figure 67c this activates a series of levers which in turn move the pin-barrel horizontally for the appropriate series of pins to be set in position. The other points to be noted from the illustration of the movement are the method of suspending the tubular chimes, and the thick, good quality plates of the movement with a spotted finish (this finish is generally associated with marine chronometers).

£1,200+

Figure 68

This advertisement shows a weight-driven tubular chime clock manufactured by J.J. Elliott Ltd. sometime between 1911 and 1917. The trade mark and statement related to it are not without significance. Although present members of the company (F.W. Elliott Ltd.) have no recollection of a trade mark it appears that one was used "unless otherwise requested". As already mentioned, when the two firms of Grimshaw, Baxter and J.J. Elliott parted in 1921, the name of J.J. Elliott was sold to Grimshaw and Baxter and hence continued to be used by them. As this trade mark appears on clocks sold by them as late as 1927 it would appear that care has to be taken when interpreting who actually made the clock and when. It is not known with certainty who manufactured clocks for Grimshaw and Baxter in the 1920s although it was possibly Williamsons of Coventry.

GRIMSHAW, BAXTER & J.J. ELLIOTT Ltd.

29 to 37, GOSWELL ROAD, LONDON, E.C.
— AND —
91, MITCHELL STREET, GLASGOW.

Telegrams: "GRIMBAX, BARB., LONDON."   "GRIMBAX, GLASGOW."
Telephones: 485 HOLBORN.   9241 CITY (Factory).   GLASGOW : 7889, CITY.

English Clock Manufacturers.

FACTORY. *(The Up-to-date Clock Factory of London).*——
Little Grays Inn Lane, London, E.C.

J.J.E.

ENGLAND

Regd. Trade Mark.

This Trade Mark appears on all Clocks of our Manufacture, unless otherwise requested, and is a guarantee of Best English Material and Workmanship.

"Elliott" Clocks have a world-wide reputation for sound construction, superior workmanship, and general reliability.

They are made of best material only, and each movement is guaranteed against original defects.

Every "Elliott" Clock you sell will be a good advertisement for you as well as for ourselves—your name on the dial, and our trade mark on the movement will stand as a recommendation for all time, because "Elliott" Clocks do not wear out.

"Elliott" Clocks are not cheap clocks—best quality articles never are—but they are what we claim them to be—the best in the world.

Recommend an English Grandfather or Bracket Clock for presentations.

We have a large variety of "distinctive" Cases in Oak, Mahogany, Satin, Walnut, Thuya, and Amboyna Woods—all of our own manufacture.

No. 26.
Carved Mahogany Case, Movement Chiming Quarters on 8 or 4 Tubes, 3 changes at will, hours on tube or gong, hand pierced, brass mounted Dial on silvered base, silvered circle, raised gilt figures.
£89 10 0
Subject usual Discount.

RAILWAY DIALS AND SHIPS' CLOCKS
FOR ALL CLIMATES ARE ALSO SPECIALITIES.

Courtesy of F.W. Elliott Ltd.

113

Figure 69

Two further examples of clocks made by J.J. Elliott sometime after 1909. These illustrations are taken from the trade catalogue of Grimshaw Baxter and J.J. Elliott Ltd. and show clocks made by J.J. Elliott. The variety of choice of styles, woods and movements together with prices is of great interest. They were far from cheap clocks starting at £89 10s. when a working man's wages at this time were 30s. per week, and it is understood that a number were exported to America at the time of manufacture. Since then they have become choice collectors' pieces in that country.

An extract from an Elliott manual below gives details of fitting and setting up instructions for Elliott clocks.

"The tubes should next be suspended from the tube rail. These are hung according to size, starting with the shortest tube on the right-hand side looking at the clock. Loop the cord at the top of the tube from slot to slot in the tube rail as shown in this diagram:

"The longest tube of all is the hour tube, and this is suspended from a separate bracket on the left hand side of the movement. Make sure that the tubes do not touch each other when hanging, as this will result in a "jangle" of the chimes. If they do touch, adjust each tube in turn by holding the bottom and moving slowly from side to side so that each swings clear of the other. Adjust the chime hammers by bending the stems so that the heads are $1/16$ins. away from the tube when at rest. The hammer heads must not lie on the tube, as this will result in a double note being struck and a dull tone. It is important that the hammers strike the tubes squarely and centrally.

"These clocks are fitted with a chime sequence corrector, so that if the chimes get out of sequence as a result of the clock running down and stopping, the chimes being repeated, or the hands being moved without waiting for each quarter to chime, etc., etc., the chimes will automatically correct themselves."

ENGLISH (LONDON MADE) GRANDFATHER ♦ CLOCKS.

No. 1.
Height 8ft. 11ins.
Handsomely Carved Mahogany or Oak Case.

No. 1090.
Height 7ft. 9ins.
Mahogany or Oak Case.

Nos. 1 and 1090 —8-day Best English Movement, Dead Beat Escapement, Maintaining Power, Brass Cased Weights, Compensated Pendulum. The Chimes can be changed at pleasure by indicator hand on dial, also hand to shut off Chimes, making Clock strike the hours only. There is a further action to shut off Hour Strike. making Clock silent. Dial Corners and Centre finely Hand Pierced and Engraved. Silvered Hour Circle with Raised Gilt Figures. The Tubes are well tuned and heavily nickelled.

	No. 1.			No. 1090.		
	£	s.	d.	£	s.	d.
Chime on 9 Tubes, giving at will St. Michael, Whittington, and Westminster Chimes	170	0	0	72	0	0
,, ,, 9 ,, ,, ,, Whittington and Westminster Chimes	168	10	0	70	10	0
,, ,, 5 ,, Westminster Chime or 9 Gongs	160	0	0	62	0	0
,, ,, 8 Bells and 5 Gongs giving at will Whittington and Westminster Chimes	158	10	0	60	10	0
,, ,, 5 Gongs Westminster Chime	155	0	0	57	0	0
,, ,, 8 and 4 Bells giving at will Whittington and Westminster Chimes	154	0	0	56	0	0

Mercurial Pendulum £8 0 0 extra.   Plain Brass Mounted Dial with Cast Corners, £3 0 0 less.
Movements chiming on Tubes can be made, if desired, to strike the hours on a Gong at same price.
Cases specially manufactured for India and other tropical climates at a slightly increased cost.

G. B. & J. J. E. Ltd.

Courtesy of F.W. Elliott Ltd.

Figure 70

This advertisement for clocks manufactured by Gillett and Johnston of Croydon that appeared in 1921, does not really do justice to their products. In common with other manufacturers of this date they also manufactured "the more expensive and massive designs with quarter chiming movements". Their 1906 catalogue stresses "with correct design, sound and perfectly seasoned wood, skilled carvers and wood workers, and *no piece work*, we are able to supply the finest procurable specimens of English Grandfather Clocks, while the workmanship of the Movements is in every way in accord with the high finish of the case". At this date their eight-day grandfather, in solid oak or walnut, hand carved, brass engraved and silvered arch dial, striking the hours and quarters on deep toned gongs, was priced from £80.

This firm was, and still is, a noted manufacturer of church bells, carillons, and turret clocks. Many famous bells have been founded by them including the Bourdon Bell of the carillon of the University of Chicago (weight seventeen tons), with many a church or public building either in England or important cities abroad housing one of their turret clocks. This side of their business remaining extremely active to present times.

£1,000+

Croydon Chiming Clocks.

THERE is no longer any need to associate Grandfather Chiming Clocks with ungainly proportions of cases.

The charm of the flat trunk cases of a hundred years ago which disappeared with the advent of tubes has been revived in the latest Croydon Clocks, owing to the design of the movement making it possible to reduce the width from back to front by nearly three inches, even when using tubes of the largest diameter.

The result is a Clock of pleasing and dignified proportions, to the charm of which is added the beauty of grain and colouring of picked figured Mahogany, polished to exactly the right degree of gloss without being glassy, and relieved by richly lacquered brass mounts.

Inside the case the highly finished nickel steel pendulum, the plated tubes, brass cased weights, brass pulleys and steel lines form by no means the least attraction.

The patent compensated pendulum with its rigid support and correct suspension, the dead beat escapement, maintaining power and pinions of twelve on the going train, combine to ensure timekeeping equal to that of a watchmaker's regulator. The pendulum nut is designed so that it cannot be accidentally turned, and as the bob is adjusted on a special fixture in the Factory these Clocks can be depended upon to keep correct time from the beginning and require scarcely any further regulating.

The tubes are nine in number, of pure tone, accurately tuned and the chimes played are the Whittington and Westminster Quarters, the hours being struck in each case on the deep ninth tube.

Early delivery can be given of all standard designs of Chiming and Striking Grandfather Clocks, and of Chiming, Striking and Timepiece Mantel Clocks.

We also make
TOWER CLOCKS AND CHURCH BELLS.

Gillett & Johnston, Croydon.

Telephone Nos.: CROYDON 2028-2029.   EXHIBITION MEDALLISTS.   Established 1844.

117

Figure 71

A similar clock to that shown here appears in the 1900 catalogue of S. Smith & Son, Limited, 9 Strand, London, with the following description:—

"'The Savoy' Grandfather Clock, in Splendidly Carved Oak Case, with Bevelled-Edge Plate-Glass Door, Best Quality Movement, showing Phases of the Moon and the Seconds on the Dial; There is also a Small Dial at the Right-Hand Corner, with a Hand, which, by Turning, effects a Change of Chimes either on to the Westminster Set of Four Gongs or the Cambridge Set of Eight Bells. The Hour is struck on a Very Fine-Toned Gong. The Small Dial on the Left is for the purpose of making the Clock Silent.

£75
Fitted with Nine Tubular Bells, £10 extra;
or with Five Ditto, £5 extra
Repeating Action £1 extra.
Height 8ft. 3in; Width 2ft. 0in. Depth 1ft. 4in."

This particular example has a month movement, chiming on five tubular bells, with maintaining power and a dead-beat escapement. According to the catalogue the dial was signed 'Diamond Merchants Jewellers and Silversmith'. Although not the de luxe model with nine tubular chimes and apparently needing some restoration carried out, this clock realised £1,450 in the saleroom in 1977. There is no doubt that these Edwardian chiming clocks are gaining in price and in view of their size it is surprising that they command a higher figure than older, smaller traditional longcase clocks, even if they do have a more complicated chime and strike.

Figure 72

9ft. 1in. The catalogue description for this incredibly ornate longcase clock was that it was "A good mahogany Long-case clock, the brass dial with rococo spandrels and silvered chapter ring, with subsidiary seconds, Whittington/Westminster and Chime/Silent dials, the movement striking on gongs, with a carved cresting inlaid with foliage and corbel supports, the glazed waist door with carved astragals, the plinth inlaid with a hanging basket of flowers and moulded block feet." There are no maker's marks on the backplate, but it is remarkably similar to the case of the clock made by Pleasance and Harper Ltd. of Bristol and shown in Figure 73. The price reached in the saleroom in 1977 was £2,200 and shows clearly the effect of overseas demand for highly ornate pieces regardless of age.

£1,700 – £2,200

72

71

Courtesy of Messrs. King & Chasmore   *Courtesy of Sotheby's Belgravia*

Figure 73

This is an illustration of the reproduction Louis XVI Grandfather Clock that appeared on the Pleasance & Harper Ltd. stand at the British Empire Exhibition at Wembley in 1924. It is described as follows:—
"The case is of solid carved mahogany with inlaid rosewood panels of correct period design. It has glass panels in front and sides, mounted with ornamental lattice carvings, and the dial is brass, with raised mounts and gilt figures. The height is 8ft. 6in. The movement is of best quality and finish, with dead-beat escapement, and the weights are gilt. An important feature is a specially adjusted seconds pendulum, built on scientific principles to ensure accurate timekeeping. The clock can be fitted with Whittington and Westminster Chimes and chimes every quarter of the hour on 8 and 4 Harrington tubes. It also strikes every hour on an extra large and deep-toned tube. The clock can be supplied with any set of three chimes; Whittington, Westminster, Canterbury, Magdalen, Guildford, etc. The value of this Louis XVI Clock is about one hundred and twenty guineas. This firm makes a speciality of Grandfather Clocks in all styles. For safe transit, care is taken to pack in special cases for despatch to any part of the world. An actual photograph, in natural colours, will be sent free, on request to this firm at 4, Wine Street, Bristol."

£1,700 – £2,200

Reproduction of Louis XVI
Grandfather Clock,
by Pleasance & Harper Ltd.

Figure 74

This advertisement by H. Williamson Ltd. appeared in the very early 1900s. It shows a three train striking longcase clock in outline very similar to a mahogany example of c.1780, but decorated with Sheraton type designs of inlay which are particularly apparent on the base.

£900 – £1,000

123

Figure 75

7ft. 2in. This mahogany cased longcase clock with a silvered dial and subsidiary dials for seconds, chime/silent and choice of Whittington or Westminster chimes on nine rod gongs, has no identifying maker's marks but was manufactured at the beginning of the twentieth century. It fetched £900 in the saleroom in 1977.

Figure 76

6ft. 2in. This caricature of a longcase clock with a two train movement was made sometime during the 1920s or 30s and could, at a generous stretch of the imagination, be considered a collector's piece by virtue of the exceptionally curious assortment of styles and designs. The combination of oriental scenes on the painted panels, the exaggeratedly narrow trunk and the dial predictably engraved 'Tempus Fugit' culminating in putti riding on eagles must be unique! The price fetched in the saleroom in 1977 was a generous £320 (the pre-sale estimate was £80-£120!). Only the spurious 'Thos Tompion London Fecit' is missing to make it a fine example of an horological joke.

75

Courtesy of Sotheby's Belgravia

76

125

Figure 77

As homes became smaller the demand for the larger longcase clocks striking on tubular chimes diminished, and in an attempt to compete with the smaller, cheaper German clocks striking on rods, Elliotts introduced in 1932 the 'Imperial' range. This name continued to be used until around 1946 or 1947. The examples in this illustration have the Westminster Chimes on rods.

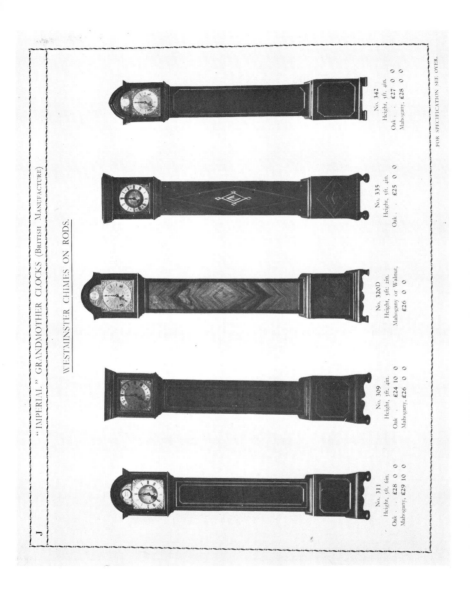

"IMPERIAL" GRANDMOTHER CLOCKS (BRITISH MANUFACTURE)

WESTMINSTER CHIMES ON RODS.

No. 311
Height, 5ft. 6in.
Oak . . £28 0 0
Mahogany, £29 10 0

No. 309
Height, 5ft. 4in.
Oak . £24 10 0
Mahogany, £26 0 0

No. 320D
Height, 5ft. 2in.
Mahogany or Walnut,
£26 0 0

No. 335
Height, 5ft. 4in.
Oak . £25 0 0
Mahogany, £28 0 0

No. 342
Height, 5ft. 4in.
Oak . . £27 0 0
Mahogany, £28 0 0

FOR SPECIFICATION SEE OVER.

Courtesy of F.W. Elliott Ltd.

127

Chapter VI
BRACKET and SHELF CLOCKS

Bracket Clocks, Boardroom Clocks and
English and European Shelf Clocks

The restrained style of the English Regency bracket clock continued into the early Victorian era and many examples from this period are highly desirable. By the mid-1800s, however, a complete polyglot of case styles had emerged. Some were faithful replicas of earlier styles, while others can only be described as over-embellished monstrosities. Unfortunately, it is usually the latter that are referred to as typical examples of Victorian clockmaking in England, with little regard for the fact that there were also on the market small, more elegant examples by makers such as Barraud and Lund, Vulliamy, Dent, etc. The only point to remember is that the demand for clocks by these makers far outstripped their output and, therefore, it was common practice for them to purchase some movements from makers in Clerkenwell – Thwaites and Reed or Moores being the two most quoted suppliers. Perusal of the Day Books of both of these makers confirms the practice, together with the fact that their marks can often be found on the dial plate or inside the barrel. Thwaites and Reed (previously Ainsworth Thwaites) have been in business since 1808 and John Moore and Sons (previously Handley and Moore) since 1824 until the end of the century. In a small leaflet of theirs dated 1886 (reproduced in the December, 1968, issue of *Antiquarian Horology*) they state that up to 1877 they had made 15,180 house clocks.

So long as their size is not a deterrent, the large so-called Boardroom or Directors' two or three train clocks of the late 1800s have much to commend them. In common with the longcase clocks of this period the chimes are usually those of Westminster, Whittington or St. Michael, and on bells and/or gongs. Circular tape gongs were used to strike the hour as this note was somewhat more reminiscent of the deep tone of Big Ben than that produced on a small bell. As can be seen from the examples illustrated these were far from cheap clocks. The solid cases being ebonised, mahogany, rosewood or oak either plain, carved or inlaid with brass, ivory, etc. The dials were silvered or brass with gilt brass overlay and small subsidiary dials for Strike/Silent, Chime/Silent, Fast/Slow rise and fall adjustment or choice of chime. The names on the dial being with few exceptions those of the retailers. Most of the movements were English with fusee and chain on both going train and striking train. Although, as can be seen from the examples in Figures 87 and 93 some German clocks of this type were imported. It must be stressed, however, that the movements made by Winterhalter and Hoffmeir were excellent movements often incorporating a fusee and chain, and are frequently mistaken today for English movements by those who do not realise the significance of the letters 'W. & H. Sch.' stamped on the backplate.

In 1901 there was a famous test case regarding the use of foreign parts by manufacturers and yet still citing their products as 'Made in England'. After this date a new Merchandise Mark Act came into force and "precluded any British watch or clock factory from using more than sixpennyworth of material" if they wished to continue claiming their product to be British. Obviously the corollary of this was that more foreign goods had to identify themselves. The demand grew for a cheaper chiming clock and about 1890 rod gongs were introduced. The rod gong slowly superseded the more expensive bells and circular tape gongs; although sneered at by most collectors their tone is not unattractive. Prior to the First World War and again between the Wars large numbers of these movements were imported from Germany and cased here. According to one account the chime rods and strike gongs for the clocks made in the Black Forest area of Germany, at the beginning of this century were made in two small factories (Wagner, Schwenningen and Johan Filtner, Villingen) "by crude hand methods". The rods were mainly of phosphor bronze with a few of German silver. The former was reputed to produce a better note. The rods were cut to the required length and tapered at one end. Brass bushes or nuts were then forced onto the tapered end which was then screwed into a block. The tuning was done by reducing the length of each rod until the required sound was achieved, with a good musical ear being the only guide. The spiral gongs were made from a flat section of wire coiled on a hand coiler and then turned by reducing the length until the required effect was achieved. Apparently it is extremely important that these rods and spiral gongs are kept free from rust otherwise they lose their tone. After gentle removal of the rust with wire wool or a glass pencil (obtainable from clock and watch material suppliers) it is necessary to reblue them. This is a simple but skilled process, involving the heating and cooling of the metal to specified temperatures. The coloured fluid sold to colour the exterior of parts that should be 'blued', i.e. clock hands, etc., is not a satisfactory substitute as it is not the colour that improves the tone but the changes that take place during the heating.

After the First World War many small clock factories opened in England determined to compete with the cheaper pre-war German clocks. Makers, such as Gillett and Johnston and J.J. Elliott, of high quality clocks having been largely unaffected by the competition as their products were aimed at a different market. Some of these newly formed companies survived and others did not. It has been possible to trace the history of a few of these and there should be a certain amount of interest in the products from factories known to have existed for a short period only, as well as those who continued to flourish.

The name of Grimshaw and Baxter has already been mentioned in association with J.J. Elliott Ltd., makers of longcase and bracket clocks, etc. After this partnership broke up in 1921, Mr. Baxter and H.W. Williamson Ltd. of Coventry amalgamated their clock factories and introduced into their range the 'Astral' and 'Empire' movements. Prior to this Williamson's had their factory at Salisbury and, having persuaded one of the leading men to come from the Hamburg American Clock factory in Germany to advise on mass production methods, they were able successfully to manufacture a wide range of cheap and high grade longcase and bracket clocks. Unfortunately the factory was gutted by fire. The firm moved to Coventry but during 1931 succumbed to the general economic problems and were absorbed by the English Watch and Clock Manufacturers Ltd. which was taken over by Smiths Ltd. in 1934.

The 'Newbridge' movements were manufactured by Hortsmann Clifford of Bath, Somerset. The introduction of their range of gas controllers in 1921 led them to extend their range of products to clock movements. All of their advertisements lay great emphasis on the fact that their clocks were the outcome of *precision* mass production and that all parts were fully interchangeable.

'Tasty Bracket Clocks' was the appellation given in 1921 to one style of clock manufactured by the Hirst Bros. & Co. of Roscoe Street, Oldham! Their Tameside factory had been built in 1919 at Dobcross, Nr. Oldham, for the manufacture of cases and movements built up of standardised parts. Their clocks bear the trade name of 'Tameside'.

It is interesting to learn that the Garrard Clock Company of Swindon opened in 1915 in order to manufacture munitions for the war. After the war they turned their attention to motors for gramophones and then finally clock movements. One of their advertisements claims a range of five hundred case styles!

Many of these small companies were eventually absorbed by what is now known as Smiths Industries and most of their history and archives lost in the take-over. It is not generally known that the Enfield Clock Company of Tottenham, London, prior to becoming part of the Smith empire after the Second World War had been founded by August Schatz and a few associates. Immediately prior to the war they brought over machinery from Guttenbach in the Black Forest of Germany and commenced production. Their clocks were excellent clocks and retailed well.

The variations in the case styles of these clocks are far from inspiring. It would only be makers such as Gilletts and Johnston, F.W. Eliotts Ltd. and a few others that would make their own cases. The remainder of manufacturers would purchase them in bulk from a case maker. It is known that in 1933 Hodkinson & Son of London had a total output of 80,000 cases. It is possible to obtain a very rough approximation of the date of these late clocks by the designs of the cases. Most readers will be familiar with the surge of mock Jacobean oak or veneered oak furniture and fabrics that were popular during the 1920s. Coinciding with this fashion was that of Japanese lacquer work "executed by native craftsmen on our own premises". Examples of these various styles will be found in Figures 100 to 102, which include the faithful 'Napoleon Hat' design.

As most factories were endeavouring to achieve a standardisation of parts and production methods there is not a great deal of difference in the movements. However, a few interesting variations can be found in the designs used by the different manufacturers of self-correcting chime devices — an innovation that had obviously become necessary in order to obviate unwarranted complaints after customers had attempted to 'adjust' them. Many movements now had provision for the removal of the barrel without having to dismantle the whole movement. Anyone wishing to study these finer points in detail should consult repair books written in the 1930s and 1940s, *The Modern Clocks — Their Design and Maintenance* by T.R. Robinson or the *Practical Watch and Clock Maker* magazines. These frequently described in detail the 'new' movements as they appeared on the market.

For those who cannot afford the earlier bracket clocks there is a case to be made out for these later pieces. It cannot be ignored that they sound well! At the moment the price of these post-1920 clocks is being influenced by furnishing trends, but if they are ever to be considered potential collectors' pieces they must be in excellent and original condition. The quality of the movements does vary and if possible those with solid pallets against those with strip pallets, etc., are to be more desired. It is only necessary to pause for a moment and reflect as to which type or quality of component would have cost more to produce, and therefore have been a more expensive item originally, to assess what will also be prized as a collector's piece in the future.

Figure 78

This is a good example of a rosewood bracket clock of about 1850, striking on a bell with a repeating mechanism. The silvered dial is signed 'Brockbank & Atkins, London.'

Figure 79

A plain but highly desirable bracket clock in walnut case striking on a gong. Both the dial and backplate are signed 'Dent 33, Cockspur Street, Charing Cross, London'. Edward John Dent (1790-1853) was associated with Lord Grimthorpe in the designing of the Westminster Clock (better known as Big Ben), with his stepson Frederick finalising the work after his death, from premises in the Strand, London. The other brother, Richard, having been bequeathed the Cockspur Street premises. The two businesses merged in 1921, when they moved to their present address in Pall Mall, London. See *Edward John Dent and his Successors* by Dr. Vaudry Mercer for a full account of the Dent family business.

Figure 80

A fine example of an eight-day striking clock in an overtly neo-Gothic styled rosewood case and matching stand. The legend on the dial (E.I. Dent London 655) would indicate that the clock was made by Edward John Dent, c.1845.

Figure 81

A further example of a bracket clock by Dent, in a walnut case, with
quarter striking and repeating on eight bells or four gongs.

82

Courtesy of Sotheby's Belgravia

Figures 82, 83, 84 and 85

These clocks usually stood on small matching brackets in offices, boardrooms, and possibly libraries or halls. Comparison of the two examples in Figures 82 and 83 provides some points of interest. The similarity in design of the two mahogany cases leads to speculation as to whether they were manufactured by the same casemaker. The similarity ends here. The example in Figure 82 has a brass dial signed 'Thompson and Vine, London'. These were retailers known to have been in business in 1890 at 85 Aldersgate Street, London, E.C. The two train movement strikes on a gong. The example in Figure 83 has a painted dial with a centre alarm disc while the movement has a fusee with a chain. It is extremely unusual to find such a movement with an alarm in this quality case. The clock in Figure 82 sold for £130, and it had been estimated that the other example would fetch a little more, however it remained unsold probably through not reaching the reserve price.

The remaining two examples were in mahogany and walnut cases respectively. Again the names on the dials are those of the retailers. Both were striking, that in Figure 84 on a gong, and both fetched the sum of £140.

83

84

85

Figure 86a

There is little doubt that this solid oak cased clock with its motto of 'Tempus Rerum Imperator' carved on the plinth was intended for anything but a boardroom! In common with many of the quality cases of this period the fretted sides are held in place by turn buttons and can be readily removed. The chapter ring and rings on the three subsidiary dials are silvered but the rest of the dial and overlay are gilt brass. The dials are Chime/Silent, choice of Whittington or Westminster Chimes and Fast/Slow adjustment through the dial arch. By turning the pointer on the appropriate dial the whole bar upon which the pendulum is suspended is raised or lowered thereby adjusting its effective length. Although there is no maker's mark visible on the backplate (there may well be on the front plate or in the barrels) there is no doubt that this is an English movement with fusees and chains. For comparison see the example in Figure 87. The quarter chimes are on four or eight bells depending upon chime chosen, with the strike on a gong.

£700 – £850
by virtue of excellence of quality and complications of mechanism

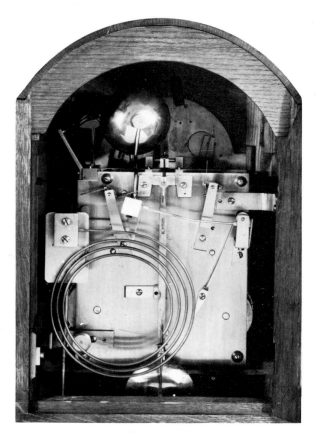

Figure 86b

Movement of clock shown in Figure 86a. Points to note are the general sturdiness of construction, nest of bells from back to front above the movement and coiled tape gong. The flat-topped knob at the bottom left-hand corner can be removed and reinserted in the threaded hole to the left of the pendulum rod — this is to hold the pendulum in place while the clock is in transit.

87a

Figures 87a and 87b

22½in. high. The case of this clock is extremely ornate and with its
ebonised wooden case and lacquered brass cast mounts and brass dial is
reminiscent of the design of much earlier bracket clocks. It is,
therefore, somewhat of a surprise to find that the movement is rather
puny for the size of the case and is actually of German manufacture, as
can be seen in Figure 87b. Striking is at the hour and half hour on a
single gong, and provision has been made for repeat at will. It has not
been possible to trace the maker's mark that can be clearly seen at the
bottom of the backplate. The value of this clock would lie in its
decorative quality rather than quality of movement.

£450 – £600

88

Figures 88 and 89

These illustrations show two clocks made by A. and H. Rowley of London, there having been a firm of this name since 1808. This name appears in many advertisements of clockmakers in the trade journals of the later half of the nineteenth century as well as among the list of exhibitors at the various Exhibitions. The International Inventors Exhibition of 1885 list A. & H. Rowley of 180 Grays Inn Road,

£500+

89

London, W.C., as having the following items on display:—

1. Large chiming clock with newly invented automatic figure work and perpetual calendar.
2. Clock with improved chiming on bells and gongs in newly designed Gothic oak case.
3. Lever clock, striking the ship's bells including the dog watch.
4. Parts of clocks showing the stages of manufacture.
5. Various chiming and other clocks with all the most modern improvements.

£400 – £450
the example in an oak case realising a lower price than
a similar clock in a mahogany or rosewood case.

Figure 90

This is an extremely attractive maplewood bracket clock of the mid-nineteenth century, striking on a gong. The silvered dial is signed 'Marsh – Maker to HRH the Duchess of Gloucester – Dover Street, Piccadilly.' It is also signed on the backplate.

Figures 91a and 91b

What appears to be a simple kitchen clock has, on closer inspection, several interesting features. The softwood case is veneered with mahogany and the painted zinc dial has the name of the retailer, 'Camerer Kuss & Co. 56 New Oxford Street', inscribed on it. This firm was established in 1788 when one of the present owner's descendants came from the Black Forest area of Germany in order to open a clockmaking and importing business in London. Initially they specialised in typical Black Forest clocks but soon expanded to include all types of timepieces. The only change made to the name of the firm is the substitution of the letter 'C' for that of 'K' in the name 'Cuss'.

This clock was an attempt to offer a reasonably priced but nevertheless better quality example than the average German and American kitchen clock of this date. Examination of the backplate (Figure 91b) reveals the initials 'W. & H. Sch.' These are significant and indicate that this movement was a product of the firm Winterhalter and Hoffmeir of Neudstadt in the Black Forest area of Germany. The plates are well made and the movement generally lacks the machine stamped-out appearance of most of the German and American mass produced movements of this period. This manufacturer has long been recognised as having produced some very fine quality clocks — longcase, bracket clocks, dial clocks — which rival those of many English makers of the late nineteenth and early twentieth centuries. In many instances it is only upon observing the letters 'W. & H. Sch.' stamped on the bottom of the backplate or movement that positive identification is possible. £30—£60 by virtue of manufacturer of the movement. If merely unidentified German make price would be about £10 less.

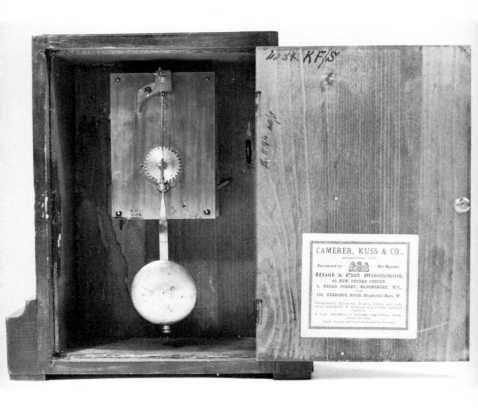

CAMERER, KUSS & CO.,
ESTABLISHED 1765.

Patronised by   Her Majesty.

Watch & Clock Manufacturers,
56, NEW OXFORD STREET,
3, BROAD STREET, BLOOMSBURY, W.C.
AND
186, UXBRIDGE ROAD, Shepherd's Bush, W.

Chronometer, Repeating, Duplex, Lever, and every
other description of Watches and Clocks carefully
repaired.
A large assortment of Chronometer and Carriage Clocks,
always on Sale.
Clocks cleaned and kept in Repair by the year.

91b

92a

Courtesy of Kingston Antiques

Figures 92a and 92b

This is a handsome rosewood bracket clock, with good quality brass caryatids, pineapple finials and feet. To all outward appearances a pleasant late nineteenth century or early twentieth century English clock. However, upon looking at the movement it is quickly realised

that it is German and actually manufactured by Winterhalter & Hoffmeir (W. & H. Sch. on the backplate). It would appear that the case is of English origin made to house an imported movement. A common occurrence at this time. Although not one of their best movements it is an extremely attractive and well made clock. Again a recognised German manufacturer of repute.

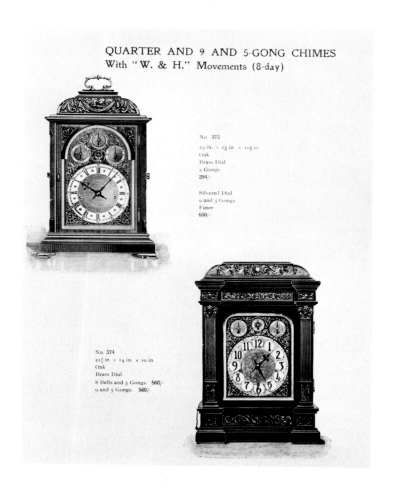

QUARTER AND 9 AND 5-GONG CHIMES
With "W. & H." Movements (8-day)

No. 375
23 in. × 15 in. × 10½ in.
Oak
Brass Dial
2 Gongs
294/-

Silvered Dial
9 and 5 Gongs
Fusee
600/-

No. 374
21½ in. × 14 in. × 10 in.
Oak
Brass Dial
8 Bells and 5 Gongs 560/-
9 and 5 Gongs 560/-

Courtesy of F.W. Elliott Ltd.

Figure 93

Two examples of clocks manufactured by Winterhalter and Hoffmeir of
Neudstadt, Germany and imported by Grimshaw, Baxter and J.J.
Elliott Ltd. sometime after 1909. At the prices shown here they must
have been a serious challenge to the English clockmakers. English clocks
of a similar nature were being offered in the same catalogue at
approximately twice the price.

Courtesy of Sotheby's Belgravia

Figure 94

19¾in. high. It is not uncommon to find lacquered cases to clocks manufactured in the 1920s — the oriental influence was, however, attributable to our association at this time with Japan and not China and showed itself in much of the furniture, and other designs of this period. This is a particularly handsome example with a silvered dial and striking the hours on a gong. Small decorative bells hang from the pagoda style top of the case. There are no identifying marks on the backplate of the movement and this clock could have come from a number of manufacturers including B.T. Greening Ltd., of Hatton Garden, London, E.C.1., who are known to have exhibited similar cased clocks at the Empire Exhibition at Wembley in 1924. This clock was sold by auction for £380.

95a

95b

Courtesy of Kingston Antiques

Figures 95a and 95b

A highly decorative and ornate three train bracket clock attributed to F.W. Elliott Ltd., with silvered dial and subsidiary dials. The chime is either the Westminster, Whittington or St. Michael on bells or gongs.

Figure 96

The point to note in this full-page advertisement of an 'English (London Made) Bracket Chiming Clock', that appeared in the Grimshaw Baxter and J.J. Elliott Ltd. catalogue sometime after 1909, is that it was offered with "Chiming on 8 and 4 Nickelled Tubes" as well as the more usual gongs or bells. Although it is stated that the case was some 30in. in height and 15in. wide the inclusion of tubes would have been no mean feat. It is a magnificent example, and it may well be that this clock was intended for the overseas market. India, in particular, was an ardent supporter of the English clockmaker at this date, and many makers offered to adapt the construction of cases and movements to withstand the warmer climate.

No. 35.—Finest Mahogany Case, with finely Chased and Gilt Brass Mountings well Lacquered, Fine Hand Pierced Dial, with Silvered Circles, Raised Gilt Bevelled Arabic Figures.

Height 30ins.   Width 15ins.   Without Bracket.

						£	s.	d.
8-day Fusee and Chain Movement, Chiming on 8 and 4 Nickelled Tubes				...	...	73	0	0
„	„	„	„	„ „ 8 Bells and 4 Gongs	...	66	0	0
„	„	„	„	„ „ 8 and 4 Gongs	... ...	69	0	0
„	„	„	„	„ „ 4 Gongs ...	... ...	63	0	0
„	„	„	„	„ „ 8 and 4 Bells ...	... ...	62	0	0

In each case the Hour is struck on a deep-toned Gong.

Engraved Silvered Dial, £2 0 0 less.   Bracket to match, £19 0 0

G. B. & J. J. E. Ltd.

Courtesy of F.W. Elliott Ltd.

97a

Figures 97a and 97b

The case of this clock is mahogany, quite unembellished but of pleasing proportions with small bun feet and silvered dial. Although no maker's marks are apparent, the words 'Made in England' together with a serial number do appear on the backplate. The movement is three train chiming the quarters and striking the hours on gongs. The mechanics of this can be readily seen in the back view. The quality is far superior both of case and movement to the example shown in the following illustration.

£90 – £150

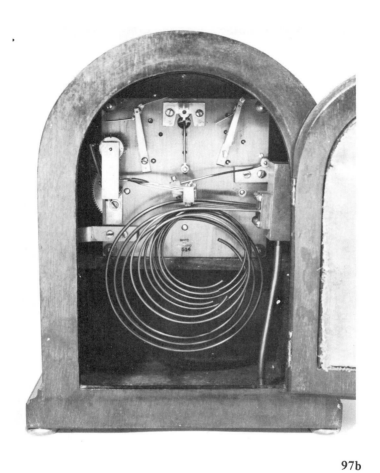

97b

98a

Figures 98a and 98b

The case of this example is oak veneered on soft wood, with added oak beading. The silver anodised dial has a small Chime/Silent lever to the right of the numeral three. As can be seen in the back view the foreign-made (?German) three train movement chimes the quarters and strikes the hours on rods mounted on the base of the case. As the demand grew in the 1930s for smaller cases the hammers were often slung from the base of the movement, instead of, as illustrated here, on the backplate.

£20+

98b

Figure 99a

This is an example of one of the clocks manufactured for the domestic market during the 1920s by the Horstmann Gear Co. Ltd. of Bath. This particular example, the 'Montmorency', in a mahogany inlaid case — had a fourteen day striking lever movement (as shown in Figure 99d). Other models would possibly have had the alternative pendulum movement shown in Figure 99c.

The history of this firm is not without interest and it is felt that any of their clocks would be extremely desirable examples of this era of English clockmaking. Gustav Horstmann, after serving an apprenticeship with Dejean, a pupil of Bréguet, came to England in 1853 and one year later established a clockmaking business in Bath, which continued as a retail establishment until 1925. Joined by his three sons, and aided by his inventive genius (he had some hundred patents to his credit) the firm prospered. After his death in 1893 the firm strayed a little from the field of horology and finally, in 1904, the Horstmann Gear Company Limited was launched to manufacture and market a car gear box. This did not prove to be a commercial success, but the youngest son designed and the firm produced the Horstmann car which continued to be manufactured until about 1930. The firm is known, however, the world over, for their screw gauges and time controllers used mainly in the gas industry. They are still one of the most important manufacturers and many a street light or domestic boiler has a timer made by this Company.

It is, however, the clocks manufactured by this Company in the 1920s that are of interest to the collector. Having decided to apply the same methods of production as they did to their timers, they started in January, 1921, to manufacture their pendulum movement. By the end of the year a striking version had been added, and by early 1923 a further model with a lever escapement was included. It would appear that, having made some 3,500 movements, production ceased around 1928 with the tooling and remaining parts sold to a London firm sometime during the Second World War.

From a contemporary catalogue it is possible to ascertain that they manufactured some thirty case designs for shelf clocks, one drop dial wall clock ('The Bungalow' Miniature Clock Dial with a pendulum movement) and one round dial wall clock. The case designs were typical solid Edwardian mahogany cases, oak pseudo-Jacobean and others more reminiscent of earlier bracket clock designs, including some with

162

99a

Courtesy of the Horstmann Gear Co. Ltd.

oriental lacquer cases. These were the most expensive and were sold to the trade at £5 18s. 4d. with strike or £4 13s. 4d. without. Additional features, again at trade prices were:—

Solid Bezel	5s.
Enamel Dial (standard one being silvered)	1s. 6d.
Ball Feet	1s. 6d.

Exceptional quality of case and movement as well as documentation of manufacturer would make the valuation of this clock £90+.

Figure 99b

Trade mark of Horstmann Gear Co. Ltd. of Bath.

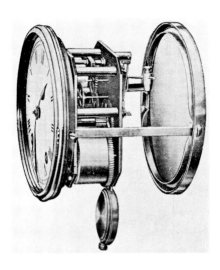

Figure 99c

This is an illustration of the pendulum movement manufactured by the Horstmann Gear Co. Ltd. under the tradename of 'Newbridge' between 1921 and 1928. The official specification states:—

"The movement is made to fit cases 4½in. aperture. Owing to precise production methods all parts are interchangeable, spares being sent by return.

DIALS. – Flat or raised zone, silvered, engraved with either Arabic or Roman figures. Enamelled dials fitted at slight extra cost.

PLATES. – Solid brass with pillars screwed at back.

WHEELS. – Machine cut of substantial thickness.

PINIONS. – Solid steel, cut, hardened and polished.

BARREL. – Cut wheel, polished brass tube, fitted to wheel with splines.

ESCAPEMENT RECOIL. – French type, eccentric adjustment, solid steel pallets.

SUSPENSION SPRING. – Permanently held in crutch.

PENDULUM. – Brass weighted bob, steel rod regulated by nut. Can be hooked on by amateur.

STRIKING MECHANISM. – Of the rack type, so that the hours always follow the hands, and can be repeated without disturbing the sequence. The hands can be turned back without disarranging the striking mechanism. This is invaluable for summer time. The hammer lifting is from a star wheel, instead of a pin, and the strike is on a deep-toned cathedral gong."

Courtesy of Horstmann Gear Co. Ltd.

Figure 99d

This is an illustration of a lever movement manufactured by the Horstmann Gear Co. Ltd. under the tradename of 'Newbridge' between 1923 and 1928. The official specification states that "this movement is similar to the pendulum model, but the pendulum is replaced by a Swiss straight line double roller lever escapement, having a non-magnetic compensating hair spring. The escapement is fitted with a shield to exclude dust. This model can be fitted in all cases". This particular example is a striking model, but the movement could be just a timepiece. The points to note are the distinctive lattice finish on the backplate and the trade mark, of which a larger example can be seen in Figure 99b.

Figures 100 and 101

Two examples of run of the mill pre-Second World War case designs. That in Figure 100 is intended to suggest a Jacobean style, and would fit in well with the catalogues of Jacobean furniture, c.1924, which were particularly popular at that point, although the decorative dial centre and hands do not make for easy time telling. The example in Figure 101 is more suggestive of the art deco theme and has a plain silvered (anodised) dial. Both have Chime/Silent levers on the outer edge of the dial. It has been suggested by one contemporary that the striking and chiming clocks proved to be a constant source of irritation to those wishing to listen on their wireless sets to the nine o'clock news. Evidently the event of the day in many households! The solution was either to set the clock fast or slow or purchase one with a Chime/Silent lever. These clocks have been very much under-estimated in recent years.

Figure 102

The majority of these 'Napoleon Hat' shaped clocks are oak veneered, although this is in good quality mahogany with a silvered (anodised) dial with Silent/Chime lever at the three o'clock position. Other quality features are the clever use of multi-wood veneers.

£40+, the quality of the case playing an important role

100

101

102

Pendel-Uhr.

Pendulum clock
Walnut brown

Echappement a balancier
Noyer brun.

Brittannia.

Height 18 inches	Hauteur 455 mm	
Scale ¹/₄	¹/₄ de la grandeur naturelle	
	1 Day	**30 heures**	**1 Tag**
Nr. 360 alarm,	a reveil,	Wecker.
Nr. 360/1 time	sans reveil,	Gehwerk.
Nr. 360/2 alarm	sonnerie	Wecker mit
& strike,	avec reveil,	Schlagwerk.

Figure 103

Two pages from the 1895 catalogue of August Schatz of Triberg,
Germany showing shelf clocks manufactured by them at this date.

Pendel-Uhr.

Pendulum clock
Walnut brown

Echappement à balancier
Noyer brun

Wellington.

Height 16½ inches
Scale ¼

Hauteur 415 mm
¼ de la grandeur naturelle

1 Day	**30 heures**	**1 Tag**
Nr. 361 alarm,	a reveil,	Wecker.
Nr. 361/1 time,	sans reveil,	Gehwerk.
Nr. 361/2 alarm & strike,	sonnerie avec réveil,	Wecker mit Schlagwerk.

Courtesy of August Schatz & Sohne

104a

Figures 104a and 104b

18in. high. This is an unusual German cuckoo clock — most examples are wall hanging with weights. Until the second half of the nineteenth century, few bracket cuckoo clocks were manufactured. The movements are either thirty- or fifty-hour with a going mainspring

104b

barrel, with some examples combined with a double fusee. As can be
seen from the back view the plates are wooden, the pendulum and
wheelwork brass and the circular round wire gong is fixed to the door
of the case and not the back of the movement. Similar clock with fusee
sold in 1977 for £450. Without this feature price would be in region of
£250–£350.

American Shelf Clocks

Although clocks of varying types and complexities had been manufactured in America for many decades, the tribute for initiating the manufacture of movements on a large industrial scale must go to Eli Terry (1772-1852) of Connecticut. With the aid of water power, machinery and standardisation of parts, he accomplished the apparently impossible task of producing some four thousand wood movements for grandfather clocks within four years. The next stride forward in this growing industry was the introduction by Chauncey Jerome (1793-1868) of a *cheap* brass movement. So successful was his method that he was forced to find new and larger markets for his wares. This combined with the fact that these movements could be transported long distances far more successfully than the older wood movements led him to consider England as a possibility. In 1842 he sent his son and Epaphroditus Peck to England with a shipment of wooden cased shelf or wall clocks similar to those seen in Figures 106 and 108. They were invoiced at a dollar and a half each with twenty per cent duty payable on arrival, and were intended to sell in England at twenty dollars each. The British Customs decided that the shipment had been deliberately undervalued and according to the then current law purchased them for the declared value plus ten per cent, thereby hoping to teach Jerome a lesson. He sent a further shipment which was treated in the same manner, but the Customs allowed the third cargo to pass through. Other American factories followed suit and for some time their clocks flooded our market. Until around 1850 these were nearly all weight-driven one- or eight-day movements, but some smaller and more compact types were also manufactured with brass springs. After this date steel springs proved more suitable and became cheaper to produce.

Although scorned by many collectors, there is a great deal of interest to be found in American clocks. Unfortunately we do not see many of the rare examples in this country, but only those imported for the cheaper end of the market. Once it is realised, however, that the attraction of these clocks lies in studying the production methods employed by the various manufacturers, as they devised ways of making them at economical prices, so the interest grows. They also have the added virtue of being of sufficiently sturdy construction to allow the amateur repairer a certain amount of scope he could not hope for in more delicate mechanisms. The immense variety of designs of these clocks and the large number of manufacturers appearing and disappearing in what was an extremely competitive business makes it impossible to cover the subject here. However, a few typical examples of American clocks manufactured after the mid-1800s appear in the illustrations here and in the following chapters. Examples are usually readily identifiable and a list of suitable reading material for anyone wishing to pursue the subject has been included in the bibliography.

Figure 105a

10in. high. This is an extremely stalwart-cased American movement and it can only be assumed that the movement was imported and cased here. Apart from the door the case is of solid oak, veneered with oak and with small gilt metal feet. The bezel is thin pressed brass, the dial painted zinc and the hands thin pressed metal with regulating arbor above Figure XII. The door has the original labels — the first stating that the clock was of American manufacture (by Waterbury Clock Co., Waterbury, Conn., U.S.A.) and that the model was called the 'Enfield'. The other label gives the Directions for Setting the Clock Running and Keeping it in Order, i.e.

"Remove the paper, or packing wire holding the Pendulum Rod and hang the Ball on the Rod. Be sure that the paper or packing wire is taken out of the Clock. The best should be equal and regular, and will be so if the Clock is set in a LEVEL position.

This Clock is fitted with our "No 30 A-2 MOVEMENT" — EIGHT DAY SPRING, STRIKING THE HOURS AND HALF-HOURS.

TO SET THE CLOCK, use the long or MINUTE hand only; NEVER TRY TO TURN the short or HOUR hand. The MINUTE hand can be turned in either direction without injury to the Clock.

The Clock can be made to strike to correspond with the position of the hands by carrying the minute hand forward to the figure. If then backwards to the figure VIII and back and forth between these figures until the right hour is struck.

THE CLOCK IS FITTED WITH OUR PATENT REGULATOR, whereby it can be regulated without touching the Pendulum by means of the small arbor just over the figure XII. If the Clock goes SLOW turn it to the RIGHT. If FAST turn to the LEFT.

If for any reason the Clock should not regulate satisfactorily from the front it can be regulated the same as any ordinary clock by raising or lowering the Pendulum ball itself. Raise the ball to make the Clock go faster, lower it to make it go slower.

The Clock should be wound REGULARLY once a week."

Intact labels would enhance the price. £50 — £60

Figure 105b

Movement of the Waterbury clock. The points to note are the Brocot-type suspension adjustment, open springs, thin wheels, round

105a

105b

wire gong (hours are struck on the gong and half hours on the bell), and fancy gilt lead bob. Also shown is the original double ended key to both wind the movement and adjust the suspension.

Figure 106a

15in. high. This is an example of a typical Gothic twin-steeple American shelf clock in a veneered softwood case with a fully glazed door. This example has decorative gold tracery on a black background but other examples are common with a tablet in the lower half of the door containing a scene, spray of flowers, bunch of fruit, etc. The dial is zinc painted white with black numerals.

£65+

Figure 106b

Movement of American clock shown in Figure 106a. The points to note are the shape and method of fixing the dial, alarm disc surrounding the centre arbor for the hands, the position of the alarm bell (screwed to the back of the case), the general mass produced appearance of the movement and the label pasted to the back of the case describing the clock as a 'Small Sharp Gothic One Day Timepiece' and stating that it was manufactured by Jerome & Co., New Haven, Connecticut, U.S.A. This was the trade name used by the New Haven Clock Company in the second half of the last century.

107a

107b

Figures 107a and 107b

15in. high. Further example of a small Gothic styled American clock in a veneered softwood case. This example, however, has a decorative tablet with a rural scene. The name on the dial is merely that of the retailer — the manufacturer being the Waterbury Clock Company of Connecticut, U.S.A. Details of the movement can be seen in Figure 107b. Painted tablet would add further £5 to basic price of clock of this type.

Figure 108a

18in. high. This is an example of another American thirty-hour alarm clock in a veneered softwood case manufactured by Jerome & Co. of New Haven, Connecticut. Again the decoration takes the form of gold tracery on a black background, but in this instance an aperture has been left through which can be seen the mock mercurial pendulum bob. This has been simulated by a piece of silver-coloured metal tube in place of what would, in a genuine mercurial pendulum, be a glass jar partly filled with mercury.

£60 – £90+

Figure 108b

View of the interior of the clock shown in Figure 108a. The points to note are the alarm bell that has been brightly gilded, the mock mercurial pendulum and the fact that, in place of the manufacturer's label, the interior is lined with black paper to set off the two features already mentioned. The small label on the back of the case describes the clock as 'One Day Foutenoy, Time Piece Alarm, Jerome & Co., New Haven, Connecticut, U.S.A.'

Figure 109

8in. high. Veneered softwood clock manufactured by Seth Thomas, Plymouth Hollow, Connecticut, U.S.A. with a small mirror in the lower third of the glazed door. Most American clocks have paper labels pasted in the back giving instructions for use and incidentally providing the name and address of the manufacturer. The latter can often assist in dating a clock. It is known that Plymouth Hollow was renamed Thomaston in 1866 and so this particular example must have been made prior to that date. This is a thirty-hour timepiece, but other examples have been seen with the additional feature of an alarm mechanism.

Early example £50+

Chapter VII
SMALL CLOCKS

The following brief selection of clocks have little in common apart from the fact that they are not Bracket Clocks or Shelf Clocks. Since 'Fancy' or 'Boudoir' are the words used to describe them in contemporary catalogues, possibly their manufacturers had the same difficulty over classifying them. It is felt that they all have some attractive characteristic to offer the collector. Apart from the Strut Clocks of Thomas Cole, only passing reference is made to them in modern literature, but they are all worthy of closer examination and are not quite so straightforward technically as external appearances would imply.

Figure 110

10in. high. This is a compact and attractive clock in a solid mahogany case which has been decoratively veneered, with added cast brass mounts. The white porcelain dial is marked to imitate a thirteen piece dial of French design. When enamelling was first introduced it was a technically difficult and expensive process and so each segment was painted and fired individually. Long after it was a necessity the custom continued as it was considered decorative. The name on the dial is that of the retailer 'Howell & James Limited, To the Queen, London'.

According to J.B. Hawkins in his book *Thomas Cole and Victorian Clockmaking* this firm was referred to in most Directories as 'Warehousemen'. He goes on to say that they were styled Howell & Co., from 1836 to 1840, after which they became Howell, James & Co. He makes no mention of Howell & James Limited. It had been hoped to be able to trace the years that the Company were suppliers to The Queen, but it has not been possible to ascertain that they actually ever held a Royal Warrant! It is known that they marketed the clocks manufactured by Thomas Cole until his death in 1864. The example here has 'Made in Paris' stamped on the movement and other examples of clocks imported from Germany have been seen bearing their name. It would appear that they were retailers of a wide variety of goods.

General elegance of case, together with good quality French movement would bring the price to between £250 and £275.

Figures 111a and 111b

6¾in. high. An Edwardian timepiece in a solid mahogany case with a little decorative inlay. The pillars and small bun feet are cast brass. The dial is of a high quality white enamel, with black Roman numerals and blued steel hands. The features to note in the view of the movement are:—

a) the cylinder escapement

b) the externally mounted barrel of an easily detachable type to facilitate simple repair

c) the Japy trade mark and 'Made in France' stamped on the backplate (Figure 111b). (Further details on this manufacturer can be found in Chapter I with regard to the manufacture of marble-cased clocks.)

Until recently these clocks had little commercial value but with the prevailing fashions in interior decorating they are slowly rising in price. There are many similar examples on the market and when contemplating a purchase only those of a high quality should be seriously considered, i.e. solid case, any decorative feature on the case which would have taken a little more labour or material at the time of manufacture and a French or English movement.

£60+

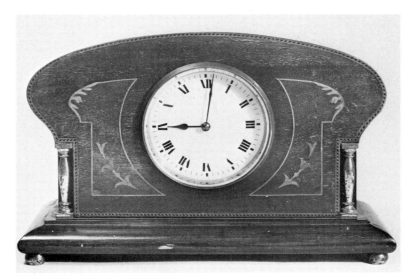

111a

111b

187

Figure 112

13in. The case and figure of the little Dutch girl are of a non-specified metal that has been left to acquire an imitation bronze patina. The pin pallet movement has an off-centre wind as described when discussing Figure 120b. There are no maker's marks but it is probably of German manufacture. Judging by the sentimentality of the design and the nationality of the figure it would be logical to assume a date in the late 1920s or early 1930s. Although of no great horological merit, it is a pleasing piece and worth acquiring as typical of the period.

£50

Figure 113

6¾in. high. The great advantage of any clock case with substantial silver mounts or decorative panels is that they carry a hallmark which provides a date for the clock. It is doubtful if these small clocks would qualify for a replacement movement having been substituted. This example is in a silver and tortoiseshell case (Birmingham 1912) and sold in 1977 for £120. Although an attractive timepiece the price would have been enhanced by the value of silver.

Figure 114

The clocks on the facing page are a selection of small clocks attributed to the London maker Thomas Cole (1800-1864). It is known that he supplied a number of the leading jewellers with finished clocks, but as was the custom it was the name of the retailer that appeared on the dial of these pieces as demonstrated by the example below. This has the name 'Tessier & Sons, London' appearing on the dial but the name 'Thos. Cole' on the backplate. The clocks constructed by Cole after 1855 usually carry the punchmark 'Thos. Cole'. He is best known for

Courtesy King and Chasemore

Courtesy of Keith Banham

his small thirty-hour oval or rectangular strut clocks which often include additional features like thermometers, calendars, etc. As most examples of his work are numbered (commencing c.1846 with number 500 and ending upon his death in 1864 at 1900) it is possible to gain some indication of the volume of his output. His life and work have been extensively documented by J.B. Hawkins in his book entitled *Thomas Cole and Victorian Clockmaking*.

Wide price range spanning several hundreds of pounds depending upon documentation of provenance and complications of movements.

Figure 115

It might be said that the clocks in the illustration were intended as the poor man's answer to that shown in Figure 193 in a fine Coalport case. Those shown here are from a page of a catalogue of Grimshaw, Baxter and J.J. Elliott some time after 1909 and the cases would have been the product of one of the continental factories that specialised at this time in cheap ware for exporting. These clocks vary in quality and amount of decoration and can be extremely attractive. The movements were thirty-hour pin pallets although some of the larger cases did have an eight-day movement. Many of the movements have not worn well and it has been noted that the original movement has frequently been replaced by a small mass produced modern Swiss movement obtainable from any clock and watch material dealer. So long as the purchaser is aware of the substitution it is possibly more beneficial to have a non-authentic working clock than a fully authentic non-working example! However, untampered with examples can still be found, with and without their side ornaments. It may be noted from the 1914 catalogue of the Ansonia Clock Company that they also offered similar clocks. Their models, however, include hour and half-hour striking on gongs, and/or visible Brocot escapements. It is possible that a few may have reached this country, but as they carry the Ansonia trade mark, as shown on page 211, they would be readily identifiable.

Movements: thirty-hour, £10; eight-day, £20. Complete with side ornaments, £10—£40.

Attractiveness of case plays a dominant role and general price would range from £10—£70.

CHINA CLOCKS.

LEVER MOVEMENTS. COLOURED DECORATIONS.

No. 219/1001 Green and Gold. Fancy Dial. Height of Clock, 9ins. Height of Candelabra, 7½ins. 1-day Lever Time ... 10/- the set of 3 pieces.

No. 1335/9615.—Light Green, Brown Edging, Coloured Flowers. Fancy Dial. Height of Clock, 6½ins. Height of Vases, 5½ins. 1-day Lever Time ... 9/- the set of 3 pieces.

No. 1335/9676.—White and Gold, with Colours. Fancy Dial. Height of Clock, 6½ins. Height of Vases, 6ins. 1-day Lever Time ... 10/- the set of 3 pieces.

No. 1533/5296.—Royal Blue and Gold. Fancy Dial. Height of Clock, 6½ins. Height of Vases, 6ins. 1-day Lever Time ... 14/- the set of 3 pieces.

G. B. & J. E. Ltd.

Figure 116a

8¾in. high and 6¾in. high. Superficially these two French timepieces appear to be similar; both have veneered drumhead cases, white card dials and Bréguet-style hands with spun brass press-on covers. Both movements are stamped with the initials 'V.A.P.' and 'Breveté S.G.D.G.' Many writers refer to 'V.A.P.' as being an abbreviation for Valogne à Paris — a maker known to have been working there after the mid-1800s. However, Tardy in his *Dictionnaire des Horlogers Français* says that 'V.A.P.' was the trade mark of Maison Pierret-Borel et Blin of Paris around 1900. In view of the fact that the movement with an alarm in Figure 116d (overleaf) and similarly marked is identical to that in *La Pendule Française,* also by Tardy, and attributed to Victor-Athanase Pierret (1806-1893), the latter assumption is more likely to be correct, the trade mark having been taken from Pierret's initials. He was an important maker of alarms and a further example of his work can be found in the skeleton clock illustrated in Figure 140. He came to Paris in 1800, and eventually opened a factory to manufacture clocks of his own design; he retired from active business in 1865 and sold a half-share to Borel but continued his researches until he died in 1893. The movements of these two clocks are, however, completely dissimilar, Figures 116b and 116c (see next page). The third example, Figure 116d (also overleaf), has the additional feature of an alarm mechanism. Although basically using the traditional drumhead case, the materials used vary and other examples have been seen in white alabaster, onyx or brass. The dials in the examples shown here are of card, but in some instances the dials were of white enamel. Although it does not carry the mark 'V.A.P.' the carriage clock in Figure 57 is most certainly a 'V.A.P.' type of movement.

Even though they are not of superb workmanship these movements are basically sound and have the virtue of offering some variations to the collector. It is doubtful if there is any difference in value between a basic pendulum type and a balance wheel example, but obviously a more decorative case or the additional feature of an alarm would increase the price accordingly.

£60 – £80 depending on quality of case
£15 additional feature of an alarm

116a

116b

195

Figure 116b

The movement of the larger of the two clocks shown in Figure 116a has a 'V.A.P.' movement but with a lever escapement. The escape wheel and lever are between the plates, but the balance is on a small separate platform on the back plate. The double ended key fits the winding arbor and the square for setting the hands.

Figure 116c

The movement of the smaller clock in Figure 116a has a deadbeat anchor escapement which was widely favoured in French drum clocks from the middle of the nineteenth century.

Although frequently referred to as 'tic tac' escapements this is not in this instance true. A 'tic tac' escapement has pallets embracing two teeth only and these movements most certainly do not conform to this definition. The solid spherical bob is screwed onto the pendulum rod which is in turn attached directly to the pallet arbor, i.e. no crutch. As the pendulum is self-setting this should on no account be firmly fixed but left just friction-tight. The original paper label with instructions for use adds to the intrinsic and academic interest. The annotations are those of the repairers.

Figure 116d

The movement in this black ebonised case of similar design to those shown in Figure 116a, is of standard 'V.A.P.' balance wheel pattern with the additional feature of an alarm mechanism. An identical movement is illustrated in *La Pendule Française,* by Tardy. As with many alarms of this period the pointer was set to indicate the number of hours you wished to elapse before being awakened and not set to point to the hour at which you wished it to ring. The small bell is set between the plates behind the balance wheel. The spun brass cover is pierced in order to allow the bell to sound freely but this has been covered by a piece of thin silk to prevent the intrusion of dust.

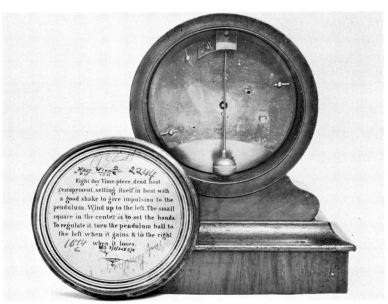

Eight day Time-piece, dead beat
escapement, setting itself in beat with
a good shake to give impulsion to the
pendulum. Wind up to the left. The small
square in the center is to set the hands.
To regulate it, turn the pendulum ball to
the left when it gains & to the right
when it loses.

116c

Eight day Timepiece detached lever,
wind up to the left, the small square in the centre is to set the hands.

116d

Figure 117

13in. high. The frame of this clock is a good quality, heavy brass casting, with an ivorine dial, recessed gilt-metal centre and delicate hands. The movement is, however, German having as it does the Junghans 8 star trade mark stamped on the backplate. The layout of the movement is identical to that shown in Figure 118b. As the unusual arrangement of spring and winding necessitated further labour and parts it must be assumed that it was carried out in order to infer that it was an eight-day movement and not a thirty-hour.

£35 – £40

118a

118b

Figures 118a and 118b

3½in. high. An identical clock to the example in this illustration appears in the 1913 catalogue of Gamages of Holborn, London, priced 3s.11d. The case is of nickel with a coating of copper, the dial of celluloid with Arabic numerals. Looking superficially at the back it could be assumed that the movement was an eight-day variety with concentric centre wind. It is, however, a thirty-hour movement with the spring positioned off-centre with gearing to enable it to be wound centrally, as can be seen in Figure 118b. Although not marked with any trade mark or manufacturer's name, the layout of the movement is identical to that in the cast brass frame shown in Figure 117.

£20

Figure 119

3½in. high. This clock is unusual in so far as it has a centre seconds hand. The cast iron base, supporting a gilt metal drum movement with a decorative finish, makes an attractive contrast. The dial is celluloid. The thirty-hour movement has off-centre wind (as is to be expected), but instead of a centre hand-set, this is off-centre concentrically with the winding arbor, yet another small but interesting variation in design.

Price of many of these small clocks varies according to knowledge of the vendor.

£25+

Figure 120a

7in. high. This clock gives the impression upon first being handled of having a heavy cast brass case; however, on closer inspection this is not true. The case is of spelter and has been filled with plaster prior to being gilded in order to add to its overall weight and to retain its shape. The little drum movement is held in place by the plaster only, as can be seen in Figure 120b. The celluloid dial has an attractive gilt-metal centre.

Appearance would attract a price of £20

Figure 120b

The movement of the clock in Figure 120a was never intended to be repaired, and it was only with care and tenacity that it was possible to remove the back cover without causing damage. However, to do so was rewarding as it was then possible to note that the movement which gives the appearance of having an eight-day movement with a spring across the entire width does, in fact, only have a thirty-hour spring that has been positioned off-centre with a concentric hand-set and wind.

Figure 121a

3½in. high. This small timepiece, in the form of a chariot pulled by a dog driven by a winged cherub, was manufactured by the Ansonia Clock Company of America. Originally founded in 1850 in Connecticut, they moved in 1879 to New York, where they had their second disastrous fire. A new factory was built in Brooklyn in 1881 and within two years they had expanded sufficiently to open sales offices in New York, Chicago and London. Around this date they started to produce large numbers of novelty and figurine clocks, as illustrated in Figure 177. By 1914 they were exporting to over twenty countries, but after the First World War they found that the demand for their products was declining. In 1929 they went into voluntary liquidation and production ceased. Most of their machinery together with some of the dies and patterns were sold to the Russian Government.

In this example of one of their clocks, the drum holding the movement is nickel, but the little dog and the cherub are gilt metal. The dial is celluloid and has the Ansonia trade mark as shown on page 211, together with the name of the Bournemouth retailer. The words 'The Ansonia Clock Co, New York, United States of America' appear on the lower perimeter of the dial. This address would indicate a date after 1879. The backplate carries the date of the patent covering the design of the movement (23rd April, 1878).

Novelty value £45+

Figure 121b

The movement of the timepiece shown in Figure 121a and manufactured by the Ansonia Clock Company of America. Note the spring across the entire width of the movement, but observe that, unlike the examples manufactured by the British United Clock Company, the arbor remains still while the spring barrel rotates. It is important not to wind these clocks in the wrong direction as this sheers the two small tabs completely off in some instances and, at best, irretrievably damages them (see Figure 121c). Provision was made for their replacement as can be seen by their presence in the clock and watch material dealers' catalogues of the day. These thirty-hour Ansonia movements come in a wide range of cases of varying qualities.

121a

121b

Figure 121c

This illustration shows in detail the inside of the back cover housing the spring. As this is rotated, the slots engage with the tabs on the movement (small detached tab shown beside the spring barrel).

Figure 122a

These three small clocks were manufactured by the British United Clock Company of Birmingham between 1885 and 1909. The largest example shown here has a good cast brass frame and is possibly an early example as the dial shows the patent number (Patent Number 13538) and not the name of the manufacturers. This patent was taken out in 1887 by Mr. Edward Davies, the Manager of the Company. The other two examples have similar movements. The case of the imitation carriage clock is of nickel and is of poor quality when compared to many of the other clocks produced by this Company. The method of retaining the glass in the metal frame was patented in 1891, which provides some indication of when production of this particular case design commenced. All three dials are of white card and carry the Company's trade mark. An enlarged view of this is shown in Figure 122d.

The history of the Company is not without interest as they played an important role in the history of the changes occuring in the manufacturing methods of English clockmakers during the closing years of the nineteenth century. The Company was formed in 1885 — Manager Edward Davies and Secretary John Fisher — with their factory first at York Terrace, Hockley Hill, Birmingham, and after 1891 at Leamington Road, Gravelly Hill, Erdington, Birmingham. They were one of the few manufacturers who realised that factory methods were here to stay and that the demand for cheaper clocks had to be met and not ignored in the pious hope that it would go away! The factory at Gravelly Hill was three-storeys high, covered 1,250 square yards and employed 250 hands, of whom 150 were girls. Everything, from their tools to the balance springs for the clocks, was made by them. Machinery was installed and the standardisation of parts was introduced — a selection of which can be seen in the pages of the Watch and Clock Materials Catalogue in the Appendix. Their products received awards in Adelaide (1887), Melbourne (1888), Sidney (1888) and, at the French International Exhibition of 1889, they received a Prize Medal and the following comment from their French competitors: "Good conception of calibre, sound workmanship in their tools, and excellent taste in the decoration — qualities which place them at once above their American rivals."

Unfortunately they did not survive. There are several possible reasons for this. Although they were sufficiently perceptive to recognise

that changes in production methods must come and had adapted accordingly, they failed to realise that quality must also be lowered if they were to compete successfully with the ever increasing flow of cheap clocks from Germany. They introduced other and larger movements and cases. "All kinds of plain and fancy lever clocks" appears in their advertisements and other comtemporary catalogues have been seen with English dial wall clocks carrying their trade mark. However, by 1909 they had succumbed and there is no further record of the Company. It is considered that any of their clocks would be of interest to the collector, but perhaps the most desirable are the small clocks housing the movement patented in 1887 (see Figures 122b and c) as these are the clocks most typical of the Company's aims and ambitions.

Price would increase with vendor's realisation of technical interest of these movements.

Carriage type, £20+   Round, £30   Large, £45+

Figure 122b

Side view of the movement manufactured by the British United Clock Company in direct competition with those manufactured by the Ansonia Clock Company of America, but of a much superior quality and to a better design. This can be seen by comparing this movement with that in Figure 121b. The British United design is superior in so far as the arbor rotates while the spring barrel remains fixed, whereas in the Ansonia design the arbor is fixed and the barrel rotates. However, as it rotates it twists askew and, as it does so, loses much of its power with friction against the sides of the case. A full view of the spring in the British United clock movement can be seen in Figure 122c.

Figure 122c

View of the back of the clock manufactured by the British United Clock Company showing the spring taking up the complete width of the barrel. Note the clumsy jobber's repair using a screw to fix the outer end of the spring in place of a barrel hook.

Figure 122d

Trade mark of the British United Clock Company.

122b

122c

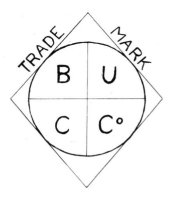

122d

Chapter VIII
ALARM CLOCKS

It is recorded that it was an American, one Levi Hutchins of Concord, New Hampshire, who, needing assistance in awakening early each morning, devised in 1787 the alarm clock. Interesting though this version is, it is more accurate to state that timepieces with alarm devices are one of the oldest forms of clocks and date from the fourteenth century. Man has always required more than his own biological clock and none more than the medieval monks with their need to have regular hours for prayer both day and night. Initially relying upon the manual ringing of bells, they eventually devised a simple clockwork mechanism which gradually over the centuries came to incorporate the telling of the hours and minutes as well as acting as a reminder of a pre-determined time. Inevitably their use spread outside the monastery walls and they became the 'toy' of the rich nobleman. It is rather amusing to consider how, during the centuries when the accuracy of clocks and watches was dubious, man preferred to depend upon these mechanical devices rather than his own acumen. Apparently gullibility for a novelty is not a recent human trait. Centuries passed and what had been an amusing possession became a necessity. The industrial revolution of the 1800s, and later the advent of the railroads, with the need for railway time, made punctuality vital to the working man. The old night-watchman and his cry needed to be replaced. This urgent demand had to be satisfied by the clocks that the workers could afford. Fortunately the technological advances that were forcing this social change were also capable of producing such a clock. The English clockmakers were extremely adverse to any of the mass-production methods introduced by their American and German competitors and so most of the examples available for illustrations are from these countries. This stubbornness to accept new ideas struck the death-knell for the English trade. Even when the First World War interrupted imports, the full implications were not realised. It is astounding that a country that had led the world horologically could voice the following comments in the columns of the leading trade journal of the day — the *Horological Journal* for November, 1918:—

"*Dearth of Alarm Clocks* Is an alarm clock a necessity or is it a luxury? Whatever may be the opinion of people who rely on this little piece of mechanism to recall them to another day's doings those in authority over us have decreed that the alarm clock is something we can do without. Only a few are coming in, from Japan. The result is that the alarm which before the war could be bought for 3s.6d. or 4s.6d. now sells at £1 or 25s. In the Woolwich area munition workers are unable to procure an alarm clock at any price and the jewellers are urging those who apply to make representation to their employers with the object of securing the importation of American clocks. If the clocks are not forthcoming from some quarter it is feared that there will be a good deal of time lost during the coming dark mornings. In some districts a 'caller-up' is employed — a system which works well where numerous workers living in a tenement require calling up at the same hour."

During the Second World War, through the serious problems caused by the lack of timing devices for munitions, the lesson was learnt. In 1945 under the guidance of Sir Stafford Cripps (then President of the Board of Trade) successful efforts were made to resuscitate the horological industry in this country.

The American manufacturers, with their well established production methods using machinery and standardisation of parts, naturally included clocks with alarms in their range. The reprints of many of the firms' catalogues that have been published in recent years provide invaluable sources of information. Some of the American companies are listed overleaf together with their dates and, in some instances, trade marks.

Ansonia

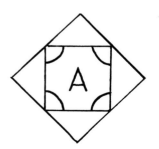

New Haven
U.S.A.

Seth Thomas

Ansonia Clock Company (1850-1929)
New Haven Clock Company (1853-1959)
Seth Thomas Clock Company (1853 to the present)
Waterbury Clock Company (1857-1944)
E. Ingraham Company (1857-1967)
William L. Gilbert Clock Company (1886-1964)
E.N. Welch Manufacturing Company (1864-1903)
Many of the wooden-cased shelf clocks made by these firms could, for extra cost, have an alarm included. Examples are shown in Figures 106b and 108b.

The following illustrations give some idea of the diversity of designs even in the small metal-cased drum alarm clock. The cases were nickel-finished, nickel-plated, oxidised copper with plain or hammered finish, brightly enamelled, plush (velour fabric finish), enamel and nickel with mother-of-pearl inlay, etc. Dials were either painted, white card or paper with inset dials for the seconds or alarm. The luminous dial appeared in America in the early 1880s. The Terry Clock Company of Pittsfield, Mass., claimed in their 1885 catalogue to be the exclusive manufacturers of 'Luminous Clocks' at that date (see Figure 124); patents for this process had been taken out in 1882 and 1883 respectively. The effect was achieved by mixing phosphorous with a small amount of radium. By the beginning of the 1900s several other manufacturers were advertising clocks with black card dials and luminous hands and numerals. The Ingersoll Company belonged to this latter group. This Company was founded in America in 1881 and in 1892 "startled the World with the 5s. pocket watch". In 1905 they opened a London office which eventually in 1930 became a separate entity under the name of Ingersoll Limited. Their factories are now at Ystradglnlais in Wales. The Second World War brought many problems and they were one of the firms taking advantage of the Government's post war offers of financial assistance to the horological industry. Mr.

E.S. Daniells, the Chairman of the London office, originated the luminous watch dial immediately prior to the First World War, and it was but a logical step to use the process on the dials of alarm clocks when these were introduced to their range of products in 1918. The process (a mixture of radium and bromide) was given the name of 'Radiolite' and its use was continued for many years. An example of an Ingersoll alarm clock is shown in Figure 126.

The majority of the movements used would have been thirty-hour, with wire or lantern pinions. The exceptions tended to be movements housed in larger wooden cases that were intended as dual purpose clocks: decorative by day and utilitarian by night. These usually had an eight-day movement with the alarm train needing to be wound each night. Expressive and amusing names were used to indicate the character of the ring of the alarm — 'Bugaboo', 'Rattler', 'Drone', and 'Wasp' all appeared in the Waterbury Clock Company catalogue for 1908. Most firms offered three alternatives — an intermittent ring (the New Haven Clock Company in their catalogue of 1906 claims to have marketed the 'Tattoo Alarm' the 'Original Intermittent Alarm Clock'), a long continuous ring or a shorter standard ring. The bell or bells were fitted externally, and some manufacturers used the casing as the resonator.

Although commencing factory methods at a later date than the Americans, the clock manufacturing area of the Black Forest in Germany made strenuous and highly successful efforts to compete. The making of clocks in this region had always been a cottage industry; the local populace making wooden weight-driven movements and cases when they could not find work on the land. The clocks were decorative, reliable and cheap and England had been a major importer. However, this market was temporarily lost to the Americans. In 1842 Chauncey Jerome sent his first consignment of factory-made clocks to England. The Germans could not compete at this period from the point of view of price or quantity. Eventually in 1861 Erhard Junghans of Schramberg decided to concentrate upon the clockmaking side of his business — the other being the manufacture of straw hats, etc. Together with his brother-in-law he formed a small company for manufacturing clocks by factory methods in place of the old unorganised methods.

Naturally there was a certain degree of local resentment at first but the venture prospered, and after his death his widow and sons carried on with the business. Various members of the family from both generations visited or worked in America primarily to observe first hand the 'American-style' and they both advised and arranged for the shipment of up-to-date equipment and machinery. As they so closely followed the methods and designs of the Americans, it is frequently only possible to ascertain a clock's origin by the trade mark it carries. The trade mark of the Junghans' Company is particularly helpful in so far as it changed several times through the years and it has been possible to ascertain the dates of these changes. It usually appears on the dial or stamped on the movement.

The first Junghans' trade mark in 1877 was an eagle with outspread wings poised on a furled flag. Between 1882 and 1888 this was changed to a star with two eagles and a flag.

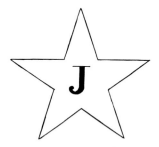

Trade mark after 1888

Left and right: trade marks after 1890.

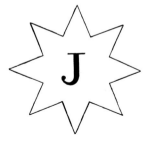

Another German firm — the Hamburg American Clock Company — formed in 1874 by Paul Landenberger and Philip Lang initially under the combined surnames, produced a similar range of clocks. These two men had worked with Junghans' widow but had decided to set up in business on their own after finding that she rigorously adhered to her husband's maxim that no outsider could participate financially in the company. They became worthy competitors of Junghans, but finally, after a few years of collaboration, merged with them in 1930. Their trade mark was a pair of crossed arrows. The American hold on the European market waned in the 1930s and the vast majority of alarm clocks imported into this country came from Germany.

Hamburg American Clock Company
trade mark

Although the French did mass produce an alarm movement and included a plain metal drum case in their range (as can be seen from the advertisement shown in Figure 135a), these were not imported into this country in such vast quantities as those from Germany. Many of their earlier examples are of particular interest in so far as they have an unusual escapement with a short pendulum and spherical bob. A similar escapement was frequently used with a silk suspension on other early French clocks. Commonly referred to as a 'tic-tac', the features of this escapement are:—

1. Anchor escapement with the pallets encompassing two teeth only

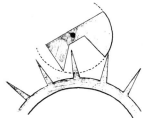

2. Impulse received on alternate swings of the pendulum
3. Pendulum fixed to the pallet arbor without any suspension spring or crutch
4. Short 'busy' pendulum usually with a spherical bob

Some of the movements that at first sight appear to have tic-tac escapements (they comply with points 3 and 4 above) actually have the pallets encompassing more than two teeth (e.g. 7) and so should more accurately be described as 'anchor' escapement. The tic-tac was not a particularly effective or robust escapement and one finds references to it in 1889 as "the defective tictac" and again in 1914 "a very unsatisfactory kind of clock, fortunately no longer made and passing rapidly out of use". Some interesting variations of case designs for these movements are shown in Figures 136a, 137, 139a.

One alarm clock that was unique to France is the clock shown in Figure 140. Hardly credible but nevertheless true is the fact that, during the Great Exhibition of 1851, it is claimed that 10,000 miniature French skeleton alarm clocks manufactured by Victor Athenase Pierret of Paris were sold.

During the 1880s and 1890s, spurred on by the wish to appear *au fait* with the then modern technical advancements, some manufacturers contrived to introduce the use of electrical power into their clocks. Many patents were taken out for clocks that adhered to the traditional clockwork mechansim for the going train, but devised systems by which the bell was rung by electricity. The source of the current being first wet and later dry battery cells. This made a rather cumbersome object as can be seen by looking at the example in Figure 142. It would appear that few examples reached the production stage or proved to have any long term appeal. Magazines of the day such as *Work* abounded with advice as to how the home handyman could convert his ordinary timepiece into an alarm clock, with the addition of an electric bell!

The only common factor between the clocks described in this section of the book is that each incorporates an alarm mechanism of some type. It is a novel theme and could be extended to include oven timers and automatic tea-making machines. This does mean therefore that it is impossible to give any general advice regarding points to be wary about or details of minor repairs. The same general principles apply here as do whenever contemplating a purchase:—

a) Does the clock work?
b) Does the alarm mechanism still function adequately?
c) Is it undamaged? It is useful to have a mental check list of points to notice, i.e. edges of veneer on cases, delicate scrolls, etc., to ensure that the most extreme parts have not been knocked. Also whether feet, winding knobs, keys, etc., are present. These small points are easily overlooked in the excitement of a purchase.
d) Using the same method ask yourself if it 'looks right'. Evaluate whether any parts have been replaced by incorrect substitutes, i.e. odd hands.

If the clock is extremely rare or the chances of finding an undamaged example are negligible, it is feasible to contemplate purchasing an example with a few minor defects. However, if the clock being offered is in the cheaper range it needs to be virtually perfect to qualify as a collector's piece.

Figure 123

6¼in. high. A simple pin pallet movement housed in an unpretentious wooden case. The case is soft wood veneered in stained oak. The dial is paper — a fact to be borne in mind when cleaning the movement so as not to discolour it with cleaning fluids. The merit of this clock lies in its place in the evolution of dual-purpose alarm clocks. The intention being that it was presentable on the kitchen shelf by day but could be of utilitarian use at night — an asset for those who could only afford one clock in the house. This is an early type (bells mounted externally) with a cottage-industry type case. There are no identifying maker's marks on the movement. Valued as collector's piece as example of early alarm. No horological merit.

£15 − £20

Figure 124

This illustration is taken from the 1885 Illustrated Catalogue of Clocks manufactured by the Terry Clock Company of Pittsfield, Massachusetts. At this date the Terry Clock Company (under the management of the grandsons of Eli Terry) claimed to be the sole manufacturer of luminous clocks (? in America):— "If placed near the bedside at night, the time can be readily seen in the darkest night, without the aid of artificial light". Although not essential for the dials to be left in bright sunlight during the day it was necessary for them to be exposed to light for a certain length of time in order to "maintain the phosphorescent light". As stated by Chris Bailey in the historical section of his book, it is as well to remember that the phosphorescent properties of these clocks will have deteriorated with time and their dials will no longer be luminous. The two patent dates given on the dials are interesting. That of 1882 taken out by the executrix of William H. Balmain of Eversley, Ventnor, Isle of Wight, England, was for a self-luminous paint. It would appear that the first application for this patent had been filed in England in 1877, with others following in Italy, Spain, Austria in the ensuing years. The second date 1883 refers to the patent for "rendering paper uniformly luminous on its surface" that had been taken out by William Trotter, Jr. of Oyster Bay, New York, USA. Apparently there had been some technical difficulties in avoiding uneven patches of the luminous paint when applying it to the paper and card dials.

£15+ on the English market

METEOR ALARM.

ONE DAY TIME ALARM.   LUMINOUS DIAL.

THEY SHINE ALL NIGHT.

TIME VISIBLE IN THE DARK.

ONE-HALF SIZE.   4 INCH DIAL.

ONE DAY . LEVER . TIME . ALARM. $3.15.

This Clock is made in Hammered Metal, and is called Meteor Alarm Embossed Gilt. $3.15.

For illustration of finish see page 26.   Nickel finish 15 cents extra.

6

Figure 125a

12in. high. It is relatively rare to find a wall-hanging alarm clock, and this is rather a handsome example in a solid wood case, that is hinged to a backboard upon which are mounted the two alarm bells. The bezel is sturdy and the glass bevelled — both indications of quality. The dial is of paper with an inset alarm dial. Paper and card dials were used extensively even in some comparatively high quality clocks. As cost of production was of prime importance, it is possible that this was an influencing factor. The crossed arrows on the dial indicate that the clock was manufactured by the Hamburg American Clock Company of Germany (1874-c.1930). The retailer's label is intact and is shown in Figure 125b. Both label and ability to trace the vendor enhance the price of this clock. As this has some visual appeal, expected price would be £35+.

Figure 125b

Retailer's label inside the alarm clock in Figure 125a. It gives both his name (W.E. Watts of Nottingham) and instructions regarding care of the clock. It has been possible to trace the dates this man was in business (1874-1920).

125b

125c

Figure 125c

Interior view of 'Thunder Alarm' shown in Figure 125a. Note the thin stamped brass strip backplate, lack of cover to the spring, serviceable wheelwork, etc., all typical of a functional mass produced movement of this era.

Figure 126

7in. high. A later dual-purpose alarm clock identifiable as having been made by the Ingersoll Company. This company had been founded in America in 1881, but the London office became a separate entity in 1930. They had introduced alarm clocks to their extensive range of watches in 1918. 'Radiolite' was the registered trade mark of the clocks and watches luminised "with genuine Radium-Bromide which is a Radio-Active Self-Luminous Compound". The case had been made in England and is more aesthetically designed and better made than the previous example. The base is of solid oak, and access to the clock is through a hinged flap at the back. The robust nickel-cased alarm clock was made in Italy by Fratelli Borletti of Milan for the Company. This would have been an intermediate design as later examples in the 1940s appeared again with the movement as an integral part of the case – usually a Bakelite case of pleasing design and as an indication of the changing social face advertised as "should meet with grand public response, particularly from people living in small flats or combined rooms".

As this clock is not highly attractive, its value lies in its relative rarity (as few would have been treasured and stored to the present day) and its role in the evolution of alarm clocks. Price is virtually dependent upon how much the particular example is wanted by the potential purchaser.

£20+

Figure 127

3½in. and 2½in. high. These are two small German alarm clocks. That on the left is in a copper on brass case, with a white enamel dial and spade hands. The back of the case has knobs for winding and setting the hands or alarm, with a silent/alarm lever. The crossed arrow mark stamped on the movement indicates that it was made by the Hamburg American Clock Company of Germany (1874-c.1930). Upon comparing this with the example shown in Figure 125a, also from their factory, the full range of their products is recognised. A small neat movement in a better than usual quality case and dial, so this clock would be worth a few pounds more than the usual drum alarm.

The even smaller clock on the right is also German but, although it is known that it came from Wurtenburg, there is no indication as to the name of the manufacturer. The case is oxidised metal, and the dial again of enamel, with luminous hands and numerals. The pointer for the alarm is blued steel. The alarm shuts off by lowering the carrying handle. The most interesting feature of this clock is that it is wound by winding both clockwise and anti-clockwise. This is made possible by an opposing ratchet mechanism on both time and alarm barrels — the movement being in two tiers rather than in the usual side by side arrangement. This immediately makes it a collector's item and also illustrates why it is necessary to examine closely an article before dismissing it as being of a standard range.

£30+

Figure 128

11½in. high. A nicely produced, oval wooden base, with elegant mouldings and surround, make this a desirable and unusual alarm clock. The white card dial with inset seconds and alarm dial also has the Junghans eight point star with a capital 'J' trade mark denoting a date after 1900. The 3½in. diameter alarm bell is mounted under the movement on the wooden base and has an internal hammer. After this date it became more usual to use the case of the clock as a bell and eventually to house the bell inside the case.

£30+

Figure 129

15½in. high. Veneered softwood case with decorative beading and turned finials. Full glass door to front. White painted dial with skeletonised centre to show alarm setting dial. The decorative pendulum is a cheap imitation of the two jar mercurial pendulum often found on expensive clocks. The effect in this instance being achieved by two cylinders of polished steel. The movement is typical thirty-hour with striking of alarm on a bell mounted on the backboard of the case. Although very similar to many manufactured by the various American factories of this period, this was made by the Junghans factory in Schramberg, Germany. Evidence of this is found in the trade mark below the figure 12 of a five-pointed star with a capital 'J' in the centre. This dates the clock as prior to 1890. This particular clock was sold by T. Coombes, Watchmaker and Jeweller of 117 Walworth Road and 109 Westminster Bridge Road, London. According to Directories he was at these addresses after 1880. A nice piece of collaborating evidence. It is details like this that, when traced and recorded, can add the odd pound or two to the value of each item. In good condition and in working order this would fetch upwards of £70+.

Figure 130a

7¾in. high. This thirty-hour drum alarm, in a brass case, is supported by two side pillars which also act as standards for the two highly polished steel bells, firmly mounted on a wooden kidney shaped base. The decorative chapter ring is celluloid, with inset gilt metal centre — a similar style to those found on French movements. The bells are struck alternately with an external hammer. The Junghans' trade mark appears stamped on the movement as can be seen in Figure 130b, and indicates a date of manufacture after 1890. It is noted that a similar clock appears in the catalogue of the American Company of William L. Gilbert dated 1901-1902. It is referred to as the 'Dewey Long Alarm', and although the external appearance (apart from finish on bezel and dial decoration) is identical, it would appear that the American clock was of a higher quality finish, with a more solid construction, an ivory porcelain dial and a movement with a seconds hand. No great quality involved but unusual appearance has appeal.

£35+

Figure 130b

Interior view of the drum alarm illustrated in Figure 130a. This particular movement was introduced in 1875 and continued to be used unchanged for fifty years.

Figures 131a, 131b and 131c

6½in. high. The style of this clock case — thin brass front, nickel-finished sides with glass panels — must have been extremely popular as at least two American and two German manufacturers used it for their movements. In 1879 Seth Thomas and Junghans used it to house either a musical alarm or strike movement, while the New Haven Clock Company model had either an ordinary alarm or strike movement. A catalogue of Adolph Scott of Birmingham, which appears to have been published c.1910, had the following offer which refers to these clocks as carriage clocks:—

	BBC and other Makers	HAC Guaranteed Goods
1-day Time	5/4	6/4
1-day Alarm	6/8	7/-
1-day Strike	7/8	8/-
1-day Musical — 1 air Alarm	10/-	11/6
1-day Musical — 1 air Strike	10/6	13/-
1-day Musical — 2 air Alarm	11/-	13/-
1-day Musical — 2 air Strike	11/6	14/-

HAC refers to the Hamburg American Clock Company, but it is not certain who the other makers were.

The example illustrated here has a gilt front, nickel finish to the rest of the case and glass panels at the sides. The dial is of card with seconds and alarm dials. Although 'cheap and nasty' as regards finish of the case and movement these clocks are eagerly sought after and the present prices would be in excess of thirty times the original cost.

The movement (Figure 131b) is thirty-hour with the musical barrel and comb housed in the base as shown in Figure 131c. With a clock such as this, it is sensible to hear the music played through to determine whether it has one or two tunes and also in order to detect any broken or missing pins on the barrel or teeth on the comb. It is doubtful what repairs could be carried out as the original was so poorly made.

£60+ depending upon musical variations

131a

131b

131c

229

Figure 132

8in. high. This is an intriguing clock with some curious features. The dial is of exceptional quality — ivory porcelain with a recessed centre and inset seconds and alarm dials — similar to those found on French movements in marble, four-glass cases, etc. The case is of lacquered brass with simulated jewels embossed around the bezel. Each boss is 'faceted' and painted red. There are no maker's marks either on the dial or stamped on the movement. The movement, although perfectly adequate, is not of the high standard of the dial and could have come from either a German or American factory. Reference has been seen in some American catalogues to models having a jewelled bezel for an extra charge. Rather splendid to wake up to this of a morning!

£30+

Figure 133

5½in. and 3¾in. high. Two nickel-cased pin pallet alarm movements made by the Western Clock Company Limited of Peterborough, Canada. This Company was founded in 1885 under the name of United Clock Company in Illinois, USA. Unfortunately they were bankrupt within two years, but under new management recommenced business in 1895 as the Western Clock Manufacturing Company and by 1903 claimed to be making one million alarm clocks a year. They became the Western Clock Company prior to 1925 and in 1936 were again renamed, but this time adopting their trade mark 'Westclox'. This had been their formal trade mark since 1909. The name 'Big Ben' first appeared in 1910 and was retained as each new model appeared and so knowledge of the changes of name of the Company and appropriate dates are invaluable when dating these particular clocks. 'Baby Ben' is particularly neat and has been recognised as a collector's item for many years in America. They are not often seen on the market and this will be reflected in the purchasing price.

£15+

134a

134b

Figures 134a and 134b

This American table alarm clock was made by the Parker Clock Company, Meriden, Connecticut, USA. The Company is known to have been trading since 1890. The drum of the clock movement and base are made of brass. The bell is steel. The alarm is operated by an independent mechanism in the base (see Figure 134b). Alarms made by this Company tend to use the same clock movement but vary the style of base, number of bells, etc., to provide a variety of styles.

£30+

135b

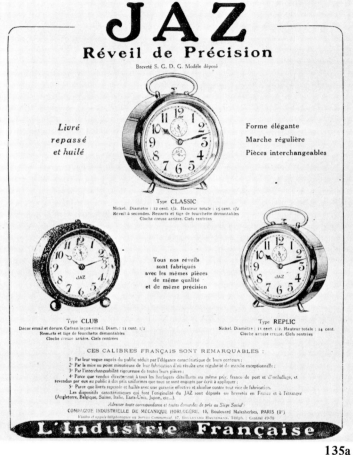

135a

Figures 135a and 135b

This advertisement for alarm clocks manufactured in France by Compagnie Industrielle de Mécanique Horlogère appeared in magazines, journals, etc. around 1924. 'Jaz' the trade mark of this company was registered in 1919 and continued to be used until 1941 when a parrot (as in Figure 135b) was introduced.

Figure 136a

The value of this timepiece is greatly enhanced by the fact that the movement is housed in a well finished bronze figure holding a bell and torch. The dial is stamped on his ample stomach, with two spade hands and a pointer for setting the alarm mechanism. Winding and hand setting are through the cloak at the back. The cloak is removable (two small screws hold it in place) to allow access to the movement. When the predetermined hour is reached the whole arm holding the bell swings thus ringing the bell that is suspended from the hand. £350+ as a decorative piece, without additional merit of telling the time and sounding an alarm.

Figure 136b

Rear view of Figure 136a with cloak removed. This is a typical French tic-tac escapement of the late 1800s of simple construction, a single barrel arbor producing the necessary power for both the alarm and time mechanism. There are no identifying maker's marks.

Figure 137

2½in. high. Small French travelling alarm clock in a brass case, with a white enamel dial, black Roman numerals, steel trefoil hands and a pointer for the alarm.

This clock is not to be confused with 'the Alarm Clock with two Springs' patented by T. Maurel of Paris in 1868. This example has the alarm and time off a single barrel. It is possible as the style of hands and dial are so similar to the model by Maurel that this was a later copy. There are no maker's marks. Although collectable and an interesting example this clock would not fetch as much as one by T. Maurel.

£30+

Figure 138

View of back of movement of the small French travelling alarm shown in Figure 137. It has a tic-tac escapement (anchor encompassing two teeth), together with a short pendulum and spherical bob.

Figure 139a

2½in. high. Rare small lacquered-brass case French alarm with stamped Arabic numerals and small centre pointer for setting the alarm. There is neither bell nor gong as the alarm hammer strikes the casing. This is purely a timing device as it is necessary to set it not at the hour one wishes to be awakened, but at the total number of hours between the time of setting and the time of awakening, e.g. at 10.0 p.m. the alarm is set to ring at 7.0 a.m. the next morning by moving the pointer to the numeral 9, as there are nine hours between 10.0 p.m. and 7.0 a.m. The movement is wound by turning the whole of the back cover anti-clockwise.

£60 – £70

Figure 139b

The movement has a tic-tac escapement (anchor encompassing two teeth) and an extremely unusual pendulum. One other known example has a similar escapement, but with a conventional spherical bob placed between the back and front plates. This second example had a partially legible label reading 'Maison Brevete a Paris, La rue Vivienne, horologerie boites à musique, reveils.'

Figure 139c

It has not been possible to trace the trade mark of a cockerel and letters A R, but it is likely to be that of Antoine Redier (1817-1897) a prolific maker of alarms for the English market. It is interesting to comment that Japy Frères also used a cockerel as one of their marks, but of a different configuration. Figure 139c shows the cockerel trade mark inside the alarm in Figure 139a.

139a

139b

139c

239

Figure 140

The small French alarm clock shown in this illustration has many interesting and desirable features. They were introduced into this country at the Great Exhibition in 1851 by their maker Victor-Athanase Pierret (see pages 194 and 216 for further references to this maker). It is stated in the Jurors' Report that, "The Jury, however, agreed to mention some small alarum clocks by M. Pierret, of Paris, on account of their cheapness, and because alarums really are, for certain purposes, useful articles of household furniture." A rather grudging award when noting the fact that some 10,000 were sold during the Exhibition! Their price at this date was 25s. Many of them carry the oval stamp on their base plate advertising the fact that their maker had received an Honourable Mention, but it is not clear whether this was after the Great Exhibition or after the Paris Universal Exhibition of 1855 when he received a further Honourable Mention. This mark has frequently been mistaken for the name of the maker, M. Honourable! This example has the name 'R. Holt et Cie — A Paris' appearing on the frame and dial, and would be the name of the retailer or importer — it was common practice to imply French connections and this would indicate that the clock had been made in Paris.

The frames of this example are plain, but others have been seen with decorative engraving. The ebonised wooden base has brass stringing. The points to note are:—

a) The alarm bell (a true bell shape and not the usual hemi-sphere), is housed in the base and is wound by pulling the small cord just visible on the right hand side of the base.

b) The alarm is set either manually by removing the dome or by pulling the cord on the left that protrudes through the small hole in the side of the base. This pulls the ratchet toothed alarm disc round via a pawl, tooth by tooth.

c) The tail of the hour hand acts as an index against the alarm disc to indicate the time of ringing.

d) The dial is porcelain, through the centre of which can be seen the alarm disc and motion work.

e) The ratchet wheel above the numeral twelve regulates a rise and fall mechanism for adjusting the length of the pendulum and thereby regulating the clock.

f) It is just possible to discern the silk suspension — a method much favoured by early French makers. It is often troublesome as temperature and other atmospheric changes readily affect it.

Figure 141

1½in. high, 3⅛ diameter. The alarm mechanism shown in this illustration was patented in 1823 by William Gossage (1799-1877), an eminent industrial chemist. According to J. Fenwick Allen in his book *Some Founders of the Chemical Industry*, Gossage, wishing to begin his studies at an exceptionally early hour, invented this device in order to ensure that his tutor was also awake! It was produced commercially with this particular example bearing the serial number '266', although it must be remembered that few manufacturers commenced numbering at '1' in order to make their output appear larger. This example has an outer protective box of japanned tin — black on the outside and red within. The alarm mechanism itself is housed in a silver plated case with pierced sides. This is on the left and viewed immediately from above in order to see the large bell that entirely fills the bottom half of the case. The top view shows the top plate under which is the movement. This drops into the lower half of the case and is secured by small pins at the side. This top plate is also of silver plate and carries a small plaque bearing the words 'W. Gossage — Patent' and the Royal Coat of Arms. The small dial visible through the crescent-shaped aperture is enamel on copper. The right hand view shows the instructions pasted to the bottom of the outer protective case. Before reading them it is necessary to understand that this is not an alarm clock, but an alarm mechanism for attaching to a watch. This was by no means a completely new idea as further examples of similar devices can be found. Clocks were still a comparative luxury whereas many men carried a watch.

"Instructions for Setting Gossage's Patent Alarm. First determine the number of hours between the time of setting and that of going off. (Thus, if it is set at 10 and is to go off at 4, the number would be 6.) Bring this number on the dial to the index point. Wind up the Alarum by the square in the middle then attach the Watch to it by inserting the projection pipe into the wind-up part of the Watch. If, in doing this, the number should be moved from the index, it may be brought back by turning the Watch, either to the right or the left.

N.B. The Alarums are furnished with Moveable Pipes of different sizes, so as to fit any Watch. In selecting a Pipe for the Watch, care should be taken that it is of sufficient size to let the Watch rest on the top of the Alarum.

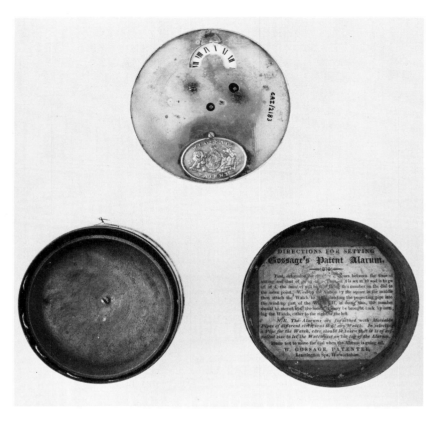

Please not to move the dial when the Alarum is going off

W. GOSSAGE PATENTEE

Leamington Spa, Warwickshire"

Further details of another example can be found in an article 'Gossage's Patent Alarm' by Cedric Jagger that appeared in *Antiquarian Horology* for December, 1959. Needless to say these alarms are choice collectors' pieces and have of recent years passed through the salesrooms for £200—£400.

Figure 142

The patent for this clock was taken out by M. and S. Turton of Tiplow in 1888 but the patent rights were purchased from them by Fattorini & Sons of Bradford (not to be confused with Thomas Fattorini (Skipton) Ltd.). For further details of the Fattorinis see text accompanying Figure 143. According to the account of this clock in the *Horological Journal* for December, 1888, it was not solely intended for use as a morning alarm. A handle at the back of the clock could be used to ring it at will — "a merchant can signal for one or all of his clerks, a teacher for his classes, or dismiss his pupils", etc. There was a double bell — one housed on the side of the box housing the electric battery and also the mechanical alarm which was within the casing of the clock. This was one of if not the first electric alarm clock.

Figures 143a, 143b, 143c

11½in. high. This alarm clock is a magnificent example and, by the volume of noise achieved by it ringing both on bell and gong, speculation is aroused as to whether it was intended to awaken the living or the dead! The case is of walnut, with a cream celluloid dial (this needs close examination to detect that it was not ivory coloured porcelain), brass bushes to the winding holes and a recessed gilt metal centre with alarm disc. As indicated by the details on the label found pasted to the base of the case (Figure 143c), this particular model was marketed by Thomas Fattorini of Skipton, Yorkshire although a similar clock was sold by Fattorini & Sons of Bradford, Yorkshire. The two firms had a common ancestry springing from a watchmaker/jeweller, Antonio Fattorini, who settled in England after the Battle of Waterloo (1815).

Two separate business houses emerged — one in 1827 and the other 1831 — which to this day operate completely independently of the other: Thomas Fattorini (Skipton) Ltd., and Fattorini & Sons of Bradford. The latter among their other achievements designed and manufactured the Trophy Cup for the Football Association.

The patent for the clock illustrated in these photographs was taken out in 1901 by Joseph Arrigoni, a cousin of Thomas Fattorini. He was the retail shop manager at the Caroline Square premises and was also a qualified optician. The patent mentions an eight-day movement, but later a fourteen-day movement was introduced. This was offered to the public for 25s. or "Send 5/- Today ... pay the balance by 4 subscriptions of 5/6d per month".

About the same time Fattorini & Sons of Bradford were marketing a similar alarm called the 'Automatic Caller'. This had an oak case, eight-day movement, also rang on a bell and gong and also reset itself each night. The patent for this had been taken out in 1892 by T. Wood, but by 1897 the patent rights had been purchased by Fattorini & Sons. It was sold in 1902 for 26s. and the advertisement stressed that it was 'John Bull's Own Work' and 'English Manufacture'. The country of manufacture being a topical subject at this date as the previous year there had been legislation to ensure that clocks and watches marked as being made in this country must actually be made here and not just foreign movements assembled or cased in England and then sold as 'Made in England'. It had been noted on close scrutiny that the movement of the 'Bugler' Alarm Clock illustrated here (Figure 143b) bore the trade mark

143b

143c

of the Hamburg American Clock Factory of Germany (crossed arrows). It would appear that although it was an English patent owned by the firm of Thomas Fattorini, the movements were made abroad and probably cased here. This was common practice to minimise the cost of import tax and transporting cases as well as movements from abroad. Fascinating device worth £100+ for sheer volume of sound.

Chapter IX
WALL CLOCKS

Vienna Regulators

The original Vienna regulator manufactured by the master clockmakers of Austria from the end of the eighteenth century and well into the nineteenth, were excellent timekeepers and, therefore, frequently used in public buildings. The cases of the early examples made during the Biedermeier period (1815-1845) were simple and followed the classical lines popular at this time. The white enamel dials were plain and one piece, although some had a decorative brass edge. The movements, apart from the wheels, would have been hand made and examples can be found that run for a year, a month or a week. Any strike work was usually on gongs which were fitted to the backplate of the movement. This could be full strike with repeat or just striking on the hours and half hours. Full strike was with the quarters *first* (four blows at the hour, one blow at a quarter past, two blows at half past and three blows at a quarter to the hour), with the hours struck *after* each appropriate quarter strike. Some four thousand makers' names have been listed but to date little has been written on the subject. It is doubtful whether examples of the very early Vienna regulators are to be found in this country, although some excellent later pieces made by these makers do appear occasionally. The original Vienna regulator continued to be made in diminishing numbers until the end of the last century. Those manufactured after about 1850 had far more ornate cases with additional carvings, pillars, etc. The early elegant hands were now replaced by ornate pierced examples and the dials were manufactured in two pieces with an intervening brass ring between the two sections.

What do appear frequently, and are quite erroneously referred to as 'Vienna regulators', are the later German made copies. They neither come from Vienna nor are they precision timepieces. From the 1850s clock factories began to develop in several areas of Germany and inevitably copies were made of the superior Austrian clocks. The quality of these clocks vary — those made by the Lenzkirch factory in the Black Forest area for example are held in high esteem, while many others bear all the signs of mass production. One peculiarity of these German made 'regulators' is that the seconds dial although marked for sixty seconds, actually has the hand calibrated to complete its circuit in forty five seconds. Apart from a very few exceptions these German clocks have two piece dials.

Two manufacturers known to have made these clocks are Aug. Schatz and Sohne of Triberg and Gustav Becker of Freiburg. Becker was a prolific manufacturer and according to the history of the firm as recounted by Karl Kochman, he originally manufactured these timepieces for offices etc., but about 1860 began to produce more ornate striking models for domestic use. Although he received many awards for his achievements, he found that the fierce competition of the cheaper spring-driven 'regulators' produced by the makers in the Black Forest area forced him also to manufacture movements of this type. His clocks prior to 1880 had been weight-driven. His trade mark was an anchor with the letters GB. This either appeared on the dial or stamped on the backplate.

The original Vienna regulators were precision timepieces and as such are finely poised and adjusted. It is, therefore, necessary to ensure that the movements are kept well cleaned and polished to eliminate any friction caused by dust or dirt. The German factory-made examples are far more robust as can be seen from the pages shown in the Appendix devoted to parts for them.

It is as well to be aware of the fact that there have been kits available in America for some time for assembling your own Vienna regulator, and it has been recently noted that reproduction movements and dials are being imported from Germany into England. One manufacturer of these modern copies being J. Kieninger of the Black Forest area of Germany.

Courtesy of Derek Roberts Antiques

Figure 144

6ft. 1in. This large example of one of the comparatively early Vienna regulators has an elegant mahogany case with one piece dial and centre sweep seconds hand. The graduated enamel regulating plate can be seen at the base of the case on the back board, but it is not possible to discern the two small screws at the sides of the case for levelling the clock against the wall.

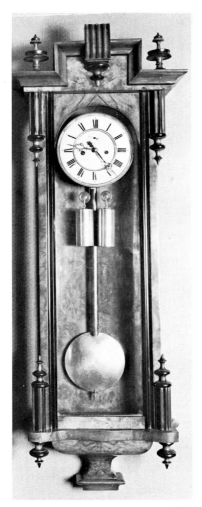

Figure 145

This is a Vienna regulator of a later date as indicated by the shaped case and two piece dial. Note the attractive use of the walnut veneer both on the back board and the bottom section of the case. These clocks have frequently lost their top pieces.

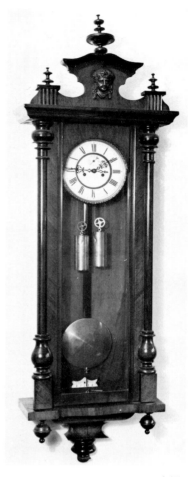

147a

146

Courtesy of Derek Roberts Antiques

Figure 146

This example is a timepiece only. The shaped door and two piece dial indicate a later date, with overtones of art nouveau styling.

147b

Figures 147a and 147b

4ft. 1in. The German weight-driven clock (left) is in an elegant mahogany case with decorative turned finials, carved mask and pillars reminiscent of the style used on the later Vienna regulator cases. Note the two piece enamel dial with subsidiary seconds dial. The pendulum has the conventional wooden rod and spun brass bob. Striking is on the hours and half hours. Note in the rear view that the gong is not mounted on the backplate of the movement, but on the back board of the case.

Examples with elaborately turned finials and superstructures like this are less popular than ones with cleaner lines, such as Figure 145.

£150+

148a   148b

Figures 148a and 148b

3ft.10in. A German spring-driven eight-day regulator in an ornate walnut veneered case. In place of the more usual fully glazed door only the dial has a convex glass with another small glazed aperture through which to view the pendulum bob. The conventional pendulum has been replaced by a mock compensated one. The two piece dial is of cream porcelain with a subsidiary seconds dial. Compare this good quality spring-driven movement with that shown in Figure 150b and note that the example in Figure 148b is fastened onto a removable wooden base board, has solid plates, an encased spring, ting-tang striking on two gongs and bears a German patent number stamped on the backplate.

£160+

No. 1747.—Brass mounted Dial.
Length 55½ins.   Width 19ins.
8-day Strike ...   ...

No. 1641.—Length 52ins.   Width 18½ins.
8-day Strike   ...   87/6

No. 1798.—Length 55½ins.   Width 19½ins.
Brass mounted Dial, Ivory Circle.
8-day Strike on Steel Rod Chime

Courtesy of F.W. Elliott Ltd.

Figure 149

The page shown in this illustration is from a post-1921 catalogue of Grimshaw, Baxter and J.J. Elliott Ltd. and shows a few of the 'Vienna Weight Regulators' sold by them at this time. 'G.B. movements' would indicate that they had been manufactured by Gustav Becker of Germany.

£200+ each

255

Figure 150a

2ft.8in. This illustration shows an example of a German spring-driven regulator from the Black Forest area. The case, although attractively carved, is made of stained and varnished soft wood. The dial is of zinc and brass sheet overlaid with painted card. The pendulum is of a mock compensated design.

£150+

Figure 150b

Although the case is attractive (see Figure 150a), the 'pressed-out' movement of this clock is immediately seen to be from the lower end of the range of mass produced German regulators. Note that the gong (and indeed the movement itself) is mounted to the back board of the case. The coarse wheelwork, thin plates and open spring, together with the imitation grid-iron pendulum are all typical features. Compare this movement to that shown in Figure 148b. Although both mass produced the difference in quality is immediately noticeable.

257

Figure 151

This is an unusual brass dial weight-driven regulator with a calendar aperture, seconds dial, date and phase of the moon. Striking is on a gong. A similar styled clock was made by Lenzkirch of Germany in 1926. There are no identifying marks on the movement apart from a repairer's date of 1921. It is nevertheless an interesting and attractive piece well worth acquiring.

Figure 152

This illustration has been included in order to emphasise the importance of studying fully any timepiece available and not to make sweeping assumptions. This movement comes from one of the cheap mass produced German 'regulators' made by Junghans (name appears stamped on movement), but it is noted that it has an extremely unusual rack striking mechanism. In place of the more usual toothed rack, this example has pins arranged at right angles to the arm. Although not adding greatly to the monetary value of a piece with such a feature it would make it a desirable collector's piece.

Dial Clocks

Although there were various wall clocks prior to 1770, the English dial clock as we know it today dates from about this time. The earliest cases were solid mahogany, with a concave surround and flat bottomed box behind the dial to house the movement. A small door at the side was made to enable easy access to the fixed pendulum and verge escapement, with another at the base giving access to the pendulum bob for any necessary adjustment. Except for a few scattered examples the anchor escapement replaced the verge, which led to some changes in the shape and design of the cases. In order to accommodate a larger pendulum the base of the box was curved and in some instances lengthened. These are generally referred to as 'drop dial' or 'trunk clocks'. The lower section can be decorated with stringing, inlay, veneering and in some instances the pendulum is visible, but in other examples it is enclosed by a small mirror or panel.

After 1850 the wooden surround tended to be convex, although by this date other shapes, for example hexagonal or octagonal, also appeared. About the same date the cheaper spun bezel (the earliest examples had been cast brass) also appeared. Until 1875 the glass was retained in place by plaster, but at this date examples began to appear with a sight ring (an inner brass ring). However, it was still necessary to use plaster to retain the glass in place. Early this century the spun bezel with a sight ring that could be sprung in became more common. The dials of the clocks manufactured after the mid-1800s were of iron — painted white — either flat or convex, although a few examples can be found with the older-type silvered brass dials. Boldness and clarity would be the most noticeable characteristics of the painted dials. At this date the names on the dial will be those of the retailers — the makers of the movements being content to omit their names or at best stamp them on the dial plates. Thwaites and Reed were one supplier to the trade during the nineteenth century, details of others will appear with the appropriate illustrations.

With very few exceptions these clocks manufactured after 1850 will have anchor escapements, although some can be found still using a verge or deadbeat escapement. In typical English tradition the movements will have a fusee and chain or steel wire. It is possible to ascertain whether the movement has the original line by counting the fixing holes in the barrel. One indicates that a chain was used, whereas the presence of three infer a steel wire or gut. It would not necessarily be true to state that one was any earlier than the other as it was noted, for example, from a 1921 catalogue: "New feature — the 8-day movement now made with chain". Although there are some examples with strike, seconds, alarm or calendar work the commonly found dial clocks are timepieces.

So far the clocks described have been *English* dial clocks, but inevitably they were copied in large numbers by the American and German manufacturers. German manufacturers such as Winterhalter and Hoffmeir (see pages 147-152) included them in their range and made some models with fusees, but almost without exception those manufactured by other makers omitted the additional mechanical refinement of the fusee. Many German movements were imported and cased here and therefore outward appearances can be deceptive. Movements, backplates and, if possible, dial plates should be noted to arrive at a positive conclusion!

One gains the impression from the catalogues of American manufacturers that the majority of their movements were housed in cases of the drop dial pattern with varying shaped surrounds. They did not favour the simple English-style dial clock, but added either on the same dial or on a second dial calendars, barometers, etc. Strike work was far more common than on the English counterparts.

Further detailed information concerning these clocks can be found in the book on *Dial Clocks* written by R.E. Rose. Although the majority are of no great horological merit the English examples in particular are good solid clocks that deserve higher praise than being referred to as 'just' schoolroom or kitchen clocks. Few of these late examples have been tampered with unduly — dials may have been repainted but in this case no great harm has been done. Most handymen can cope with any repairs that may be necessary to the cases, and it is still possible to obtain hands, springs, etc. from material dealers.

Figure 153

An example of an English dial clock in an attractive case, with a carved mahogany surround and trunk. The painted iron dial is signed Grosvenor, Ellesmere. The date of this piece is c.1870.

£100+

Figure 154

This appears to be another example of a plain timepiece manufactured at the beginning of this century similar to that shown in Figure 157. However, on closer examination it is realised that it is a highly sought after collector's item as it is of one month duration. Note the convex surround, spun brass bezel and sight ring.

Figure 155

This is an extremely attractive timepiece with 12-inch painted iron dial, octagonal surround and elaborate trunk. The case is part oak and part papier-mâché inlaid with mother-of-pearl. It is an unusual design for an English dial clock, but one which was used extensively in America.

£150+

Courtesy of Ruislip Antiques, Alfies Antique Market

Figure 156

2ft. 4in. An inlaid American 12 drop dial clock with eight-day striking
movement. This is a typical case style for these clocks.

157a

157b

Figures 157a and 157b

This is a typical mahogany dial clock as used in offices, shops, etc. at the beginning of this century. This example has the added interest of having been part of the shop fittings of Playle Bros. of 137 Northcote Road, London, S.W., who were in business as watchmakers from around 1906. In the movement (157b) note the fusee and that although the rest of the wheels are crossed out, the hour wheel is not — this was common practice as it was not usually visible. Although it cannot be said that this clock is horologically exciting, it is an excellent example of a good sturdy English fusee timepiece and can only appreciate in value. Price depends on size of clock. A small (8in.) example, £200+; large (12-18in.) £100+. Ebonised examples £40—£100.

Figure 158

This is an illustration of a rather curious movement viewed from the dial plate (i.e. dial has been removed). Note the uncrossed wheels, open spring, only means of access through dial and lastly the trade mark. A movement of this quality could only be American or German and this is the trade mark of the New Haven Clock Company of Connecticut, but it has also had the words 'British Manufacture' stamped around it. Possibly the case was made in this country.

No. 501.—Oak, Walnut, or Mahogany Case.
8-day Time, 10 and 12in. Dial, **19**/-. 8-day Strike, 12in., **26**/-
8-day Time, 14in. Dial, **32/6.** 8-day Strike 14ins., **39/6**

No. 502.—Oak, Walnut, or Mahogany Case,
12in. Dial.
8-day Time, **21**/-. 8-day Strike. **28**/-

No. 503.—Oak, Walnut, or Mahogany Case,
12in. Dial.
8-day Time, **27**/- 8-day Strike. **34**/-

E. Ltd.

G. B.

Figure 159

This illustration shows three styles of dial clocks manufactured by the British United Clock Company (for further details of this maker see page 206). They appeared in a trade catalogue published c.1910.

Price here depends on size and whether the case dial surround is ebonised or wood. Ebonised £100+; wood £150+.

BRITISH RAILWAY or OFFICE CLOCKS.

SOLID OAK CASES.

Going-barrel, 8-day, Croydon 11-jewel lever movement; escapement mounted on top of movement. Front wind and regulation.

	No. 7841. Spun Bezel.	No. 7842. Solid Bezel.
6in. enamel dial	86/-	93/-
8in. ,, ,, ...	92/-	101/-
10in. ,, ,, ...	94/-	106/-
12in. ,, ,, ...	100/-	113/-

EXTRAS.

	6in.	8in.	10in.	12in.
Chromium bezel	3/-	3/-	5/-	6/-
Mahogany case	2/-	2/-	3/-	5/-

Nos. 7841 and 7842.

SOLID OAK WALL TIMEPIECES.

Solid bezels; convex glasses; silvered dials; 8-day Croydon lever movement, going-barrel, with 11-jewel escapement mounted on top of movement. Front wind and regulation.

		£ s. d.	
No. 7847	4½in. dial, Oak case ...	4 15 0	Mahogany
No. 7848	6in. ,, ,, ...	6 0 0	cases, 6/-
No. 7849	8in. ,, ,, ...	7 6 0	extra.

Nos. 7847, 7848 and 7849

"IMPERIAL" STANDARD OFFICE CLOCK.

Finest grade fuzee and chain movement, bridged motion work. Oak or Mahogany cases.

Dial size.	Spun bezel. No. 7857.	Solid bezel sheet glass. No. 7858.	Solid bezel, plate glass. No. 7859.	Extra for short drop.	Extra for Teak; Round.	Drop.
	£ s. d.	£ s. d.	£ s. d.			
8in.	8 10 0	8 15 0	9 0 0	16/-		
10in.	8 12 0	8 17 0	9 2 0	16/-	19/-	19/-
12in.	8 12 0	8 17 0	9 2 0	16/-		
14in.	10 10 0	11 0 0	11 7 0	28/-	22/-	34/-
16in.	13 10 0	14 0 0	14 15 0	40/-	34/-	46/-
18in.	15 10 0	17 10 0	18 10 0	50/-	46/-	64/-
24in.	24 0 0	25 10 0	27 0 0	130/-	80/-	160/-

Wind and Set Hands at Back, 50/- extra.

CROYDON SPECIAL DIAL CLOCK; hinged box; fuzee chain movement; Oak or Mahogany case.

No. 7845 (10in. dial), £7 10s. 0d.; No. 7846 (12in. dial), £7 15s. 0d.

Nos. 7857, 7858 and 7859.

Courtesy of F.W. Elliott Ltd.

Figure 160

This illustration shows a selection of dial clocks manufactured by F.W. Elliott Ltd. sometime between 1932 and 1946.

Cuckoo Clocks

The clockmaking industry in the Black Forest area of Germany had originated as a secondary winter occupation for the farming community, but in 1850 a great spur was given to the industry by the establishment at Furtwanger of a clockmaking school. The following account was written by Miss Seguin:—

"Formerly, and until within the last fifteen years, every portion of the works of these Black Forest Clocks was made by hand, and each workman began and finished his own Clock in his own cottage, being assisted in his labours by the different members of his family. Now, this hand and individual labour is, to a great extent, done away with, being supplemented by large establishments, where a hundred or more men are engaged, in which machinery is employed, and the labour is subdivided into at least a dozen processes. The men work twelve hours, are paid from a shilling to half-a-crown a day, and women are employed as polishers of the cases. The old hand-labour system is maintained only in a few remote villages, and for the inferior kinds of Clock.

"Since the introduction of machinery the Black Forest Clocks have been, it is said, not only cheaper but more accurate, although it is certain that some of the old wooden Clocks, made a hundred years ago, are still in use, having withstood the various changes of temperature, and the wear and tear of a century, with scarcely any diminution of their powers.

"One peculiarity of the Black Forest Clocks, is that they are almost all made to be fastened against a wall, not as chimney timepieces, and thus they are used throughout Germany, where, in truth, it would be difficult to find a place for timepieces, as chimneys do not exist there.

"The favourite form is the cuckoo-clock, and a variety of other mechanisms is also introduced in the more elaborate specimens. It would be difficult, indeed, to say that any result was impossible to the inventive genius of these Black Forest Clock-work makers.

"In the ninety-two parishes which form what is called the Clock-country, are over 1,400 master Clockmakers, who employ some 6,000 workmen. Altogether, about 14,000 people, including women and children, are occupied in this one industry. The number of Clocks manufactured yearly in this district is calculated at two millions, valued roughly at one million sterling."

The Americans, with their cheaper factory-made shelf clocks captured for a while at least the English market that had previously been supplied by the German clocks. However, the Germans rallied and began to use factory methods themselves, and, as well as manufacturing copies of the American, English and French clocks, adapted their own traditional designs to the new methods. The Black Forest cuckoo clock was, according to legend, invented by Franz Anton Ketterer of Schoenwald about 1730 to 1740, and is still popular to this day. Apart from the pinions and perhaps a few pieces of wire, the entire clocks were made of wood, although gradually brass wheels were introduced and by the end of the nineteenth century only the wooden plates were retained. About 1850 the cuckoo clock as we think of it today was introduced — the case having a sharp-angled gable roof, and being in the form of a box with a flap at the back for access to the movement housed within. The variations that are shown in the illustrations in Figures 161 and 162 are not without interest.

The points to note when considering a purchase are first to inspect the case carefully for damaged or missing parts. Frequently made of pine and having become brittle with age only too often the carvings have been broken. Secondly, ensure that your cuckoo can still 'cuckoo' and the bellows have not been perforated. Although the Appendix lists a comprehensive range of parts for these clocks it is doubtful if they can be obtained today and patching bellows can be a tedious task. Lastly, never be tempted to improve upon the basic design of the movement as, although to all intents and purposes it appears a very bodged affair, it has evolved over many years of trial and error to become perfectly satisfactory. For example a flat strip on the pendulum with a hole to place over the suspension hook could possibly stop the clock as the two hooks in the original design roll within each other and reduce friction. Similar refinements also bring problems in their wake.

Little has been written in English on the subject of these clocks apart from two articles in *Antique Collecting,* October, 1976, by Terence Camerer Cuss and the book *Black Forest Clocks* by E.J. Tyler.

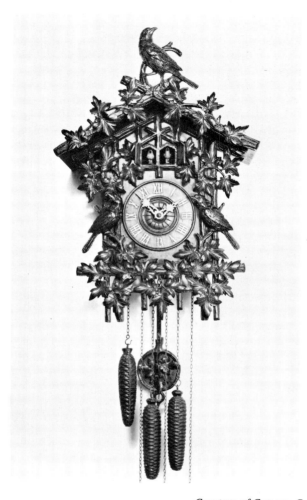

Figure 161a

This is a fine example of a cuckoo and quail wall clock, dating from around the end of the last century. The quail giving the quarters and the cuckoo the hours. It is far more common to find examples with a cuckoo alone.

£250–£350 because of double automaton.

Figure 161b

Movement of cuckoo and quail clock shown in Figure 161a. Note the steel arbors and lantern pinions with wooden plates, and the pipes and bellows above the movement.

Figure 162a

An attractive and slightly unusual cuckoo clock of around 1850 to
1875. The points to note are the gabled roof of the case, painted
mother and child scene (after 1860 transfers were commonly used),
enamel dial and steel moon-shaped hands and brass cased lead weights.
Later examples have cast pine cone weights (see Figure 161a).

£150+

Figure 162b

Movement of clock shown in Figure 162a. The points to note in this view are the gong secured to the door of the case, wooden plates and general appearance of string and bent wires! The two supporting pillars on either side are covered with coloured marbled paper. The bellows and cuckoo are housed at the top of the case. Later examples (after 1900) are more likely to have brass movements and plates.

Figure 163

A typical example of a Black Forest 'postman's alarm'. These were manufactured up until the First World War and maintained a steady popularity. The dial is glass, with the numerals and markings painted on the obverse. In this example the alarm is set by positioning the third hand at the required hour. In this instance the alarm would ring at about quarter past seven. The arrow indicates the counter-clockwise setting of the alarm. Other examples have been seen with a centre disc for setting the alarm mechanism.

Depending on decorative quality of dial surround £100–£150.

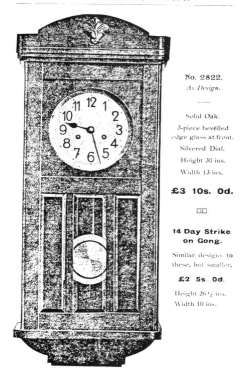

No. 2822.
As Design.

Solid Oak.
3-piece bevelled
edge glass at front.
Silvered Dial.
Height 30 ins.
Width 13 ins.

£3 10s. 0d.

14 **Day Strike**
on Gong.

Similar designs to
these, but smaller.

£2 5s. 0d.

Height 26½ ins.
Width 10 ins.

Figure 164

German wall clock appearing in the 1921 catalogue of Appleton
Limited, 29 Warrington Road, Prescot, who were at that date describing
themselves as 'Manufacturers, Importers and Wholesale Merchants of
Watches, Clocks, Jewellery, Sundries, Tools and Materials for the Watch
and Jewellery Trade'.

Very little value, perhaps £50+.

277

Figure 165

These four wall clocks appeared in the 1936 catalogue of Aug. Schatz & Sohne of Germany and were typical examples of the clocks being imported at this time. With few exceptions the cases were of oak, with solid oak mounts, bevelled glass panels of varying shapes and sizes, silver anodised dials and striking on gongs. The movements were German — Gustav Becker being one of the most prolific manufacturers. Further details relating to this maker can be found on page 249. As with any of these late clocks, to be considered as a collector's item they must be in good condition and in their original state.

Very little value, perhaps £50+.

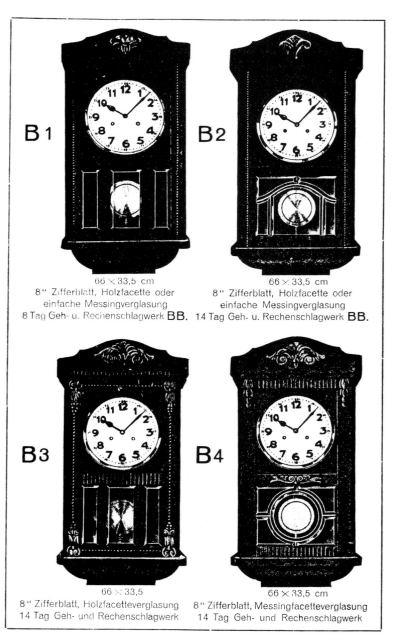

B 1

66 × 33,5 cm
8" Zifferblatt, Holzfacette oder
einfache Messingverglasung
8 Tag Geh- u. Rechenschlagwerk **BB.**

B2

66 × 33,5 cm
8" Zifferblatt, Holzfacette oder
einfache Messingverglasung
14 Tag Geh- u. Rechenschlagwerk **BB.**

B3

66 × 33,5
8" Zifferblatt, Holzfacetteverglasung
14 Tag Geh- und Rechenschlagwerk

B4

66 × 33,5 cm
8" Zifferblatt, Messingfacetteverglasung
14 Tag Geh- und Rechenschlagwerk

Courtesy of Aug. Schatz & Sohne

Courtesy of Kingston Antiques

Figure 166

2ft. 8in. This is an unusual wall clock by an interesting maker. The carved oak case has a curved door either side by which to gain access in order to adjust the pendulum, etc., and in place of the usual frets these have been filled by canework. The white enamel dial is pleasingly bold and signed 'Adam Thomson, New Bond St., London'. Adam Thomson is known to have been active in 1842 at this address and was the author of *Time and Timekeepers* a small book published in February of that year and dedicated to His Royal Highness, Prince Augustus Frederick, Duke of Sussex. A shortened translation into German by Franz Rottenkamp appeared about 1850.. The movement is of solid construction with fusees and striking on bells. The size might be a deterrent, but if space allows it has much to commend it.

Figure 167

25in. The cartel clock originated in France about 1750, but whereas the English developed their counterpart — the dial clock — on simple lines, the French continued to utilise ornate highly decorative surrounds, usually of ormolu. The case styles of these early examples were repeated and copied through the years. The example in this illustration is reminiscent of the designs used during the Louis XVI period. The movement is stamped with the name of the maker L. Marti et Cie together with the fact that they received a Medåille d'Argent in 1889, thereby indicating that the clock must have been manufactured after this date. It is an attractive piece — well proportioned and with fine detail. As the value of these clocks lies in their decorative appeal this is important.

Figure 168a

Having stated that these clocks are valued by their decorative appeal, an
exception is immediately made! The case of this example is attractive —
Napoleon III style case c.1855 with copper repoussé dial, enamel
plaques with black Roman numerals and pewter mounts, etc., but it is
the position of the winding hole that is of great interest. It is *above* the
centre arbor. The reason for this will be seen in Figure 168b.

£120+

Figure 168b

View of the movement to the clock shown in Figure 168a. As access to
the movement is difficult an aperture has been left in the wooden
backboard for any necessary adjustment to the effective length of the
pendulum. Upon looking at the movement it is immediately noted that
it has an *inverted* pin pallet escapement. The other point of interest lies
in the trade mark stamped on the backplate. It is identical to that on
the Swinging Cherub clock illustrated in Figure 184b. To a collector
these technical curiosities will greatly enhance the value.

Figure 169

24in. These clocks come from the Franche Comté region of France and are referred to as 'Tableaux Comtoise'. They are spring driven and although of simple construction are extremely robust and durable. The shape of the case can be square, oval, scalloped or plain and decorated by brass or mother-of-pearl inlay. The name on the dial is Claude Mayet à Morbier. The name 'Mayet' is associated with the origins of the clockmaking industry in this area. Legend has it that three brothers of this name founded the industry in the seventeenth century after successfully replacing a worn out public clock. This Claude Mayet would possibly be the name of a nineteenth century retailer. Due to a certain amount of renewed interest in these clocks, both as decorative and practical pieces for a small modern home, reproductions are being manufactured by firms on the Continent. Several books have been written on the subject including:— *The Morbier 1680-1900* by Steve Z. Nemrava; *La Comtoise, La Morbier, La Morez. Histoire et Technique* by Francis Maitzner and Jean Moreau.

£100+; if merely painted dial, £60+.

Courtesy of Sotheby's

285

Figure 170a

25in. This is a particularly attractive weight-driven clock made by Seth Thomas of Connecticut in a well preserved veneered softwood case with fully glazed door and colourful tablet in the lower portion.

Prices in England for these clocks bear no relation to the figures they fetch in America!

£100+

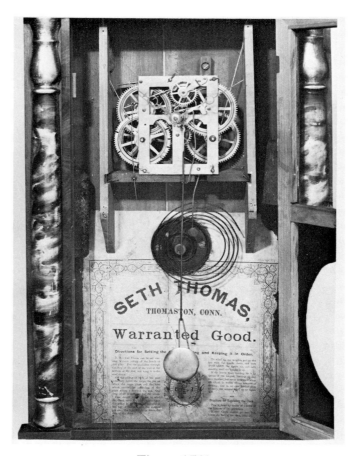

Figure 170b

Movement of clock shown in Figure 170a. The points to note are the
original cone-shape weights suspended either side of the movement, the
general poor but serviceable quality of the mass produced movement,
and the circular wire gong mounted on the back of the case. In
common with most American manufacturers of this period the maker's
label is pasted in the lower half of the case. From this it is possible to
discern the name Seth Thomas, Thomaston, Conn. As the name of the
town was changed from Plymouth Hollow to Thomaston in 1866, the
date of this particular clock must be between 1866 and 1888.

Figure 171a

17in. This is an exceptionally small American clock in an ogee veneered softwood case with a fully glazed door. The scene appearing in the tablet on the lower half of the door is entitled 'View in Rome, Italy'.

£100 because small, compared to £100+ for standard size.

Figure 171b

View of the movement of the American wall clock shown in Figure 171a. The interesting points to note about this thirty-hour spring driven movement are that the springs are brass (later examples used steel), the thin brass plates have been ribbed to give added strength and the name of the maker on the label is that of Brewster and Ingrahams of Bristol, Connecticut, USA (1840-1850).

Figure 172

25in. Weight-driven American clock in ogee veneered softwood case with fully glazed door. The building shown in the tablet in the lower half is that of the Burns Monument. The maker of this example was Jerome & Co., New Haven, Connecticut, USA (name used by the New Haven Clock Company in the last half of the nineteenth century).

It is expedient to take care when moving these clocks to ensure that the weights do not swing and break the glass door or crash downwards through the bottom of the case.

£60 – £100

Chapter X

MYSTERY and NOVELTY CLOCKS

In the early days of horology many clocks were the products of fertile minds seeking to improve upon the then limited knowledge of the art and mystery of horology with experimental devices. The clocks of Nicholas Grollier de Serviere (1596-1689), soldier, mathematician and inventor being one example, with the concepts and ideas suggested by the Marquis of Worcester (1601-1667) in his patent of 1661 being another. This patent (Patent No. 131) was the first patent relating to clocks and watches to be taken out. Further details of the Marquis and his horological inventions can be found in the Winter issue of *Antiquarian Horology,* 1976. As the centuries passed and for all practical purposes the technicalities and basic design for a clock were mastered, the necessity arose to please the wealthy customer and satisfy his desire for an unusual timepiece. So the clockmakers strove to provide such items by adding complicated chimes, automata, elaborate case and dial decoration, etc. Still later the factory methods of production, which had brought the clock within the price range of the working man, also created the problem of uniformity of design. Individuality had to be achieved in some aspect in order to overshadow competitors. Some manufacturers relied upon being the first with some new innovation or being able to add some gimmick to their range. This created the need to protect new ideas by filing applications for a patent. The flood of applications for patents to be granted for items being shown at the Great Exhibition led, in 1852, to the reorganisation and simplification of the patent system. Even amateur inventors tended to protect their devices in this manner, many of which were ludicrous and never reached the production lines, while others only enjoyed a short period of popularity, with a residue of commercially acceptable ideas remaining. In some instances the basis for these were reintroduced from previous areas and adapted to current manufacturing techniques and materials. One example of this is the clock in Figure 188a illustrating the rack or gravity clock. Others were considered by their inventor to fill "a long felt want" — one example being the Memorandum Clock of John Davidson shown in Figure 187.

Frequently the patent dates or numbers appear on the clock and provide an invaluable piece of documentation, for these can be traced at the Patent Office in order to ascertain the name of the inventor, occupation, location and, if not already quoted, the date the invention was patented. Although this can only establish the earliest date from which an article was manufactured it is nevertheless invaluable.

As the following clocks are so diverse in concept, quality and design it is impossible to provide any specific guidelines as to features to seek or note except in the accompanying text with each illustration.

Figure 173

The mystery of this clock lies in the fact that there is no apparent connection between the pendulum held firmly in the hand of the bronze statue and the movement in the marble pedestal. With a high power lens it can be noted on careful inspection that in this example the bronze ring upon which the figure stands rotates by 1/40th of an inch either right or left with each impulse of the escapement. A full description of this interesting mechanism can be found in the *Horological Journal* for August and September, 1948. The movement is French. Similar clocks can be found with extremely ornate ormolu and coloured marble bases, and in some instances a skeletonised dial. The figures can be bronze or spelter. It will be the quality of these features that determines the price. A good bronze figure fetches several hundreds of pounds in its own right, whereas one of spelter would be a fraction of this. It must also be remembered that any restoration needed to the movement of any of these mystery clocks could be a problem as only a handful of restorers are prepared to overhaul and clean, let alone repair, this type of mechanism. It is therefore not particularly wise to purchase other than a working example unless provisional arrangements have been made together with an estimate of the cost that will be incurred with a restorer. Could realise several thousands of pounds depending on quality of figure.

Courtesy of Keith Banham

294

Figure 174

Approx. 12in. by 18in. An extremely rare novelty clock. Its invention is attributed to Nicholas Grollier de Serviere (1596-1689). He spent much of his life serving as a French soldier during which time he lost the sight of one eye. During this period he applied his mechanical and mathematical genius to the designing of fortifications, etc., but upon retiring from the army he turned his attention to a wider field which included various ingenious timekeepers. A few reproductions were made during the later part of the nineteenth century and the beginning of this. Their value would lie in their decorative quality and the general principle that lies behind the mechanism rather than being efficient timekeepers. This particular example has the 'fan' mounted behind glass in a recessed picture frame. The recess is lined and has two decorative mouldings in the top corners which have been gilded to match the outer frame. The fan itself is highly decorative. The time as shown in the illustration is 6 o'clock as indicated by the small pointer in the shape of a serpent. The fan snaps shut when fully unfolded at 6 o'clock and then slowly commences to unfold from left to right — the time always being that indicated on the left hand side. The movement in this example was mounted externally at the back of the frame.

Figure 175

The principle upon which this particular mystery clock works is attributed to Robert-Houdin (1805-1871) the French conjurer. He is not to be confused with Houdini the escapologist of this century. Houdin, born Jean Eugene Robert, was first trained as a lawyer but prevailed upon his father to apprentice him to his cousin, a clockmaker. In 1830 he married the daughter of Jacques Françoise Houdin, a watchmaker who worked with Bréguet, and continued his career of showman and conjurer as Robert-Houdin. With his own knowledge of clockwork, and no doubt with the assistance of his father-in-law, he devised many automata and mystery clocks for which he received several medals at the various exhibitions. There were two models for this clock — in one the column between the plinth holding the clock movement and the dial is of clear glass, whereas in the example illustrated it is opaque. In both there is no visible method by which the drive reaches the hands. In the example depicted here there are actually two glass dials within the bezel — one is fixed and has the hour and minute markings while the other carrying the hand is free to rotate. The periphery of this second dial has a finely toothed rim and is rotated by a carefully contrived series of rods and worm and bevel gears connected to the movement housed in the base. This example carries the name of 'Promoli A Paris' and has an anchor escapement with a silk suspension. A similar model appears in *La Pendule Française* by Tardy. The value of these clocks is governed by virtue of their being a novelty, and so it is of no great importance as to whom the makers of the movement and case are.

297

Figure 176

19½in. high. These clocks are usually of French origin and this is no exception. Although a late nineteenth century copy of those made over a century earlier it is a highly desirable piece. The figures of the three Graces support a globe with two rotating bands – one showing the hours and the other the minutes. The arrow held by the figure of Cupid serves as a pointer. Other similar examples would have an urn, or vase and be with or without figures. The quality of the figures (bronze signed or unsigned, or spelter) or the manufacturer of any porcelain decorations would be influencing factors when estimating the value of such a piece. This particular piece fetched £1,050 in 1976.

Figure 177

1ft. 9½in. high. The relevant catalogue entry for this attractive mystery clock reads "A French Bronze Patinated Spelter Mysterieuse Timepiece in the form of a scantily dressed young girl holding a timepiece aloft. . . . signed Louis Moreau and with founder's mark, on a turned socle, c.1900". The movement is housed in the globe held by the figure and both globe and pendulum swing *in toto*, a small pendulum within the globe being the true regulator. (It is interesting to compare this with the example in Figure 178 which is a later example and would have been made sometime in the 1930s; this spelter figure does not have the sharp finish enjoyed by the example in Figure 177, and in place of the globe there is a normal dial). The movement is that of a watch and runs for a week. The timepiece and pendulum swing fifty times per minute. It realised £300 in 1976. As early as 1886-87 the Ansonia Clock Company of America were advertising copies of these clocks in 'Japanese or French Bronze' finish but with eight-day movements. Later, in 1914, their catalogues listed swinging ball clocks, with 'real bronze finish', coloured balls and again, eight-day movements.

177

Courtesy of Sotheby's Belgravia

176

Courtesy of Sotheby's Belgravia

299

Figure 178

This example of a Diana swinging clock was manufactured during the 1930s, but similar models are still being manufactured in America. An alternative model is that of an elephant holding the timepiece aloft in his trunk.

£90 – £150, the quality of the figure determining the price

Figure 179

8in. high. The case of this clock is in the form of a gaily painted pottery dwarf. It was introduced in 1929 when Walt Disney films were making their debut and there is a label pasted to the base stating that the design was 'By permission of Walt Disney. Mickey Mouse Ltd.' The clock was, however, made in England and has a basic uncomplicated movement — the eyes rotate as the clock beats the seconds. Unlike the example in the following illustration the dial below is the true time teller.

£50 – £80

Figure 180

6in. high. Unlike the pottery dwarf in Figure 179 the eyes of this little dog actually tell the time. The white line running from the centre of each pupil points to the appropriate marking at the edge of the eye socket. The hours are marked around one orbit and the minutes the other. The thirty-hour pin pallet movement is housed in the body of the dog which is of brown simulated wood. These novelties were manufactured and advertised by J. Oswald of Freiburg, Germany in 1928 and 1929.

£40 – £70

Figure 181

13in. high. This is an illustration of an American 'Blinking Eye Clock'. The eyes flick back and forth with each beat of the pendulum. Several factories produced these clocks, but this particular example in a black cast iron case was made by Chauncey Jerome, Connecticut, USA, around 1870. They are eagerly sought after by collectors both here and in America.

£300+

Figure 182

This is an early twentieth century replica of a seventeenth century clock in the form of a clock 'pedlar' with a clock on his back. The movement, within the painted spelter figure, has the mark JVE stamped on it. The duration of the movement is thirty hours. There is at the moment a kit on the market to make your own 'clock pedlar' — complete with epoxy cement! The bodies of these are aluminium.

£80+

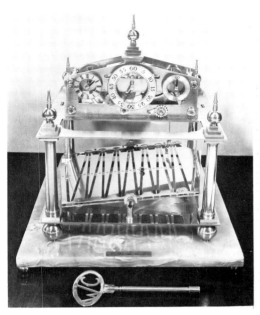

Figure 183

This is an excellent example of the reproduction of Sir William Congreve's (1772-1828) Rolling Ball Clock, based on the John Wilding interpretation which was serialised in the *Horological Journal,* 1975 and later published in book form. Although best known for his achievements in the development of rockets for military use, Congreve was also interested in devising new principles for the measurement of time. He lists in *A Second Century of Inventions*, written about 1796, some five improvements to clocks — none of which were apertaining to this particular example. He presented in 1808, an example of his Rolling Ball Clock to the Prince of Wales and this is now on view at The Rotunda, Woolwich. Reproductions of this clock have been made in limited numbers during the last fifty years by such makers as Geoffrey Bell, E. Dent & Co., and Thwaites and Reed. They were never produced on a commercial scale during the lifetime of Sir William Congreve. Price dependent on quality of workmanship put into the finish.

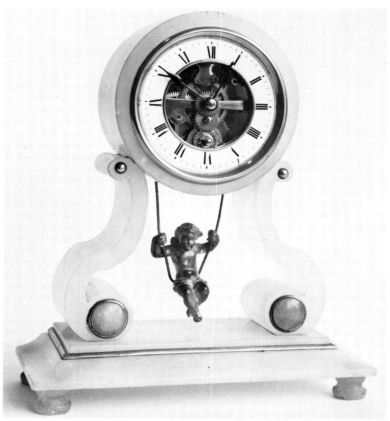

184a

Figures 184a and 184b

An interesting and attractive clock with the novel feature of a cherub
seated on a swing acting as the pendulum, which swings from back to
front instead of the more conventional side to side action. To enable
this to occur a special form of anchor escapement, patented in 1862 by
Farcot of Paris, is used (see Figure 184b). The trade mark is that of
Farcot. This particular example is housed in a white alabaster case, with
some ormolu trim and a gilt-metal cherub. The dial is attractively
skeletonised. These clocks have great decorative appeal and, depending
upon condition of case.

£150 – £250

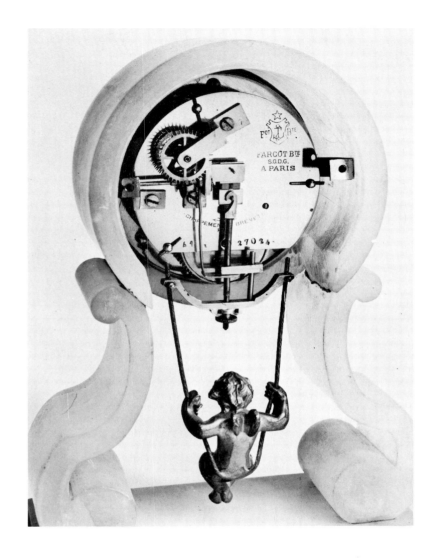

184b

Figure 185

The principle upon which this tortoise (or possibly more correctly turtle) clock works is attributed to Grollier de Sevriere of whom mention has been made in the text accompanying Figure 174. A simple timepiece is housed in the base, to which is fixed an arm carrying a magnet. As this revolves throughout the twelve hours it attracts with it, by means of the small piece of iron embedded in his stomach, the small turtle floating in the bowl of water above. The hours are marked on the chapter ring around the rim of the plate. This particular example has a handsome marble base or plinth, a silver dish and a horn tortoise. The price is dependent, to some extent, on date of manufacture, but far more emphasis is placed on the aesthetic appeal and value of the materials used.

£100 – £400

Figure 186

7½in. high. This is an illustration of a modern reproduction of a rotary pendulum clock patented by John C. Briggs of Concord, New Hampshire, USA, in 1855 and 1856. The two patent numbers (13,451 and 15,636) are stamped on the top of the plates. Although the principle behind them was ingenious they were far from a commercial success. Several models were manufactured, the first of these being in 1858 and 1860 when Abel Chandler, a clockmaker and instrument maker, also of Concord, became interested in them. They were manufactured by another American Clock Factory (E.N. Welch) during the 1870s when catalogues offered them at $2.50 for models with brass finish and $3.50 for models with nickel finish. Further details appear in *The American Horologist and Jeweler*, August, 1946, Vol. 13, No. 8, entitled 'The Brigg's Rotary' by J.E. Coleman.

£40 – £50 for reproduction

Figure 187

14in. high. The clock in this illustration is a perfect example of Victorian ingenuity and would have appeared to have a great many practical applications. It had, however, only a modest commercial appeal and was manufactured for about five or six years. The clock was patented by John Davidson in 1891. His invention was primarily the mechanism for the automatic memorandum device for use with any ordinary clock movement, so one finds examples in a variety of cases. This example is housed in a well-made oak case with brass finials and frets. The square dial is similar in concept to that of a longcase or bracket clock, being of brass with a matted centre, brass spandrels and silver chapter ring. It was intended that the revolving drum at the top should have forty eight slots and that an ivory tablet bearing the relevant message should be placed in the appropriate slot. At the appointed hour a bell would ring and the tablet drop into the small brass box seen below the dial. John Davidson foresaw his Memorandum Clock being a boon to busy financiers or nurses in the sickroom and five years later, in 1896, he took out a second patent for 'Improved Automatic Memorandum Clock'. In the second version a bell rang and the tablet had to be removed from the slot in order to read the reminder. John Davidson had come from Scotland with his wife and children about 1895 but by 1900 the automatic Memorandum Clock Company was wound up and the family returned in 1900 to Wick, Caithness. Further information regarding this clock can be found in *Antiquarian Horology,* June, 1975, in 'The Automatic Memorandum Clock' by R.K. Shenton.

Minimum of £250 depending on style of basic clock

Figures 188a, 188b, 188c and 188d

9½in. high. The principle of utilising the weight of the clock movement, as it slowly descends a notched rack, to drive the clock is not a new one. This type of clock was made as early as the seventeenth century. The clock in these illustrations, however, was manufactured during the 1920s and was first introduced at the Crystal Palace British Industries Fair in 1920. Patents had been taken out the previous year by Thomas Watson and Christopher Frederick Webb. It was manufactured and marketed under the name of the Watson Clock Company and then under the name of the Kee-Less Clock Company, both of Kentish Town, London. At this time the clock was described as "The Silent Kee-Less Clock. A revolution in Clock Construction. No Keys. No Springs. Moving Parts reduced to a Minimum giving Greater Reliability at Less Cost. Price 50/−". The example in this illustration is of brass, with a clear glass dial with white figures painted on the obverse. The front plate being painted matt black in order to make the figures and hands more readily visible. Later advertisements indicate that gilt figures, or plain or luminous dials, were also to be had. Other examples have been seen on marble or onyx bases, and one with the brass base embossed with a leaf pattern and a wreath of brass foliage surmounting the bezel. These clocks needed winding daily by pushing the drum containing the movement back to the top of the columns. Figures 188b, c and d provide detailed illustrations of the movement and case.

In 1921 patents were taken out in America and some examples have been seen which were manufactured by the Ansonia Clock Company of New York (1879-1930).

£80+ depending on material used for base, e.g. onyx, brass.

188a

188b

188c

188d

Figure 189

7in. high. The concept of a 'flying pendulum' was not new, but the version shown in this illustration was invented by Alder Christian Clausen in 1883. The clock has been aptly referred to as 'the craziest clock in the world'. The small ball on the end of the thread wraps and unwraps itself first around one post and then the other – a procedure that either enthrals or infuriates the onlooker! Originally these clocks were manufactured for one year only (1884-85) and were produced by the New Haven Clock Company of New Haven, Connecticut, USA, although sold under the name of Jerome and Company also of Connecticut. The clock in the illustration is a replica of the clock patented in 1883 and made in the 1960s in West Germany for the Horolovar Clock Company of the USA. The case is of metal, with matt black finish and brass trims. The original had an oak case with brass trims and retailed in 1885 for $5.18. It would appear that there was also a similar version of these clocks manufactured in France. The cases of the French models were similar, but of ebonised wood, with the central pillar carrying an umbrella from which hung the thread and ball. A small cherub sat crossed legged under the umbrella.

£40 – £50 for reproduction

Figure 190

5in. high. These clocks are generally referred to as 'Ticket' or 'Plato' clocks. The first name was intended to be a reference to the fact that, in place of the orthodox dial, small plates or tickets bore the figures for the hours and minutes, but the general public preferred another interpretation in that the cylindrical case was reminiscent of the lantern which Plato carried while looking for an honest man. The top ticket indicates the hours and the lower the minutes. The patent for this clock was taken out in 1902 by Eugene Fitch of New York, USA. The American Electrical Novelty and Manufacturing Company, also of New York, sold some 40,000 of these clocks, although the horological trade refused to recognise them as timepieces and hence marketing and repairing difficulties arose. The advertisements of 1904 and 1905 refer to them as the " 'Ever-Ready' Plato Clock, an ideal timeteller without hands or dial. The change of the figure every minute on the lower plate is very catchy and impressively suggestive of the flight of time. The plates can be had in any colour — white, red, blue or dark green. Price 6 dollars."

A conventional pin pallet movement is in the base of the clock. In common with most of the novelty clocks these cannot be expected to keep atomic time and it is common practice for the tickets to fall in multiples instead of one at a time, thereby really making time fly! It usually takes but a minor adjustment to the small hand or pointer holding the bottom edge of the tickets to rectify this. There were four models, three on circular bases and the fourth on a rectangular base, see Figure 191. A later model was made by Junghans of Germany and the words 'Made in Germany' appear on the base. In the 1920s a further model was manufactured in France.

£90+

Figure 191

This advertisement appeared in one of the trade catalogues of Grimshaw Baxter and J.J. Elliott Ltd. at some date after 1909.

190

"EVER-READY" NOVELTIES.

THE "CHRONOS" CLOCKS.

No. 300 —Nickel-plated or Gilt Case.
Height 4⅞ins.
1-day Lever Time, **34/-**
Similar Clock with Alarm, **37/6**

No. 314.—Mahogany Case with Gilt
Columns.
Height 6¼ins. Width 6⅞ins.
8-day Lever Time, **82/-**

No. 230.—Gilt Case, Height 5⅛ins.
8-day Lever Time, **62/-**
No. 302.—1-day Lever Time, Black
Oxidised Steel, **49/-**; Gilt Finish, **42.-**

Courtesy of F.W. Elliott Ltd.

191

Figures 192a and 192b

8in. high. This is an extremely curious item and provides an excellent lesson on the importance of being able to document a clock in order to enhance its potential value. This particular clock is believed to have been manufactured in China in the early 1900s.

The veneered clock case is typical of that period. The main dial indicates the time, with the smaller apertures showing the sun or moon (whichever is appropriate) and the character indicative of the time according to the Chinese system. The old way had been to divide the day into twelve parts, each of which had their own Chinese character. The left hand panel indicates the day of the week, date and month. The right hand panel carried a thermometer, while the bottom panel has a hygrometer and an open aperture through which the movement of the pendulum is visible. A rough translation of the instructions pasted on the door read as follows:—

1. To start the clock — wind it by the key once a week.
2. If you need to adjust the time or the date, use the key and turn it until the correct reading appears.
3. In the short months (those with 30 days) turn the date to the 31st in the evening of the 30th day.
4. To adjust the month. Use the key and turn it until it shows the correct month.
5. To regulate the clock, just adjust the hand.
6. If the hygrometer is not accurate, use the lever at the back to adjust it. The clock should stand on a small metal stand with adjustable feet so that it can be moved in order to ensure a good circulation of air. In good weather the hygrometer should read between 70 to 50.

The most interesting horological feature of this clock is the unusual construction of the escapement which automatically adjusts to keep the clock in beat even if the case is tilted through ten to fifteen degrees either side of the vertical. Apart from this the movement is perfectly straight forward and purely functional.

£55+ depending on source

318

192a

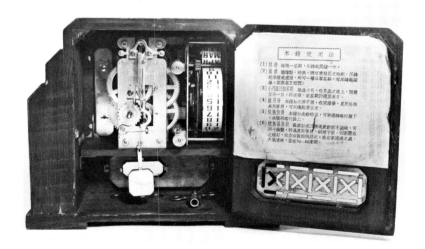

192b

319

Chapter XI
CLOCK CASES

Decorative Clocks

The majority of the clocks in the following illustrations are valued primarily for their decorative appeal and are of little interest to the horologist who refers to them as 'furnishings'. However, even a hardened clock collector may occasionally wish to purchase a piece for its decorative appeal and not solely for technical interest.

One of the factors influencing the price of this category of clock is the type of metal used for the cases or mounts.

a) Bronze — originally a mixture of copper and tin. Figures in bronze are much sought after by collectors today and it is an accepted fact that it is particularly suitable for producing sharp castings which can be finished later to a high degree of perfection by chasing, chiselling or engraving. Although by the Great Exhibition of 1851 opinion was deploring the quality of the mass produced figures, statues, mounts, etc., being made by the foundries using the sand casting methods, they are still highly desirable pieces.

b) Brass — originally a mixture of copper and zinc. Although this does not produce quite such a sharp casting it has most of the virtues of bronze and was used extensively for mounts. In fact the two metals have now become so adulterated and the proportions of their basic components so altered to facilitate casting that there is often little difference in their composition.

c) Spelter and other similar alloys — basically mixtures of tin and zinc. Although used extensively during the latter half of the nineteenth century for the sake of cheapness and the ease with which it was cast (its melting point is much lower than that of brass or bronze), it was too soft to be finished in any way. Therefore, the quality of the detail depends entirely upon the soundness of the mould. It also has the added disadvantage of being less durable than bronze and brass and cases or figures made in this material need to be closely examined. If too much zinc has been used the alloy will be soft and articles made from it will readily dent; whereas if an excess of tin has been used the alloy will be brittle and extremities may be broken or damaged. Repairs are difficult.

To distinguish between the first two metals mentioned and spelter is relatively simple as a piece made of spelter is inevitably lighter than a comparable example in brass or bronze. Also it should be possible to mark the surface lightly (microscopically on the base!) of spelter with a finger nail, while bronze and brass are too hard for this to make a mark. Each example should be judged on its merits; quality of finish and definition is often of first importance and not necessarily the choice of material. Just because it is bronze it does not have to be a superb piece any more than one of spelter has to be poor — a well executed spelter case or figure can be superior to a poor bronze example.

When used for figures, statues, etc., bronze is frequently left to acquire its own patina with age, but when used for cases or mounts it was normal to fire-gilt or mercurial gild. The latter was introduced about 1785 and produced a beautiful finish, but due to health hazards to workers coming in contact with the mercury vapours given off during the process it has been banned. 'Mercury Madness', otherwise known as 'Hatters' Shakes', was the inevitable death of those working under these conditions. Electro-gilding was introduced by Elkington in 1836; coming into more general use by 1840. 'Ormolu' is the term used to describe cases or mounts cast in brass or bronze and gilt. It is possible to have cases regilded, but care has to be taken at each stage to ensure that the interstices are well drained and that no residual fluid remains. It would be criminal to use a cheap gold lacquer on any of these cases.

Spelter pieces are also generally electro-gilded although some of the extremely cheap examples were lacquered to resemble bronze or gilt.

Other price-influencing factors are commented on in the copy accompanying the illustrations.

In most instances the movements in these cases are the round French movements as found in the black marble-cased clocks. Exceptions being the inevitable American copies. Care must be exercised in purchasing a case with the intention of adding or replacing the movement with one from another clock. Although conceding that the majority of the French movements were of a standard size, the diameters of the bezels and dials were not so constant and it is remarkable how elusive the exact substitute can be!

Many of the clocks were originally part of a garniture and protected from the dust and atmosphere by a glass shade. Although it is obviously desirable to have examples in their original state it would be foolish to refrain from making a purchase if these were missing. It is more important to ascertain that side ornaments being sold with the clock started life with it and have not been added since to enhance the price.

Figure 193

This large clock and matching stand was manufactured by Coalport about 1837 and sold by Sparks of Worcester, a notable retailer and decorator of porcelain. Although the face and sides both feature the celest ground with encrusted flowers and painted decoration in a small reserve, the reverse of the clock has been left white but with a number of finely painted floral studies. To a collector of Coalport a highly desirable piece, but although attractive to a horologist the price would deter his awakened interest in fine porcelains.

£500+

Figure 194

Two good examples of French clock garniture of gilt-metal and porcelain.

That on the right has a turquoise-blue dial painted with trophies as are the other porcelain insets on the clock and candelabra. Striking is on a gong. It is always wise when a clock and side ornaments are of such complexity of design to be meticulous in checking for damage, as the overall effect is so overwhelming that important points can be missed and the wrong valuation placed on the item in question. Missing hands or, in this example, the linked chains would be of nuisance value but not irretrievable, whereas broken porcelain panels or decapitated figures would be a disaster. It fetched £200 in 1976 and would have reached a higher price if the porcelain panels had been the product of one of the important factories.

£350+

The clock below is a nineteenth century French clock with an eight-day striking movement.

Courtesy of Parsons, Welch & Cowell

325

Figure 195

An uncommon late nineteenth century French bronze, porcelain and champlevé enamel clock garniture, with a two train gong striking movement. The backplate is stamped with the maker's name 'G. Mignon' and the fact that they had won a Medaille d'Argent at one of the Exhibitions. Its value would lie in the high quality of the work and decoration put into the case and side ornaments and it is not surprising that it fetched £2,800 in a London saleroom in 1976. These clocks can rocket in price on occasion and a safer figure would be £1,500— £2,000. A similar clock *on its own* sold in early 1977 for £780.

Courtesy of Sotheby's Belgravia

Figure 196

13in. high. In view of the decorative dial and other porcelain insets, together with the high quality of the casting, this would be a desirable piece. Many of these clocks stand on decorative bases and are covered with glass shades; these have frequently become lost or damaged, which is unfortunate as they do protect the gilding from dust and atmospheric impurities. It fetched £400 in 1977. A spelter example might make £150.

Figure 197

14in. high. An example of a pleasant compact French clock with porcelain dial and gilt-metal case. Note that the casting is not so sharp as that shown in Figure 196. It is possible to date the clock as c.1850 by identifying the maker of the movement (Popon à Paris).

£150 – £250

Figure 198

16in. high. A further example of an exceptionally high quality clock garniture. The clock is of gilt-metal and alabaster with matching candelabra. This particular example provides several excellent points to note, examine and assess before purchasing a similar clock. The two gilt columns are not upright — is it a simple matter of tightening and straightening the supporting rods that run through their centres or have these become rusted and difficult to restore? The metal swag on the left-hand alabaster column is missing, what can be done to replace it? It is often possible to find replacement finials, swags, feet, etc., of a conventional pattern in an architectural ironmongers — one well-known London example being J.D. Beardmore & Co. of Percy Street, London, W.1. It is not known, however, how standard a pattern this particular swag is. Obviously one could be specially cast but even if sufficiently fortunate to find someone prepared to do this it could prove expensive (£10 to £15) and it may be necessary to have all the parts regilded in order that the colour of the replacement and original pieces match. This particular problem has two satisfactory solutions. Either sacrifice both the swags from the candelabra and manufacture one for the clock (the resulting pin holes could be covered by small brass rosettes) or replace all four swags by a new set. As it is not an insurmountable problem it should not deter from any intentions to purchase but may influence the price one is willing to pay.

£300 – £500

Figure 199

13½in. high. The case of this mantel clock is silvered and gilt-bronze with a brass dial inscribed with the retailer's name (Elkington & Co. Silversmiths, Liverpool). This is an exceptionally good quality case both in material (bronze) and in design and has the added advantage of having a movement by an interesting maker. C.A. Richard et Cie were founded in Paris in 1848 and opened a branch in London in 1857. This branch is still trading under the name of the French Clock House Ltd. They were makers of good quality clocks including carriage clocks for which they received an Honourable Mention in the Paris Exhibition of 1889. The movement of this example of their work is stamped with their trade mark — the letters R C with two snakes entwined round a staff between them.

Over £400

Figure 200

16½in. high. This example of a French clock is in an ebonised and red tortoiseshell 'case' of Egyptian style. Many clocks from the early part of the nineteenth century have designs influenced by the rise of interest in Egyptology following the Napoleonic campaigns in Egypt. This later specimen is from the end of the century. The pendulum is a mock compensated one. The white enamel dial is recessed and signed John Hall, Paris. This is not an indication that John Hall was a Parisian clockmaker but that he had the clock made in Paris. Striking is on a count wheel that had ceased to be used in England by 1700-20 but continued to be used in France. The value of this clock would again lie in its decorative qualities and it was sold in 1977 for £240.

Figure 201

14½in. high. A further example of a metal cased mantel clock. This specimen has a brass case with two matching ornaments. The movement was stamped with the name of Japy Frères et Cie. The value of this garniture is similar to the clock shown in Figure 199. Whereas it could be said that a bronze case was superior to a brass one, this clock has the advantage of being part of a set. It fetched £260 in 1977.

335

Figure 202

17½in. high. Although a nineteenth century copy of a Louis XV case this is a handsome clock in a brass and brown tortoiseshell boulle case. Boulle is a type of inlay frequently found in French furniture as well as smaller items such as boxes, clock cases, etc. The process was first used by André Charles Boulle (1642-1732) and involves the gluing of a thin layer of tortoiseshell to one of brass, pewter or silver and then pasting a paper pattern for the marquetry over the top. This is then cut out. To avoid wastage of materials the layers of brass and tortoiseshell are then separated and two different effects can be achieved by using the brass on the tortoiseshell background and vice versa. The resulting veneer is then firmly glued to the carcase of the piece being decorated. Various hues can be given to the tortoiseshell by placing coloured foil beneath it. The mounts in this example are of gilt-metal. They are added both for decorative appeal and in order to protect the fragile edges and corners of the inlay. The repair of boulle work is not to be undertaken lightly and, bearing in mind that before any restoration can be undertaken time is spent in removing the mounts and movement, it can be a costly repair to have carried out professionally. Although, theoretically, it can be refixed by the application of heat, glue and pressure, it is often found in practice that the shell has lost much of its natural oil and become extremely fragile. Missing mounts would have to be specially cast.

Price for one this size £600—£700; one 12in. high about £400+.

337

Figure 203

The movement of this clock was *examined* by Lund & Blockley — a firm of whom little is recorded except that they carried on an extensive business in tower clocks, silverware and pocket watches in India and had possible connections with Lund of Barraud and Lund, London. They are listed as having traded in London between 1875 and 1881. As the movement has every appearance of being French they would have merely imported and checked it was in working order prior to casing. However, it is the case that is of great interest to anyone devoted to Victorian art pottery as it is a product from the Southall pottery of the Martin brothers. There is an excellent account of this pottery to be found in *Victorian Art Pottery* by E. Lloyd Thomas, but it is sufficient to say here that they manufactured jugs, vases, etc., between 1873 and 1930, although it is the work of Wallace Martin (1843-1923) with its grotesque birds and beasts that is particularly sought after. This example was sold 1973/4 for £280.

£550+

339

Figure 204

28in. high. There is no doubt that the value of this piece lies purely in its excellent quality bronze figures and general aesthetic appeal. It could even be said that the clock dial is superfluous and added nothing to the composition of the group. It most certainly has an unusual pair of hands — the head of the snake pointing to the hours, while its tail indicates the minutes. One small casting has been lost from the right hand foot, but that could be recast. It sold for £840 in 1976.

£1,300+

Figure 205

This elegant timepiece has a white alabaster case, with gilt-bronze figures, feet and mouldings; however, the quality of the castings are poor and lack definition as can be noted particularly in the hands and faces of the cherubs. It fetched £200 in 1977. It is interesting to note that as the dial is somewhat smaller than the total diameter of the movement, the arbor to the Brocot suspension has been placed outside and above the dial with a decorative escutcheon.

£250

Four-Glass Case Clocks

Although four-glass clocks are sometimes referred to as 'regulators' or 'library carriage clocks' neither term is correct. They are not to be confused with the large French mantel regulators of the early nineteenth century and their only resemblance to a carriage clock lies in the similarity of case style. There can be some superb examples with calendar dials, phase of moon, etc., but those more commonly found have the French drum movements that were produced in such abundance from the mid-1800s and have been described in the chapter dealing with Marble-Cased Clocks. Naturally there are exceptions and these include copies manufactured in America by the Ansonia Clock Company of New York (their catalogue for 1914 has some eighteen pages of 'crystal regulators'). The examples in Figures 207-211 are, however, more typical and vary only in shape and decoration.

The enamel dials can be plain or decorated with swags of flowers, with others having a recessed centre and visible Brocot escapement (see page 12 for further details of this). The majority of the pendulums are mercury compensated although some examples appear with an Ellicott pendulum. The former was invented by George Graham (1673-1751) in 1721 and works on the principle that the mercury in the jar (or jars) expands upwards to compensate for any increase in the length of the pendulum rod caused by a rise in the temperature. The mercurial pendulum used in these clocks usually has two glass jars each containing an equal amount of mercury. This is for aesthetic reasons as well as ensuring a quicker response to any temperature change. The clocks illustrated in Figures 207, 208, 210 and 211 have mercurial pendulums. Difficulty can be experienced in obtaining replacement jars and it must be remembered that mercury is a dangerous and expensive commodity. It should be possible to obtain advice if not assistance from any of the restorers who specialise in barometers.

The Ellicott pendulum is an interesting mechanism. The two outer brass rods upon any rise in temperature expand and press downwards on two pivoted steel levers. This causes the other end of the levers to push upwards thus raising the bob. This pendulum was devised by John Ellicott (1706-1772) and according to the records of the Royal Society, of which he was a Fellow, was shown to them in 1738. Figure 209 illustrates a clock based on the principle established by Ellicott.

Figure 206a

22in. high. This is a fine French mantel clock — frequently referred to as a 'Mantel Regulator' which although a not strictly accurate term does, in this instance, reflect the quality and indicate correctly the accuracy of their timekeeping. This particular example has, apart from the perpetual calendar and barometer, a rather unusual and obscure visible escapement which could at first glance be taken to be that of Achille Brocot. It is, however, attributed to Desfontaines about 1853. Comparison of Figures 3a, 3b and 206b will demonstrate the difference. The movement had a rise-and-fall regulation, a gridiron pendulum and struck on a bell. The inscription on the dial reads 'Le Roy et Fils Palais Royal Gal[ies] Montpensier, 13 and 15 Paris 211 Regent Street, London'. The connection between Desfontaines and Le Roy is interesting. According to Charles Allix in his book *Carriage Clocks*, on the 30th June, 1845, Charles-Louis Le Roy sold his business to an employee Casimir Halley Desfontaines on the condition that he continued to trade under the name 'Le Roy & Fils'. This request was complied with until 1889. 211 Regent Street was their London address between 1866 and 1875, thereby limiting the date of this particular clock to these years. Perhaps not a vital piece of information, but nevertheless an exercise in adding a little colour to the provenance of an excellent clock. It fetched £1,600 in 1977. A not unexpected price in view of the interesting escapement and the perpetual calendar work.

Estimate for the 'next one', £1,750+.

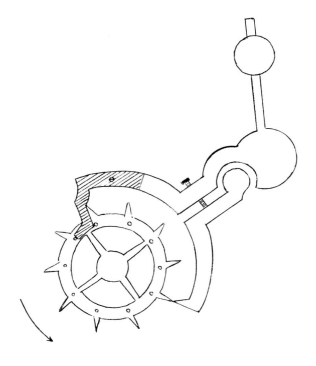

Figure 206b

Line drawing of the visible coup de perdu escapement attributed to
Desfontaines in 1853 seen on the clock illustrated in Figure 206a.

Figure 207

It is not surprising that this extremely decorative cloisonné and onyx garniture sold early in 1976 for £820, although it is basically the same clock as that shown in Figure 211 in a more attractive case. This is a good example of how the case influences the price and not the merits of the movement. However, if the movement had been American the price would have been slightly lower, but nothing of any great significance.

£1,300+

347

Figure 208

14in. high. This is a particularly good specimen of a French four-glass mantel clock, with mercurial pendulum and was manufactured in Paris for Maple & Co. of London. The movement is stamped with the name of 'S. Marti et Cie'. The decorative bevelled glass side panels are etched with swags and geometrical borders, while the case is solid brass with attractive brass castings. The *pied de biche* feet are especially pleasing. The white enamel dial is recessed with a visible Brocot escapement. The pallet stones appear to be agate. Hourly and half-hourly striking is on a bell although examples are common with striking on a gong. Generally gong striking is slightly less popular than bell striking. It is interesting to compare this with the example in Figure 211.

£300 – £500

Figure 209

9½in. high. A further example of a French four-glass clock with a plain
enamel dial, striking on a bell at the hour and half-hour, with the name
'Japy Frère et Cie' stamped on the backplate. Strictly speaking the
pendulum is not an Ellicott compensated pendulum, although loosely
based on his method of using the different coefficients of expansion of
two metal rods within the pendulum bob. The greater expansion/
contraction of one rod against the other operates a spring which raises/
lowers the bob.

£200 – £300

Courtesy of Sotheby's Belgravia

Figure 210

15½in. high. This example has the disadvantage of having a case not of brass but of gilt-metal, otherwise it is an unusual shape for a four-glass case which is interesting. This also has a 'plain' visible Brocot escapement and would have been made late nineteenth century.

£200 – £300+

Courtesy of Sotheby's Belgravia

Figure 211

17½in. high. Upon comparing this example with that shown in Figure 208 it is quickly noted that, apart from the lack of decoration to the case, this clock is less desirable for several other reasons. It is a larger clock and, therefore, not quite so versatile, the visible Brocot escapement is more functional than decorative, neither does there appear to be any maker's name on the movement. This would be a later specimen manufactured at the end of the nineteenth century. It was sold in 1977 for £210.

£300+

Art Deco and Art Nouveau Cases

This is a further group of clocks that, although of no great interest to the horologist, would be of considerable importance to the collector of art deco or art nouveau pieces. Unless, by some remarkable coincidence, an interest in clocks was accompanied by some knowledge of the artists and their work, it would be advisable to seek a specialist dealer and rely upon his assistance. As can be seen by the example in Figure 212, prices can be extremely high! However, the inference should not be taken that all clocks in art deco or art nouveau cases are worth a considerable amount of money — this is only true of the pieces by known and important artists. Naturally their designs influenced the manufacturers of clock cases and this can be seen in contemporary examples. A movement housed in a glass case signed by Réné Lalique would be worth several hundreds of pounds, but one in a similar case by an unknown maker or designer would be valued accordingly with the quality of the movement coming to the fore. The clock in Figure 243, although it has an art deco-styled case, is valued highly because it has an extremely rare and virtually unique electric movement.

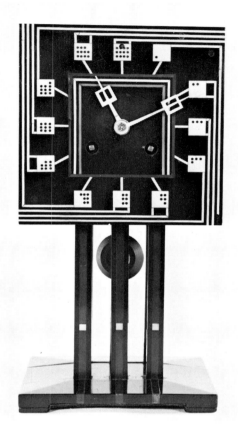

Figure 212

10in. high. The sole reason for the high price of this clock (it cost over £7,000 at auction in 1976) is that it was designed for 'Derngate', Northampton, about 1917 by Charles Rennie Mackintosh (1868-1928) the leader of the Glasgow School of art nouveau artists. The case veneered with ebony and inlaid was made in the Isle of Man by German prisoners of war. It is aptly named 'The Domino Clock'.

Figure 213

17in. high. The information offered in a catalogue entry to the effect that the design on the case of this clock appears strongly influenced by Sir Edward Burne-Jones (1833-1898), the painter and friend of William Morris, would greatly enhance the price of this item. The gilded and ebonised case is painted with scrolled leafwork and Gothic lettering, and is surmounted by stained ivory tiles finished with gilt metal minarets. The enamelled dial is signed 'W.A. Perry & Co. Birmingham' and 'Made in France'. The latter is possibly referring to the French movement. There is nothing of horological significance to affect the price of the clock. The auction price in 1977 was £320.

Courtesy of Sotheby's Belgravia

355

Figure 214

18in. high. The design of the case of the clock shown here is typical of the flowing lines of the art nouveau style at the turn of the century. The figure is of a relatively high quality casting in gilding metal that has been electro-gilded. The unglazed dial is silvered with raised stylised numerals, and ornate hands. The movement is French with the maker's name 'Marti et Cie' stamped on the backplate together with the information that this maker received a Medaille d'Argent at the 1889 Exhibition, thereby indicating a date of manufacture after this date. Striking is on a gong. As has been stated previously, the American clock manufacturers were swift to copy designs from other countries especially France, so it is particularly interesting to note that in the 1906/1907 catalogue of the New Haven Clock Company of New Haven, Connecticut, a similar clock appears as part of a garniture. The figure is identical, but the dial of the clock is porcelain, with bevelled glass within a decorative bezel. The style of the hands is *fleur de lys*. The caption to the American set reads:—

'LIBITINA SET

Clock, Height 17¼ inches; Width 9¼ inches. Vases, Height 14¾ inches

Four-inch Porcelain Dial, with Bevelled Glass. Ormolu Gold Plated Case

Eight-day, Half-hour Strike, Cathedral Gong

Clock, List Price, $26.50   Vases, per Pair, List Price $29.25

Set Complete, List Price, $55.75"

If spelter, £100—£200; if bronze £250—£400.

Figure 215

This clock was part of a garniture — the side ornaments being a pair of vases. The base of the clock is black marble with white inset pieces, while the figure is of spelter with ivorine hands and face. The resulting effect was rather attractive. The value of this clock would depend entirely upon its value as a piece of art deco, with the fact that it is a timepiece being of secondary importance. The movement was made in France (it had words to the effect of being Paris finished stamped on the backplate), but has a count wheel for the strike. Even for a French clock this is surprising on an example of this late date, and speculation is roused as to whether an old movement was utilised by the manufacturer. This would endorse the emphasis upon this being sold as a work of art rather than a clock. Examples have sold recently at auction in the £120–£160 price bracket.

Figure 216

19½in. high. The case of this clock is of ebonised wood with china panels. The style is similar to the clock designed by Henry and Lewis F. Day (illustrated in the *Aesthetic Movement* by E. Aslin). Other examples have been seen with panels reminiscent of blue and white delft tiles.

£120+, the more porcelain the better

Figure 217

There is, to the horologist, only one fascinating feature to this
particular clock and this is the fact that it realised in a 1977 sale the
astounding figure of £3,600! The movement has no particular merit,
the value being entirely dependent upon the art nouveau figure gracing
the case, which is by F. Preiss, whose work is extremely sought after.

Figure 218

The clock here and those on the following pages are a selection of the type of art nouveau clocks featured in the highly influential magazine, *The Studio*, between 1893 and 1910. Many of these models were 'one-offs', and therefore the collector is unlikely to see the actual examples. Their importance, however, lies in the enormous influence such pieces had on contemporary designs.

The prices of these clocks will depend largely on the materials used, but unless the case is by a well known art nouveau name, the value is likely to be in the £80–£120 bracket for smaller clocks, while the longcase illustrated on page 364 would probably fall in the £150–£200 bracket at auction.

These pieces rarely have any feature of horological significance and are simply cases designed to fit into the appropriate setting.

The clock above was designed by Otto Prutscher, c.1901.

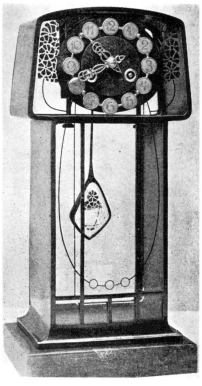

Two more clocks designed by Otto Prutscher of Vienna about 1905. He was then about twenty six, having won a Rothschild travelling scholarship. He studied in Paris and London and won a silver medal at Turin. Like most followers of the artistic movement he rebelled against the poorly made, mass produced sameness of Victorian design and concentrated on making something different, even if it was more expensive.

362

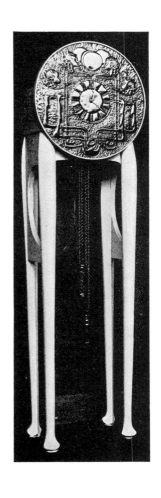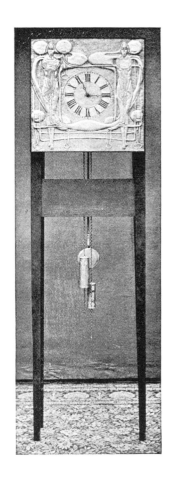

Two clocks, designed about 1897 and made by Margaret MacDonald (1865-1953) and Frances MacDonald (1874-1921), who were respectively the wives of Charles Rennie MacKintosh and Herbert MacNair.

Nothing quite like these has been on the market recently. Prices are suggested on the basis of the designers and materials used, and would probably be in the £400–£600 region.

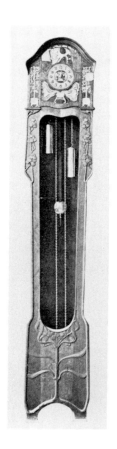

Left: A shelf clock made by the famous C.R. Ashbee and exhibited by the firm of Wylie & Lochead in the Glasgow Exhibition, 1901. Like so much of the art nouveau furniture the woodwork is solid oak and very simple, in contrast to the highly ornate carving of the standard Victorian mahogany furniture.

Right: A longcase clock exhibited in Glasgow by La Maison Moderne, but by contrast to Ashbee's clock, highly decorative. It has the typical curved lines in both the outline of the case and the decoration on the base. It was designed by F. Ringer.

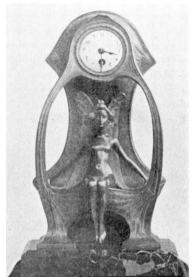

Two clocks by Albert Reimann, a young sculptor from Germany, and made about 1900. Exhibited at the Berlin Kunst Ausstellung, they were made in bronze, silver and majolica, and one can see the sculptor's approach in the designs which were then considered fairly advanced.

About £80 – £120 each

Clock designed by Otto Prutscher, c.1905.

Figure 219

The illustration right and that overleaf show a selection of marble, bronze and enamel decorative clock cases offered in the catalogue of Hour, Lavigne & Cie of 7, rue Saint-Anastase, Paris, earlier this century.

The clock, right, would be priced at about £40–£60 because it is part of a set, but has a comparatively small value; those on page 368 have a slight art deco appeal and would probably fetch £25–£40 at auction.

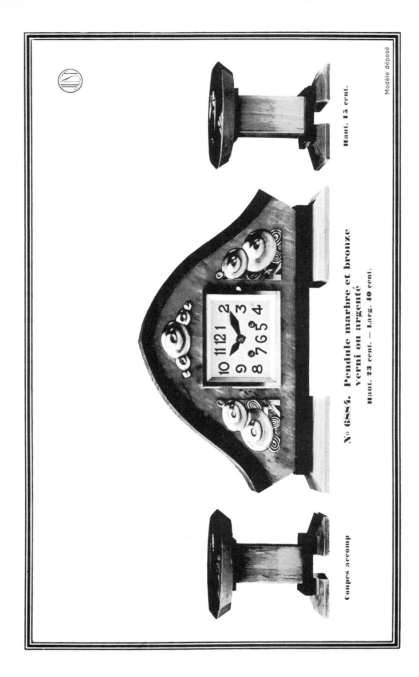

Coupes accomp

No 6884. Pendule marbre et bronze
verni ou argenté
Haut. 23 cent. — Larg. 40 cent.

Haut. 15 cent.

Modèle déposé

367

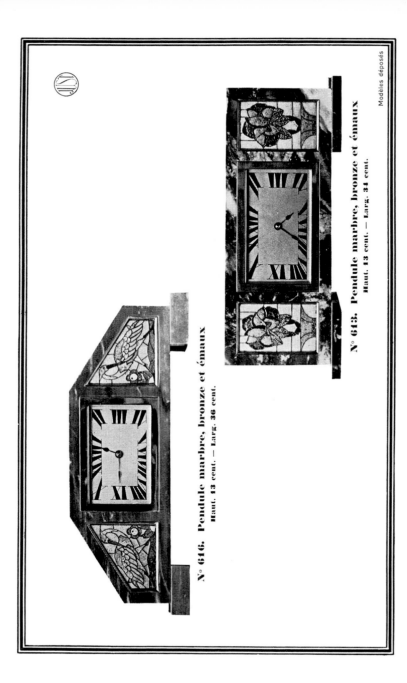

N° 613. Pendule marbre, bronze et émaux
Haut. 13 cent. — Larg. 34 cent.

N° 616. Pendule marbre, bronze et émaux
Haut. 13 cent. — Larg. 36 cent.

Chapter XII
ELECTRIC CLOCKS

Although several stalwarts have persevered and ignored the initial derision of their fellow horologists, it is only in the past year or so that examples of electrical horology have been more widely recognised as being worthy of study and collection. In 1970 the Electrical Horology Group was formed as a sub group of the Antiquarian Horological Society and, largely due to their work in this field of research, sufficient accurate information was available to form the basis upon which the exhibition held in 1977 at the Science Museum, London, entitled Electrifying Time, was built. 1977 was the chosen year as it coincided with the centenary of the death of Alexander Bain who is acknowledged as the 'Father of Electrical Timekeeping' in this country. Although as early as the sixth century BC electricity and magnetism were recognised phenomena, it was not until much later that they were fully understood and mastered. During the eighteenth and nineteenth centuries much research was carried out in England and on the Continent until finally in the mid-1800s sufficient technical advancements (magnets, reliable current sources, etc.) had been made for the practical application to be made possible. Steinheil (1801-1870), a Professor of Munich University, built a master clock which sent out impulses to drive slave dials, but the pioneer in electrical timekeeping in this country was Alexander Bain (1811-1877). During his boyhood in Caithness, Scotland, he had become intensely interested in the then extremely topical subject of applying electricity to telegraphic communications, but soon began to realise that it had a potential use in timetelling. In 1841 Bain took out his first patent (Patent No. 8783), the contents of which were to provide the foundation stone for future electrical horology for nearly a century. Other patents soon followed. Most of the extant examples of his clocks are in museums (see Figure 220), but one came on the market in 1977 and was sold for several thousands of pounds. To date, only the existence of two small models suitable for standing on a shelf have been recorded. Both are in private collections – the existence of the example appearing in Figure 221 only becoming known recently.

It had now become possible to provide the distribution of a standard time over a much wider area. In the past an extremely localised standard time had been obtained from observatories where either a time ball was dropped or a gun fired at an appointed hour each day in order that the local inhabitants could set their timepieces. Now, using the wires of private telegraph companies, and later those of the Post Office, signals could be sent further afield either to activate the timeballs electrically or synchronise secondary dials. Examples of master clocks from this period can be found in various museums and their invention is attributable to such men as F.J. Ritchie of Edinburgh (Patent No. 2078 taken out in 1872); R.L. Jones of Chester (Patent No. 702 taken out in 1857), Lund of London (Patent No. 3924 taken out in 1876) to mention but a few of the English patentees.

Possibly the most important continental pioneer in this field was Dr. Mattheus Hipp of Neuchatel (1813-1893), as the principle of his toggle was used in modified forms in many of the later master clocks and battery electric clocks. This consists of a toggle or trailer attached to the pendulum, which passes quite freely over a notched block of steel until the swing falls below a predetermined arc, whereupon the toggle is 'caught' in the notch, which depresses the block, closes the circuit, and the pendulum receives a fresh impulse from the electro-magnet. Hipp stated that he first conceived the idea of using what later became known as the 'Hipp Toggle' as early as 1834, but the first clocks using this did not appear until 1842. Examples of the original clocks are very rare in this country, the agent for them having been a colleague of Professor Wheatstone. They are more commonly found on the Continent and it is known that the firm of Peyer-Favarger & Company of Neuchatel and the Telegraphic Manufacturing Company, also of Neuchatel, were manufacturing his master clock after 1860. The backplates of the original clocks have some acknowledgement to the fact that they were manufactured to the specifications laid down by Hipp stamped upon them. This can be merely 'M. Hipp' or it can have the additional information 'Neuchatel — Swiss' and a serial number. Pure copies or variations of the Hipp toggle have always appealed to the model or precision engineer wishing to make an electric master clock. This is worth bearing in mind when assessing any unusual clock working on this principle.

The next step was to introduce systems of master clocks with subsidiary dials (slave dials) suitable for using in large factories, public buildings, etc., in order to provide a uniform time throughout the building. This had never been completely successful when using a group of mechanical clocks. It is from this group of electric clocks that the collector will be able, with varying success, to seek examples to acquire. Upon studying the patents taken out it quickly becomes evident that a great deal of ingenuity and enterprise was shown by the inventors of the day. Their main problems being to find a contact that did not wear or tarnish, thereby reducing the electrical efficiency, and a method of impulsing the pendulum but at the same time leaving it 'free'. Many of these designs never left the drawing board while many others died a natural death due to inherent faults that only became apparent after production had commenced. This is one field of collecting where the failures are often of more value than the successful examples.

Basically electric clocks fall into three main categories:—
1. Those that are electrically impulsed. When the pendulum falls below a predetermined arc an electric circuit is made and the pendulum receives a further impulse.
2. Those that are electrically rewound. The same principle but instead of the pendulum receiving an impulse a small motor is rewound which powers the clock for a further period.
3. Those that are synchronous. These are the clocks that appeared so prolifically in the 1930s as small domestic shelf clocks running from the mains. The alternating current synchronous motor was first used in clocks in 1918 by an American, H.C. Warren, but these clocks were not a practical proposition in this country until 1927 when the introduction of the National Grid assured a standard alternating current of 50 cycles. Basically these clocks were an electric meter measuring the amount of current that passed through and recording it on a dial. They attracted a great deal of criticism and scorn from the horological trade. Obviously they were adversely affected by current failures and variations and were later superseded by the modern battery movements. Trailing wires provided a further complication although many houses built during this period made provision for them by placing a small two-pin socket in the wall immediately above the centre of the fireplace surround. These clocks can barely be considered collectable now, but will become increasingly so for several reasons. As interior decorators turn to this period for inspiration and converts seek

authentic pieces to match the rest of the décor; as the introduction of quartz crystal movements expands and mechanical clocks increase in value and, lastly, as the collecting of items using early plastics increases so will the desirability of these clocks. With regards to the last point, there is a rising interest in all of the early types of plastics, i.e. Bakelite, etc., and as many of the cases for these movements were made in the 'new' materials it will not be just the horologists that make selective purchases from this range of clocks. Purchasers do need to be selective as it is only early examples or those with any technical interest that deserve to be preserved for posterity.

The following illustrations show a representative selection of master clocks by some makers. As can be seen from these illustrations they are housed in a variety of cases from the longcase style of the Bentley Earth Driven Clock (Figure 230) to the smaller wall hanging example made by the Silent Electric Company (Figure 231). Unfortunately it has not been possible to include every known type. A list of some of the known literature on the subject has been included in the bibliography, but in most instances these are contemporary references as, apart from the researches of some members of the Electrical/ Horology Group of the Antiquarian Horological Society, nothing has been published in the last thirty or so years. Obviously some examples are more rare than others. It should be possible, however, to find a good working example manufactured by the Synchronome Company and these are highly desirable pieces for many reasons — one of which is the extremely high standard of workmanship put into their manufacture. The finish on the parts being commensurate with that used in instrument making rather than the more usual mass production look of most of the other clocks of this date.

The name of Frank Hope-Jones (1867-1950) is only second in importance to that of Alexander Bain when discussing the history of electrical horology. When reviewing one of his books in 1931, Prof. Sir Charles V. Boys refers to him as "The high priest" and "like St. Athanasius, his faith is clear and emphatic . . . St. Hope-Jones". Possibly not all would subscribe to quite such extravagant praise today, as unfortunately in his enthusiasm, Hope-Jones swept all other contemporaries' thoughts to one side. However, it was he who, after some thirteen years of experimentation, patented in 1908 an electric master clock whose accuracy at that time was only matched by the most accurate astronomical regulators. Initially working with George Bennet Bowell (1875-1942) he formed the Synchronome Company at Birkenhead in 1895. This was the date of his first patent taken out in collaboration with Bowell. By 1908 the Company had moved to London and his partnership with Bowell had been dissolved. From this date onwards Hope-Jones fervently worked to make the Synchronome Master Clock the commercial success it deserved to be. Their installations included shops, government and public buildings, railway stations, etc., both here and abroad. William Hamilton Shortt, originally an engineer on the London and South Western Railway, became interested in precision timekeeping in 1906. Having met Hope-Jones in 1910, he continued his own line of research and patented his own clock in 1911. However, the early examples were not up to the standard Shortt had set himself, but by 1921 he had mastered the problems and the Shortt Free Pendulum Clock was patented (No. 187814). It was these clocks invented by Shortt (now a Director of the Synchronome Company) and manufactured by the Company that became the standard timepiece for observatories the world over until superseded by the Atomic Clock. It is doubtful if it would be possible to find one of these clocks on the open market – their location is well documented – but there are many examples of the more standard models made to Hope-Jones' specifications to be found.

It is just worth bearing in mind that in the 1930s and early 1940s the Company made available to model engineers the castings, etc., of their clocks on the condition that the end product was for personal use and not for resale, so some examples on the market might not be from the commercial run of the Company. These examples would command a much lower price than those manufactured by the Synchronome Company. Often the cases were not to standard specifications and there would not be a serial number stamped on the base of the Retard/Advance plate on the left-hand side of the movement. Hope-Jones was the most prolific writer on electric clocks at this time. Although his books were basically tracing the evolution of the Synchronome Clock, and therefore omitted many other interesting contemporary examples, they are invaluable reference books for present day collectors. With one exception – *Electric Clocks* – they have the added advantage of having been reprinted which means that those who are not too worried about owning early editions can have a cheaper working copy. The titles of these reprints are:– *Electrical*

Timekeeping, Electric Clocks and Chimes and *Electric Clocks and How to Make Them.* Both of the later books provided the details of construction for model engineers using the castings provided by the firm. It is no longer possible to obtain these parts in England.

It is possible to date approximately the movements made by this Company. Basically there were three models. The earlier models (approximately before 1930) had a smooth finish to the casting holding the movement and were without a damper for the gravity arm (see Figure 223). After about 1930 a 'crackle' finish appeared on the casting and a small damper was added to the gravity arm. Both these points are illustrated in Figure 225, although the damper is somewhat obscured by the pendulum rod.

The third model is that shown in Figure 226, and was an experimental movement manufactured in 1922. Although it eliminated some of the minor faults of the standard design it introduced others and this, together with the fact that it needed expert technical skill to set up and maintain, led to its discontinuation. Only one hundred were produced.

Other types of master clocks can be found with varying degrees of success. The sources range from the large London salesrooms to firms specialising in demolition. Generally speaking the faults are of a mechanical nature, with only minor adjustments to the pawl, count wheel, toggle, etc., necessary as often they were still in use until placed on the market. The majority of these clocks run on three volts for the master clock and one and a half for each slave dial. It is as well to familiarise oneself with the working of the example in question before assuming it is one of the exceptions and thereby burning out the solenoids with too strong a current.

One of the earliest examples of an English 'domestic' electric clock was that first patented by Herbert Scott in 1902 (Patent No. 10271). Herbert Scott was a Yorkshireman, born in Bradford in 1865, and brother of Alfred Scott the designer of the Scott two-stroke, water cooled engine for motor cycles. Initially Scott had problems finding anyone interested in manufacturing and marketing his clock. Eventually he managed to interest the Ever-Ready Electric Specialities Company who were at that time promoting a number of novelty clocks, especially those using batteries. The most intriguing feature of this clock is that the pendulum has the unusual characteristic of swinging back to front instead of the more normal side to side. This, together with the fact that the later examples have the back of the case mirrored, can be most disconcerting. Examples of the two styles — early and late — can be seen in Figures 235 and 236. These clocks were not a great commercial success and production ceased by 1912. The figure of five hundred has been suggested as the quantity produced.

One of the most commercially successful clocks was that manufactured by the Eureka Clock Company Limited between 1909 and 1914. The inventor of this clock was one Timothy Bernard Powers but the patent (No. 14614) taken out in 1906 was taken out jointly with the Kutnow brothers of New York, USA. The latter being a firm of manufacturing chemists with premises in the Clerkenwell area. Whether it was this tenuous association with horology that led them to set up a small clock factory in 1909 at 361 City Road, London, to commence manufacturing and marketing these clocks is not known. The three years between taking out this English patent and actually commencing production were spent in perfecting the design, negotiating the forming of the Company, acquiring the premises and some preliminary advertising. The Kutnow brothers utilised their expertise in the art of advertising to good purpose and even approached Edward VII, for an audience. They possibly hoped that he would accept one as a gift thereby setting the seal of approval on their product. There is no record of this occurring. By the time production had ceased in 1914 some 10,000 clocks had been manufactured. Clocks bearing a higher serial number than this are generally regarded as having been made from parts disposed of when the firm went into liquidation. Naturally the outbreak of the First World War meant that all their skilled workmen were needed for war work, but the firm had been in difficulties prior to this. If the clocks had a fault it was that they were too well made and, therefore, too expensive. Their stockists included Harrods, Knightsbridge, London, and Asprey Ltd. of Bond Street, London.

A few of the many case styles can be seen in Figures 237, 238 and 240-242. These range from those consisting of a base to house the battery and a glass dome to cover the movements, through to wall models and Sheraton balloon cases. Quality and style of case have some bearing on the price of the clock. As the main attraction of the clock is the large oscillating vertically mounted balance wheel, examples where this is completely hidden from view tend to attract a lower price than those where it is fully visible. The two exceptions to this generalisation are those in the balloon style case, or that in Figure 240.

There are no dramatic variations in the design of the movements. The first models were 'short', i.e. the balance wheel was mounted behind the dial. Upon realising that part of the appeal to the public was this large wheel the manufacturers rapidly progressed to a 'tall' movement, i.e. the balance wheel mounted below the dial. The short movements however continued to be manufactured to fit the cases requiring this type of movement. All the movements were machined to a high standard, and although some collectors place great store on whether there were two or three small ball bearings in the bearing housing this has no definite dating significance. It would appear that many of the minor variations in the methods of finish could be attributed to several finishers each with their own individual approach.

Although there may be further examples of the clock shown in Figure 243, the location of one only is known at present. It was invented by Mr. Thomas Murday in 1908 and this particular example was presented to a member of the firm who manufactured the Murday Clocks — the Reason Manufacturing Company of Brighton — in gratitude for his assistance in a court case. Two years later, in 1910, Murday took out a further patent (No. 1326) in which he replaced the pendulum by a large balance wheel. See Figure 244. This is again an extremely rare clock. It is not known with any certainty as to how many were manufactured but as production commenced immediately prior to the First World War one would suppose that this, apart from any more inherent timekeeping faults would have had a serious effect upon both production and demand.

Figure 245 shows the 'self wound' clock first patented by Frank Holden in 1909. The same movement can also be found mounted upon an oak base with a small compartment being provided for the battery and covered by a glass dome. The words 'Rebesi' and 'Regina' appeared on the dial, apparently as trade names. A later model with a large helical spring and horizontal oscillating balance appeared in 1923 — patents being taken out in England and France. It is not known where these clocks were manufactured but every indication points to it being France.

The most commonly found electric battery clock is the Bulle Clock. It was first patented in England during 1922. The initial research on this clock had been carried out by two Frenchmen, M. Moulin and M. Favre-Bulle and had reached the stage of a prototype being made immediately prior to the First World War. Both men had naturally become involved with war work and M. Moulin was killed during a military assault. Immediately after the war M. Favre-Bulle patented in his name and the widow of M. Moulin their original ideas. However, there were some technical difficulties still needing to be solved and eventually, in 1922, Favre-Bulle took out a further patent alone. Within two years, 1924, the clocks were being marketed in this country by the British Horo-Electric Co., Ltd., whose brass plates can still be found on some of the early models. To date it has not been possible to trace any manufactory in this country although there may have been some assembling and casing of movements here. The main factory was in France with outlets in various countries including Belgium and England. Production continued until the intervention of the Second World War and it is claimed that some third of a million movements were made and that these were housed in at least a hundred different case styles. Some of these can be seen in illustrations accompanying the Chapter. One of the reasons this clock was so successful was that, apart from it being a good timekeeper, Favre-Bulle realised the principal reason for the failure commercially of many of the early electric clocks was the inability of owners to find anyone interested in minor adjustment or repairs. Conventional horologists were prejudiced and hostile and in any case understood little of the principle upon which the clocks worked. Other manufcturers played into their hands by not issuing any repair manuals. Favre-Bulle provided both a repair manual for the retailer and a small leaflet for the purchaser in the appropriate language.

The case style comprising a circular base with the movement covered by a glass dome was to remain constant throughout production, only changing in size and choice of materials. The first models were on a circular mahogany base, 8½in. in diameter, with the battery housed in a vertical brass cylinder also supporting the movement. This is illustrated in Figure 247a. Smaller versions of this were soon introduced with the necessary modifications to the pendulum and supporting pillar. Provision for the batteries for these later models was made in the base. The most significant changes came in the early 1930s when more radical alterations in the design and materials of the movement slowly crept in. The wooden bases or cases were replaced by the 'new' material Bakelite, and nickel plated parts took the place of brass. The pendulum rod became a flat metal strip, a metal disc was used for the bob, and the introduction of cobalt steel meant that the use of a small magnet only $3/16$in. diameter and 2in. long could be used. Comparison between Figures 248a and 249a will demonstrate some of the mentioned changes. To anyone contemplating the purchase of any of these clocks, possibly a few words of caution would not be amiss. Beware of an apparently working example which is only doing so with the aid of too strong a battery. They should all run upon a 1½ volt battery; if one stronger than this is necessary it is because there is high resistance in the circuit due to oxidisation of the contacts or joints, or too great a variation in the magnetic field. Both can be tedious to trace and rectify. Quite often a non-working Bulle clock needs nothing more than the battery connections reversed in order to activate it. A feature of its magnet is that it has consequent poles, i.e. both ends have the same polarity, while the centre has the opposite polarity. Usually the ends are South with the centre North, but examples have been seen in which this has been reversed. Another minor repair that might be necessary on the pre-1930 models concerns the suspension. The earlier models had silk suspensions which until quite recently it was possible to purchase, but the supply has now ceased. It should be quite simple to replace this with a small piece of lingerie ribbon (and not as has been seen a piece of sticky tape).

It should be possible to regulate any of these clocks to be quite reasonable timekeepers, although there is always the 'rogue' that will not bow to logic.

Replacement shades are no great problem when needed for the small Bulle or Holden, but any required for the larger clocks do create a problem and incur expense.

Figure 220

This is generally acknowledged as being the most attractive of the master clocks attributable to Alexander Bain (1811-1877). The carved case is exceptionally handsome, and the movement well finished with gold contacts and agate insulation. The silvered dial is signed 'Alex^r Bain's Patent Electric Clock' and carries the serial number 113.

A museum piece and therefore difficult to value. One changed museums in 1977 for several thousands of pounds.

379

Figure 221

Until recently the existence of this small shelf clock by Alexander Bain was unknown, and its presence in the Electrifying Time Exhibition at the Science Museum, London, in 1977 roused great interest. The brass movement is mounted on an ebonised softwood base and covered by a glass shade in the manner of a conventional skeleton clock. The silvered chapter ring is signed 'A. Bain's Patent Electric Clock'. The contacts visible at the front of the movement and leading off through the base are operated at intervals of two hours. The reason for this is uncertain, which would imply that the clock was custom made for a specific purpose.

Unique clock and therefore value can only be guessed at several thousands of pounds. If you see one buy at any price!

Courtesy of the Director, Science Museum, London

222a

222b

382

222c

Figures 222a, 222b, 222c, and 222d

At first glance this would appear to be a typical longcase clock of the 1920s or 1930s in an oak case and with a German movement. Although the latter is correct, the clock has some exceptionally interesting features including a single electrically rewound remontoire. It is rewound by an electric motor operating on 3 volts with a small step down transformer being provided so that this voltage can be obtained from the mains supply. The mainspring of the clock has a reserve capacity of fifteen hours, should for any reason the current be interrupted. The electric motor which is used to operate the quarter striking train also winds up the mainspring every quarter of an hour. Striking is on rod gongs. This clock was introduced and exhibited at the Polytechnic Institute in Northampton Square in London, during December, 1929, and was manufactured under Patent No. 319240 by Kienzle Uhrenfabriken, Schwenningen, Germany (Figure 222c shows their trade mark). Being introduced into this country during a recession, sales appear to have been limited and the design does not appear to have proved commercially viable. The widespread introduction of the mains-synchronous chiming movements about the same time would have sealed its fate. Movement of this clock is illustrated overleaf.

£400+ depending on whether case is of oak or mahogany

Figure 222d

The side view of the movement of the clock in Figures 222a and 222b shows an arbor which can be displaced axially by a cam and lever arrangement to operate the hour striking train, and at the same time provision is made to increase the rate of striking of the hours by short circuiting a resistance placed in the motor circuit.

Figure 223

This is the standard case style later adopted by the Synchronome Co. and most other manufacturers of master clocks — oak or mahogany, of plain construction with a fully glazed door. This example has a seconds pendulum — the rod being of Invar. It is not unusual to find a sixteen pounder shell in place of the more conventional bob on examples manufactured between the two World Wars.

£200+

Figure 224

The advertisement on the facing page, by the Synchronome Co. Ltd., appeared in the *Horological Journal* in 1920, and showed their earliest case style. In a contemporary catalogue they are offered 'In Polished Oak, Walnut or Mahogany Cases with Glass Fronts' at prices between £6 and £12 12s. depending upon whether they were of the ¾ seconds or seconds variety and whether their pendulum rod was of 'Invar' or 'Invar rod (certificated)'.

Early examples in similar architectural pedimented mahogany cases £250. Later examples in ugly oak cases £80 plus.

Below: Synchronome Co. Ltd. price list in 1947 and a detail from the company's catalogue c.1925/6.

STANDARD PRICE LIST.

These Prices operative on and after 1st MARCH, 1947.

MASTER CLOCKS.

	£	s.	d.	P. T. £	s.	d.
Standard Master Clock, half-minute impulse with 7" silvered engraved dial	34	0	9	8	10	3
Standard Master Clock, without dial	29	14	0	7	8	6
Standard Master Clock, without dial or case	28	6	6	7	1	7
Master Clock with seconds switch	53	11	0	13	7	9

The following OBSERVATORIES

have adopted the

SYNCHRONOME FREE PENDULUM

to assist them in their determination of time :—

Greenwich (3)	Lorenzo Marques
Edinburgh (2)	Loomis
National Physical Laboratory	Lick
Sydney	Copenhagen
Adelaide	Warsaw
Melbourne	Batavia
Singapore	Helwan
Cape of Good Hope (2)	Tokio (2)
Nairobi	Kyoto

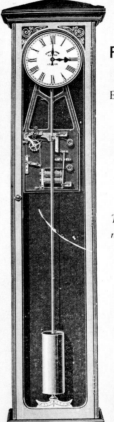

Figure 225

This is a movement from a Synchronome Master Clock manufactured after about 1930 (assessed by crackle finish to casting and presence of damper to the gravity arm). The serial number is 2388. This appears across the bottom of the plate on the left indicating the rating of the clock. Unfortunately the screw holding this in place makes reading these numbers difficult. It is known that the two clocks with the serial numbers 2386 and 2387 were despatched in October, 1937, so it has been possible to arrive at a more specific date for this particular clock of probably the November or December of 1937.

Although a later model the price would be enhanced for a collector by the documentation.

£150

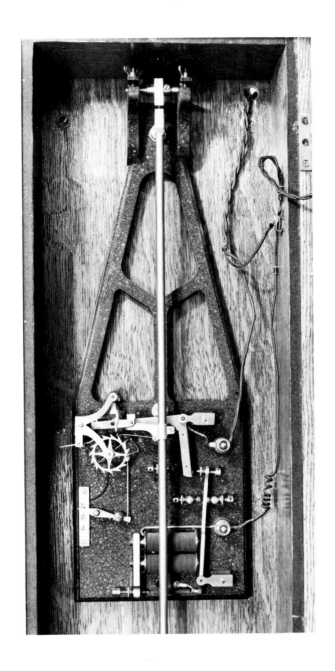

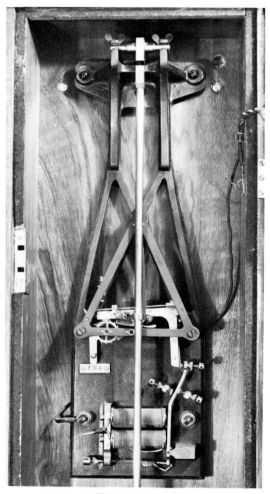

Figure 226

This illustration shows an experimental movement made by the Synchronome Company in 1922. Only one hundred were manufactured and it was discontinued as it needed expert technical skill to set up and maintain the clock. The cases housing these movements would be similar to that seen in Figure 223.

Limited quantity produced £300+

Figure 227

This is the movement used by the Synchronome Company Ltd. in their slave dials. The principle was extremely simple and was generally adopted by other manufacturers.

Slave dials are valued according to the design and quality of the case. They can be extremely handsome.

£15 – £75

Figure 228

4ft. 2in. high. A master clock manufactured by Gillett & Johnston Limited of Croydon – a firm world famous for their turret clocks and bell founding. Further details of the history of the company are on page 100. The patent for these clocks was taken out in the name of C.F. Johnston in 1921 and production has continued to the present day. The distinctive feature of these clocks is that the design of the armature eliminates noise and makes it more acceptable domestically. The cases can be in mahogany or various shades of oak. In general any master clock in a mahogany case fetches a few more pounds than one in an oak case. The pendulum is of 'Invar', with a small platform half-way down its length to hold any weights necessary for precision adjustment.

Mahogany case £200 – £300   Oak case £150 – £200

Figure 229

Movement of a Gillett & Johnston master clock.

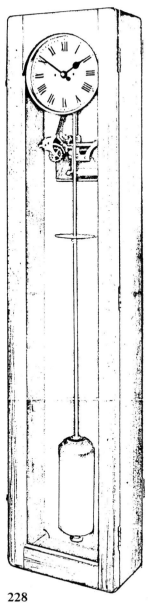

228

229

Figure 230

This master clock has the unusual distinction of having been designed for use with an earth battery (as had the earlier clocks of Alexander Bain). The energy driving the clock is obtained from a zinc carbon couple buried 3-4ft. deep and 1ft. apart in moist soil, which is said to provide a potential of approximately 1 volt at the clock terminals. The example at the Museum and Art Gallery of Leicester ran for forty years without attention on its original installation before being serviced in 1950. A more conventional modern battery can, however, be substituted! The patent for this clock was taken out by Percival Arthur Bentley in 1910 with the Bentley Manufacturing Company being formed shortly afterwards in order to commence their production. The factory was situated at Forest Gate, Clarendon Park Road, Leicester. Unfortunately the outbreak of the First World War halted the manufacture of this clock in September, 1914, but the firm moved to the Queens Road Factory, also in Leicester and undertook heavy commitments to help the war effort. The manufacture of clocks was not reintroduced and the firm was eventually absorbed into the Clore Group. This particular example is in a handsome, well made mahogany case, bevelled glass to the door, and a silvered skeletonised dial and subsidiary seconds dial. One other example is known in a superb shaped mahogany case, while others have been seen identical to that in the illustration but in oak. Two small plates appear below the contact mechanism one carrying the words 'Earth Driven Electrical Clock No. . . .' while the other states 'Bentley's Mf. Co. Leicester, England' together with the patent numbers and dates (Patent 19044/10, 3236/12 and 8464/13). There are some minor variations in the movements but as these are rare clocks there is no merit in being fussy. In common with many manufacturers, numbering of the movements did not commence with No. 1 and although this example has the serial number of 193, it is doubtful if more than about seventy were ever manufactured. Further details on these clocks can be found in the article entitled 'The Earth Driven Clock' by Dr. F.G.A. Shenton which appeared in the December, 1972, issue of *Antiquarian Horology.*

Depending on case design and whether mahogany or oak £1,500 as a minimum price. An elegant mahogany cased example could double this. Extremely rare clocks.

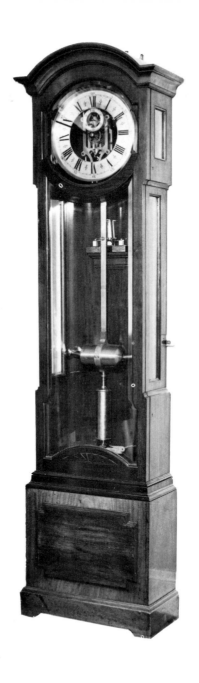

395

Figure 231

When G.B. Bowell and F. Hope-Jones parted company in 1897, Bowell continued with his researches into electrical timekeeping and took out several patents. However, in 1911, he took out, with H.T.W. Bowell, Patent No. 9287 relating to what was to become known as the Silent Electric Clock. A company was formed at 192 Goswell Road, London, and production of these clocks began. They managed to continue exporting clocks throughout the First World War and it is noted from their advertisements that a large floor standing model was sold to the Argentine Railways in 1919. Production ceased around 1925. The example shown in the illustration is the model used by the Post Office in England as well as many customers abroad. The case is oak, with a two-thirds glazed door and enamel dial in the remaining third. Other examples have been seen in a mahogany case. Note the small name label on the bottom of the door, in some instances the tradename 'Silectock' is shown. The name of the Company was derived from the fact that Bowell had successfully eliminated the usual noise emitting from the slave dials as they received their impulse from the master clock. A further example of a small neat master clock, as well as technically interesting, so in excess of £300. If in a mahogany case it could fetch a higher price.

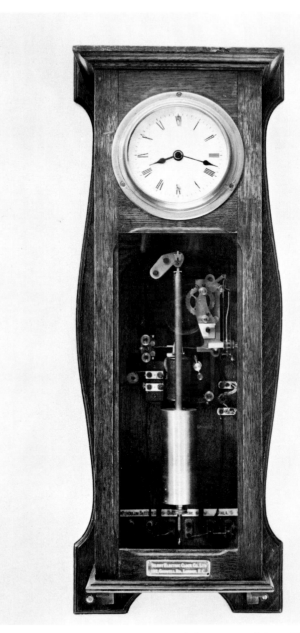

397

Figure 232

Facing page: An advertisement for the Silent Electric Clock Co. Ltd., which appeared in 1921, showing a row of the small master clocks as seen in Figure 231 and a selection of slave dials as sent to the Siam State Railways.

Below: No. 1. Standard silent 'receiving' mechanism as shown in the 1919 catalogue of the Silent Electric Clock Co.

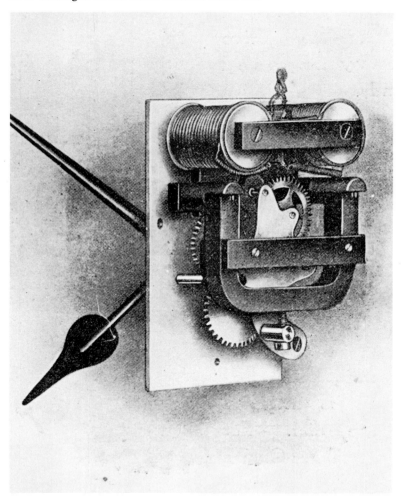

Figure 233

This is an example of a French master clock of the type used in the Eiffel Tower for transmitting signals to the Paris Observatory. Unfortunately little has been published in this country concerning these clocks, but it would appear that they were a successful and widely used type of electric movement in France. Apparently invented by the Brillie brothers they were being marketed by 1910 first by them, but later their movements appeared in clocks manufactured by other companies (e.g. Magneta, Vaucauson, etc.). This particular example has the name 'L. Leroy & Cie, 7 Boul^d de la Madeleine, Paris' which can be traced to Leon and Louis Leroy who traded from this address between 1901 and 1938. The movement is mounted on a heavy white marble slab to provide extra stability; this is enclosed by a mahogany box with a fully glazed front. Other examples have been seen in a gilt brass four-glass case. Note the good quality enamel dial, seconds hand, spheroidal pendulum bob, horseshoe-shaped magnet and coil. These clocks should run from a 1½ volt battery, and the need for a stronger current indicates that the coil has, in all probability, been damaged by the earlier use of a strong battery. Although not rare in their country of origin, these clocks are not readily found in this country in any great numbers. This, together with the fact that they are aesthetically pleasing and of a compact size, would enhance their price.

Minimum price for wooden cased example in excellent condition, with porcelain dial £350.

Figures 234a, 234b and 234c

Robert Mann Lowne, the inventor of the highly successful Lowne Electric Clock System, was born in 1840 and died in 1924, and during these eighty four years took out some eighteen patents on a variety of subjects. Further details can be found of these in the article entitled 'Robert Lowne and his Electric Clock System' by R.K. Shenton that appeared in *Antiquarian Horology* for March, 1975. His first patent concerning electric clocks was abandoned but a more successful one (No. 25374) was filed in 1901. By 1903 the Lowne Electric Clock and Appliances Company Limited had been formed and in that year he obtained a contract from H.M. Royal Arsenal, Woolwich, for a master clock to which, connected in a series on a circuit nearly six and a half miles long, were forty six slave dials. It is understood that this installation ran for some thirty years before being replaced. Further patents were taken out for minor improvements. The Company continued after the death of Robert Mann Lowne under the directorship of his two sons, but competition in the 1920s and 1930s was extremely keen and the last Lowne master installation was completed about 1933 although a maintenance service was continued on past this date. They did manufacture a synchronous electric clock, and carried out war work for the Air Ministry during the Second World War, but after this they gradually increased their production of anemometers and finally in 1960 changed the name of the company to Lowne Instruments.

The example shown here and overleaf is typical of their master clocks. Although examples have been seen with a square painted dial on the clock it is more usual to find it serving merely as a transmitter with an accompanying slave dial nearby. First impressions of the movement of these clocks cause speculation as to whether they ever worked, but as illustrated by the quoted installation at Woolwich they did and extremely successfully. The cases are of oak, although a few do appear in mahogany, the pendulum has been designed, as has all the movement, with an eye to serviceability and cost. The brass covering on the lead pendulum bob merely encloses that part of the bob which is readily visible. These are rare clocks and most certainly not for the amateur electrical horologist to become entangled in before reading the little information that appears on these clocks in the book *Electrical Horology* by H.R. Langman and A. Ball, or *Science of Clocks and Watches* by A.L. Rawlings. These clocks should work quite

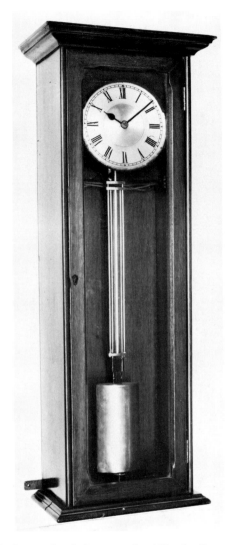

234a

satisfactorily from a 3 volt battery plus 1½ volts for each slave dial.

Possibly only appreciated by a connoisseur of electrical horology who would realise its true collecting value. To the educated collector the value would be in excess of £550. Perfect going examples rare and therefore more expensive.

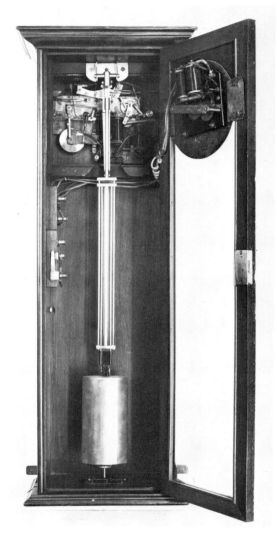

234b

The illustrations on this and the facing page show the movement of the
Lowne master clock seen in Figure 234a.

234c

Figure 235a

15in. high. An early example of an electric clock manufactured by the Ever Ready Electric Specialities Co. from patents taken out by Herbert Scott in 1902. The two large brass pillars supporting the dial and movement contain the batteries. This model on a lacquered wooden base under a glass shade was superseded by that shown in Figure 236. Upwards of £600 if with original dome.

Figure 235b

Back view of the Scott Electric Clock as shown in Figure 235a. The same movement was used in the later model as shown in Figure 236.

Figure 236

"The "Ever Ready" Electrically Propelled Clock.

Specifications

Height:	17″	Width:	11″	Depth:	7½″

Base: Solid Mahogany, Oak or Walnut.

Cover: Front and Sides — best plate glass, bevel edge
Back — Mirror of best plate glass

Dial and Hands: Plain bold designs

Pendulum: Constructed of special alloy, which is practically insensitive to temperature changes

Motion Work: Accurately machine cut on highest class precision tools.

Price: £5 5s. 0d. complete.   Refills 4s. each."

This is the official description issued by the Ever Ready Specialities Company of the clock manufactured by them from patents taken out by Herbert Scott in 1902.

The example in the illustration has a mahogany base and the name of one of the companies retailing the clock at one time — London Stereoscopic Co. 106 & 108 Regent St. London. — appears on the dial.

Other examples have been seen with a compartment in the base for housing the two batteries necessary for powering the clock.

Upwards of £600. Much would depend upon undamaged case.

Figure 237

10½in. high. The movement of this Eureka clock is of the 'short' variety, i.e. the balance wheel is behind the dial. The porcelain dial has been skeletonised in order not to hide completely the oscillating balance wheel. The base is gilt metal with the movement covered by a glass dome. The details of the manufacturer, etc., appear on the small brass plate immediately above the figure 6. See Figure 242b for further details. This is one if not the first model produced by the company.

£300+ ; if dome missing deduct £50

Figure 238

13in. high. The movement of this Eureka clock is of the 'tall' variety, i.e. the balance wheel is visible below the porcelain dial. The seconds dial is an extremely unusual feature. The mahogany base houses the battery.

£300+

Figure 239

13in. high. This is the rear view of a 'tall' movement on a rectangular thick brass base covered by a glass shade. Note the two balls clearly visible in the bearing housing behind the glass end plates. £350 if complete with dome. Example illustrated could be in excess of this as it is probably the last clock produced by the original company.

Figure 240

This is one of the most elegant case styles used by the Eureka Clock Co. Ltd. Although not an early model the shape of the case necessitates the use of a short movement. In this particular example the dial has been skeletonised but other models have been seen with a full porcelain dial. As the value of the former is slightly higher than the latter it is not unknown for examples that originally had a full dial to be skeletonised. Examples that started life skeletonised have the name plate of the company visible from the front, whereas those with full dials display this on the back of the movement. Note the three balls in the bearing housing behind the glass end plates.

One of the more elegant examples £350 plus; if dial non-skeletonised deduct £50.

Figure 241

This is an example of a clock manufactured by the Eureka Clock Co. Ltd. in a mahogany case which, although pleasant, completely hides the movement. In this instance this would detract from the value of the clock. Note the '1000 day electric clock' below the name of the Company — this is referring to the estimated duration before the battery needs changing.

Non-visible movement, so price is confined to £200 plus.

242a

242b

Figure 242a

A Eureka movement housed in a wall clock is unusual and was probably intended for use in offices and factories rather than domestically.

Unusual example so price £350 plus to a collector.

Figure 242b

An enlarged view of the small brass plate found on many Eureka models with a rating star and scale on the lower section and the name of the company, address, patent number and date together with the serial number of the clock.

Figure 243

19in. high. An extremely rare example of an electric clock patented by Murday in 1908 and manufactured by the Reason Manufacturing Company Ltd., Brighton. The mahogany case has decorative brass work and ball-and-claw feet. Only one example of this model is known to exist.

How do you evaluate a unique and documented piece? Just buy, if ever fortunate to see a further authenticated example!

Figure 244

14in. high. An example of the other clock manufactured by the Reason Manufacturing Company Ltd., Brighton, from a patent taken out by Murday in 1910. The mahogany base houses the battery, while a glass dome covers the movement. A few examples were made with clear glass skeletonised dials, but the majority of known examples have glass dials backed by white card. This is held in place by a brass retaining ring.

Example known to have realised £1,000 plus in 1977. In view of their rarity this was not excessive.

Figure 245

This example of a clock patented by Frank Holden in 1909 is in a gilt metal four-glass case, and has a silvered skeletonised dial. The alternative case style is shown in Figure 246. The movement in both models is identical.

Attractively cased so would realise £250—£300 plus.

Figure 246

View of the movement of a similar clock to that shown in Figure 245. This model has a square oak base (the battery is housed within), and circular brass ring to retain the glass shade in position. Not so aesthetic as previous example but nevertheless a collector's piece.

£200+

247a

Figures 247a and 247b

14in. high. Example of an early Bulle movement on a circular mahogany base with the battery housed in a central brass pillar. The dial has been skeletonised to provide an additional visual feature.

In excess of £180; a missing dome would detract from this value.

247b

248a

Figures 248a and 248b

10in. high. An example of a smaller Bulle clock on a circular mahogany base, which holds the battery. A glass dome covers the movement. The dial is silvered. Note the clip which holds the pendulum steady during transit. It is rare to find an example which has retained this.

£70 – £120

248b

Figure 249a

10in. high. This is a Bulle clock made after 1930. This particular example was manufactured by Exide under the trade name of 'Tempex'. Note the Bakelite base, and disc bob.

Late example – mahogany base £50 – £85+; Bakelite £30 – £50.

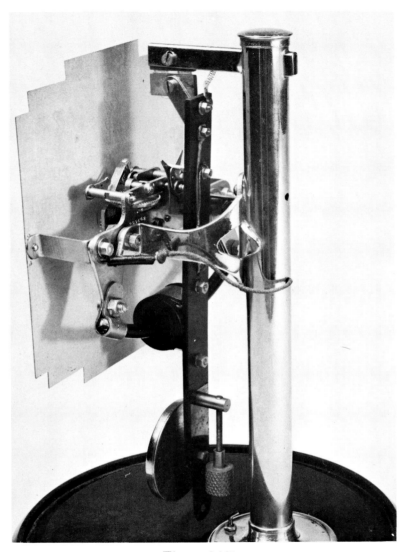

Figure 249b

View of the movement of the example shown in Figure 249a. All brass uprights, etc., have been replaced by metal plates. Note the smaller magnet.

Figure 250

20in. high. An exceptionally attractive cased Bulle clock. Brown and white marble top, bottom and columns decorated with brass reliefs and bronze lion battling with a snake enclose a conventional four-glass case. The movement is the standard type used in many of the wall clocks manufactured by this Company where the large central pillar has been replaced by a slender more aesthetic column and the battery is now housed in the base. The skeletonised dial is of gilt metal.

In the catalogue produced by the manufacturers in 1926 this example is designated: 'Modele S—Lion au Serpent, marbre skyros, sujet bronze cisele (signe Aubert). Hauteur 51cm. Largeur 32cm. Longueur du balancier 24cm. Prix unique: 1,800fr.'

Obviously originally one of the more expensive styles in the range produced. Comparative price is difficult as the whereabouts of only one other is known, but a price in excess of £600 plus could be expected.

427

Figure 251

Four pages from the catalogue issued by the Bulle Clock Company in 1926. The rate of exchange at this date was 152 francs to £1.

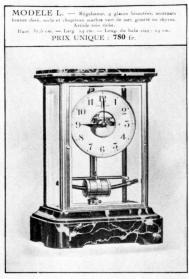

MODELE L. — Régulateur, 4 glaces bisautées, montants bronze doré, socle et chapiteau marbre vert de mer, griotte ou skyros. Article très riche.
Haut. 37,5 cm. — Larg. 24 cm. — Long. du bala cier : 24 cm.
PRIX UNIQUE : 780 fr.

La clarté de la « Bulle-Clock » illumine
l'intérieur le plus sévère.

MODELE M. — Borne marbre, façon extra soignée, avec jonc bronze doré, skyros, portor, vert de mer, onyx du Maroc.
Haut. 40 cm. Larg. 26,5 cm. — Long. du balancier : 24 cm.
(La même en forme ogive)
PRIX UNIQUE : 1.430 fr.

La « Bulle-Clock » est un objet de valeur
qui ne se déprécie pas à l'usage.

Models EE and C: rarity value would make these £100–£150 plus.
Models L and M: £100–£150 depending on case.

252a

Figures 252a and 252b

Although not readily found in England, the Tiffany Never Wind electric clock is one of the more common American varieties. It would appear that the application for the patent relating to this clock was made by George Steele Tiffany of New Jersey, USA, in 1901. Two further patents were taken out in 1904, which was about the same time that these clocks began to be widely advertised. The earlier models were cased in a wood or brass case with a door back and front. The movements were impulsed on both left and right turn of the torsion pendulum, the bob of which consisted of two balls. Later models

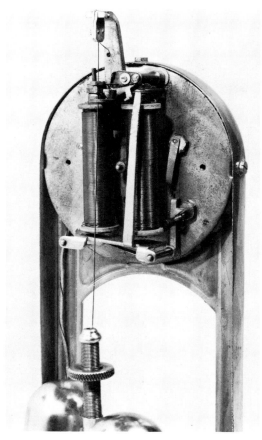

252b

produced after 1911 were on a brass circular base, as illustrated in Figure 252a, and covered by a glass dome. The movement now being impulsed only on one turn of the torsion pendulum and the bob consisting of two inverted cups. The clocks were also made under licence and so the names on the dial can be those of the Cloister Clock Company, Tiffany Never Wind Company, Niagara Clock Company, etc.

The example shown here was made by the Cloister Clock Company of Buffalo, New York, USA. Note the thin spun brass base and press brass frame and supports.

On the English market a similar clock would realise £250.

Figure 253

This is an example of a small synchronous mains electric clock manufactured by Hamilton Sangamo; this Corporation of Springfield Illinois, USA, according to Chris H. Bailey in his book *Two Hundred Years of American Clocks and Watches*, "produced an expensive electrically wound clock about 1928 and did not survive the Depression". It is not known if this also applied to the subsidiary in this country.

This particular model has a solid mahogany case, veneered and inset with circular movement, in a metal casing. The silvered dial has a central rotating disc which shows seconds. One of the problems with these early mains clocks was to convince the customer that they were working and to provide a way of detecting when variations in the current had caused the clock to stop. This was doubly important as many examples had to be manually restarted. The moving seconds dial and pointer in this instance providing the necessary visual assurance. Other makers left an aperture in the dial through which a moving line or series of dots could be seen while the clock was operating. Note the original flex and wooden plug.

Interesting examples are bound to rise in price, as they form part of the history of electrical horology. As an early named example, would realise £25.

Figure 254

This is a further example of an early mains electric clock, but this model was manufactured and marketed by Smiths English Clocks Ltd. of Cricklewood, London. It has a veneered case, silver anodised dial with an aperture showing seconds placed above the 6 position to confirm that the clock is running. The trade mark of this Company being the letters 'SEC' although the dial on this example is inscribed

Minimum of £10+

Figure 255a

15in. high. This well proportioned skeleton clock on a mahogany base under a glass shade has brass plates typical of those used in 1880/1890. It has, however, in place of the usual fusee movement an electrically rewound mechanism as patented by Chester Pond of New York, USA, in 1884. This system is commonly found in clocks marketed by the Self Winding Clock Company with movements manufactured by the Seth Thomas Clock Company of Connecticut, USA. It is both interesting and significant that in 1887 the manager responsible for the United Kingdom marketing of these clocks was Mr. Lund, who was later the founder of the Standard Time Company. It is not surprising that a few of these clocks were produced as a special line to demonstrate the 'new' electric clocks. These clocks proved to be very reliable with a remontoire hourly rewind which operated on 3 volts.

The name 'Wheatley Carlisle' that appears on the dial has been traced as referring to Wheatley & Sons, 65 English Street, Carlisle who exhibited at the Franco-British Exhibition of 1908.

Beware of amateur attempts to 'electrify' a standard skeleton movement. Only commercially produced examples have any value to a collector. £700, rising according to the merits of the basic skeleton.

Figure 255b

Movement of clock shown in Figure 255a. Note the three-pole motor which rewinds a small remontoire mounted on the centre arbor of the movement, to which is attached a contact mechanism which operates once an hour.

Chapter XIII
TIME RECORDERS

Night-watchman Clocks

John Whitehurst (1713-1788) is generally accepted as being the inventor of the 'tell tale' or night-watchman clock, although patents confirming this have not been traced to date. Born in Congleton, Cheshire, and the son of a clock and watchmaker, he commenced business for himself at Derby about 1736, but moved to London upon receiving the appointment Stamper for the Money-weights. His firm continued after his death under the management of his nephew and later his great nephew. Examples of the tell tale clocks manufactured by the Whitehursts were usually in extremely plain and functional oak or deal cases which were either floor standing or hung on a wall. They had a rotating twenty four hour dial with a set of spikes set round the periphery — one for each quarter of an hour. Upon arriving at the clock the watchman would pull a lever which pushed one of the spikes in. Hence if any pin was found protruding in the morning it was known that the watchman had neglected his duty for some reason.

As it became essential to prove either for personal satisfaction or insurance purposes that the watchman was actually patrolling a building thoroughly and regularly other methods were introduced. One of these being a portable tell tale upon which he could record his position at a certain time. Certain points on the watchman's round were selected as 'stations' and the watchman was appointed a definite time for visiting them. At each station there was an individually cut recording key firmly secured to a metal box or similar small receptacle. The watchman, upon arriving at the station, would take the key, insert it into the keyhole in the tell tale and give it one turn, thus recording upon a paper disc or tape the time and his position. The next morning upon it being opened it was possible to see where and when he had checked in during his patrol. The detectors would be made to suit individual requirements as to number of stations and time span between each recorded visit. Several examples appear in the following illustrations.

It is important when purchasing one of these portable tell tales to ascertain that it has its original set of keys, and if possible the leather pouch and carrying strap. Although still of interest without it is more a collector's item if complete.

Figure 256

3½in. An illustration of one type of night-watchman's portable tell tale. This particular example weighs two pounds and would have been carried in a leather case and strap over his shoulder. The case is of lacquered brass and is stamped on the back 'Thos. Armstrong & Bro. Manchester'. It was claimed that this model patented by Hahn in 1888 was an extremely reliable model that could not be tampered with and falsified by the watchman – an important point. The movement is a good quality lever watch movement that runs for fifty hours.

Early and complete with keys £50 – £90

WATCHMAN'S TELL-TALE CLOCKS.

AUTO UNIVERSAL TELL-TALE, No. TU 10.

Note.—By using different numbered keys from those on the watchman's stations, this Tell-Tale can also be used as an ordinary key Time Recorder. One firm to whom we sold this for a 36 stations watchman clock, is using it for checking on the engine-room and boiler-house staff. These men arrive before the lodge, where their ordinary Time Recorder is located, is opened.

6 16 20
6 18 11
6 18 3
6 18 8
6 40 13
6 40 7
6 40 15
6 42 5
6 42 17
6 42 9

Specimen
Record.

This is the most perfect and complete check on watchmen ever invented. It is THE ideal system. It is an efficient substitute for, and fulfils all the demands of, every one of the specialised Tell-Tales on the market.

It can be used for an unlimited number of stations over any length of period with any frequency desired.

Its method of operation is as simple as that of any other Tell-Tale. The record is made by brass ratchet keys, which have a raised number on the ward. The key is inserted in the clock, given a turn, and the number prints itself through an ink ribbon on to an automatically moving tape, as illustrated above. The numbers, of course, correspond with the station numbers.

The record can be detached in a moment or two of time, and can be left on for a week or longer.

The movement and recording mechanism are enclosed in a strong aluminium dust-proof case furnished with lock and key. The clock, however, can be wound up by the watchman himself from the exterior without any possibility of tampering with the interior. There is therefore no necessity for anyone but the one in charge of the clock to get at the inside, and this merely to take off the record.

It is absolutely Fraud Proof.

Figure 257

A further example of a type of watchman's tell tale clock being marketed just prior to the First World War.

£70 – £80

AUTO FIXED TELL-TALE No. SY/11.

 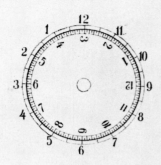

The prefatory remarks on the previous page do not apply entirely to the above Model. It is a clock for one station only, and is screwed to the one point it is desired that the watchman should visit. Its advantage over the portable form lies in its low price and the simplicity of its operation, which consists merely of pressing a button—no keys being necessary. This pierces a paper dial (see illustration above), which shows the time the point is visited.

Figure 258

This is a clock intended to be used at a fixed point and not carried by the watchman. The makers claimed that its advantage was its low price and the simplicity of its operation, which merely consisted of pressing a button, with no keys being necessary. This pierced the paper dial shown on the right of the illustration to record the time that particular point or station was visited. This model was being manufactured just before the First World War.

£50+

440

Time Clocks

The Industrial Revolution with the rapid increase of factory employment also led to the need for clocks upon which to record the time of arrival and departure of the employees. Names associated with these early 'Clocking in Clocks' are Bundy and Dey.

The Bundy clock was invented by W.L. Bundy in the USA in 1885, with production commencing in 1890 by the Bundy Manufacturing Company. A key was issued to each employee who, upon arrival at the factory, inserted it into the keyhole at the front of the clock, whereupon the engraved number on his key was recorded, together with the precise time, on to a continuous roll of paper – the entries being in chronological order of the employees' time of arrival and not their numerical order. The Dey clock was similar in appearance to that shown in Figure 260 and was invented by Alexander Dey of Scotland in 1888, and placed on the market by him and Mr. John Dey of New York in 1892. In this instance the recordings appeared in their numerical order instead of chronological order and thus obviated a great deal of work in abstracting and noting an indiviual's timesheet.

Later examples introduced the use of a card for each employee which he inserted so it could be stamped with the time of arrival or departure. This is the system generally in use today.

One English firm manufacturing these clocks was Gledhill-Brooks Ltd. The two founders being Mr. G.H. Gledhill, who had founded a cash register business in Halifax, and Mr. F. Brooks who made the original time recorder. They joined forces a few years before the First World War in order to produce these recorders. Initially the movements were manufactured for them by another firm, but as demand grew it became feasible to produce them in their own factory.

Although spring-driven clocking in clocks were extensively used, with many still in use today, they were superseded by models manufactured with electrically rewound movements or synchronous electric motors working from the mains.

One other type is the time stamp which prints the date and time – these have a multitude of uses including timing length of stay in car parks, recording the arrival of incoming mail, etc. Their advantage over a hand stamp and ink pad is that they are proof against fraudulent use, as only the supervisor having the key can open the case and adjust the mechanism. Most of these have high grade lever movements and are spring-driven.

Figure 259

Illustration from a catalogue of time clocks being marketed just before the First World War. Comments in the note at the top of the advertisement must be referring to examples manufactured by the Bundy Manufacturing Co.

£80 – £120 for an early example.
With keyboard a further £50

TIME RECORDERS: KEY SYSTEM.

MODEL B/ST. BUNDY KEY SYSTEM.

Note.—Our make of this type must not be confused with the cheaply constructed American Machines. Our trade customers will know the difference at once. Instead of movement plates and wheels of light stamped brass and wire lantern-pinions, ours is the solid type of mechanism, with solid plates and solid steel pinions, hardened and polished. This applies not only to the machine on this page, but also to all Recorders and Tell-Tales we sell.

6·01	148
6·01	149
6·02	126
6·03	141
6·03	136
*12 59	149
*1 00	141
*1 01	148
*1 01	150
*1 02	133
*1 02	126
*1 02	146
*1 03	137
*1 04	136

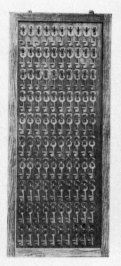

Specimen Record.   Specimen Key.   Keyboard for 100 Numbered Keys.

Heavy Oak Case. 8-Day Movement. 10-inch Bold Roman Dial.
Dimensions : Length 57-inches. Width 18-inches. Depth 6½-inches.

This machine is suitable for any kind of factory, works, store or office.

Hundreds of employees can file past the Recorder, each giving his key one quarter turn in the lock without any appreciable delay.

It is fitted with a hand shift lever which prints an asterisk against the time. This is a very useful feature, and can be used for various purposes—" out " times for instance.

P.M. times are distinguished from the A.M. by a full point at the hour figure.

The turning of the key rings a bell which indicates that the record is properly made.

Figure 260

Illustration from a catalogue of time clocks being marketed just before the First World War. The external appearance of this is similar to that manufactured originally by the Dey family in New York. Interesting collector's item but rather large.

£100+

TIME RECORDERS: RADIAL DRUM CHART SYSTEM.
MODEL E/ST.

16	6 00	8 00	8 30	12.00	1·00	5.30	6.00	8.00
17	6 00	8 00	8 30	12.00	1·00	5.30	6.00	8.00
18	6 00	8 00	8 30	12.00	1·00	5.30	6.00	8.00
19	6 00	8 00	8 30	12.00	1·00	5.30	6.00	8.00
20	6 00	8 00	8 30	12.00	1·00	5.30	6.00	8.00
21	6 00	8 00	8 30	12.00	1·00	5.30	6.00	8.00
22	6 00	8 00	8 30	12.00	1·00	5.30	6.00	8.00
23	6 00	8 00	8 30	12.00	1·00	5.30	6.00	8.00
24	6 00	8 00	8 30	12.00	1·00	5.30	6.00	8.00
25	6 00	8 00	8 30	12.00	1·00	5.30	6.00	8.00
26	6 00	8 00	8 30	12.00	1·00	5.30	6.00	8.00
27	6 00	8 00	8 30	12.00	1·00	5.30	6.00	8.00
28	6 00	8 00	8 30	12.00	1·00	5.30	6.00	8.00
29	6 00	8 00	8 30	12.00	1·00	5.30	6.00	8.00
30								
31								

Specimen Record.

Note.—The remarks made at the head of the page illustrating the B/ST, apply with equal strength to this Model. IT IS SUPERIOR TO ANY OTHER MACHINE OF ITS CLASS. We speak from practical knowledge —we have not only replaced other makes with ours, but we have also had the others at Oldham for repair.

Heavy Oak Case. 8–Day Movement.

Dimensions: Height 33 inches, width 27 inches, depth 20 inches.

This type requires neither cards nor keys—in its operation it is the simplest of all methods of Time Recording. The worker simply turns the lever to his number, depresses it, and the record is made. As will be seen from the *fac-simile*, the times are shown on a chart which is changed daily, a matter of half a minute.

Like the Model D/ST on the previous page, it has a two-colour ribbon showing ordinary times in blue, and late and overtimes in red. The necessity for a two-colour ribbon is even greater in this than in the card system.

Say there are 150 workers, each entering and leaving 6 times a day. This means 900 records, each of which must be examined daily if a single colour ribbon is used, a lengthy and eye-straining job. With the two-colour ribbon only the red printings need be picked out.

Both the " in " and the " out " positions, as well as the two-colour ribbon movement, etc., etc., are entirely automatic.

On the front of the Recorder there are plain indicators showing the colour of ribbon and which " in " or " out " column is in operation.

Figure 261

Illustration from a catalogue of time clocks being marketed just before the First World War.

£80 – £100. With card rack further £30

TIME RECORDERS: CARD SYSTEM.

MODEL K/ST, SEMI AUTOMATIC.   ONE COLOUR RIBBON CARD MACHINES.
MODEL D/ST, FULLY AUTOMATIC.   TWO COLOUR RIBBON CARD MACHINES.

Note.—The quality of their materials—the finest procurable—their superiority of construction, their improvements and advantages, combine to make these the highest developments in Time Recording mechanisms ever brought out.

Card Rack for 100 Employees.

Heavy Oak Case, 8-Day Movement, 10-in. Dial.
Dimensions : Length 57 inches, width 21 inches, depth 13½ inches.

The **Model K/ST** is semi automatic, that is, the " in " and " out " positions are changed by hand, only, however, by the authorised person, by whom it is locked into position.   But the card positions from the A.M. to the P.M., and *vice versa*, as well as from one day to the next are changed automatically.

The **D/ST** is fully automatic, and carries a two-colour ribbon, printing ordinary times in blue and late and overtimes in red.   The tremendous saving of time in making up the wages sheet is obvious—a glance at the card, no matter how hurried, will detect the red figures and, of course, only these need attention.   It never errs in this.   Absolute reliance can be placed upon it.

One of the advantages of the D/ST machine, possessed by no other machine on the market, is the detachable lever for shifting the card sheath to " in " or " out " when a workman is leaving at a legitimately irregular hour.   But after he has stamped his card the sheath RETURNS AUTOMATICALLY TO ITS ORIGINAL POSITION.   The detachable lever, of course, is in charge of a responsible person and is only handed to the workmen when properly entitled to use it.

On the front of the Recorder there are plain indicators showing the day, A.M. or P.M., and which " in " or " out " position is in operation, and, on the two-colour machine, an indicator shows the colour of the ribbon.

The record is made by dropping the card into the sheath and pressing the lever.   This rings a bell, indicating that the record has been properly made.

BOTH MACHINES ARE IDEAL FOR JOB COSTING.

Figure 262a

This illustration shows a time stamp manufactured by Blick Time Recorders Ltd. during the 1930s. Earlier models had movements manufactured by the Seth Thomas Company, USA, but by this date they were being made in England. As well as this model (The Universal) the Company also produced a range of time recorders, key recorders, radial recorders, etc.

The example shown here is in a sturdy metal box with a black crackle finish and plain silvered top. The silvered dial is signed 'Blick Time Recorders, Limited, 188 Gray's Inn Road, London, W.C.1.' The card to be stamped is placed under the handle which is then pressed down by means of a lever. Small and compact which enhances price.

£65+

449

Figure 262b

View of the fully opened Blick time stamp shown in Figure 262a.

Figure 262c

Movement of the Blick time stamp shown in Figure 262a. Note the solid construction — thick plates — and platform lever escapement.

Figure 263a

13 by 13 by 9in. This is an extremely compact time recorder made by the British Time Recorder Co. Ltd. of 149 Farringdon Road, London. The case is of plywood faced with oak veneer, with a painted dial behind a glass 'window'. This illustration shows the clock as it is normally in use, case closed and locked securely from meddling fingers. It would stand on a small shelf, but be screwed to the wall by fishplates.

£60+

Figure 263b

A general view of the movement of the time recorder shown in Figure
263a provides the opportunity to note the quality of the movement,
lever escapement, mechanism of the inking tape, etc.

Pigeon Clocks

It was not only their work people began to time but also their pastimes and sports! This was the inevitable result of many activities becoming commercialised either by centres offering facilities or by the large prize monies offered to the winners.

Although a popular sport in many countries, the breeding and racing of pigeons is considered to be the national sport in Belgium. The interest shown by the Prince of Wales (later Edward VII) and the founding of a Royal Loft at Sandringham in 1886 with birds given by the King of the Belgians provided a sufficient *raison d'etre* for an increase in the number of fanciers in this country. Next to the pigeons themselves, the most important piece of equipment when racing is a reliable timepiece which can also record the precise time of the bird's return. The velocity of the winning bird is calculated by knowing the distance covered by the bird between its point of release and its place of return (i.e. loft) and the exact time this took. The names of Alexander and William Henry Turner are often quoted in connection with the first pigeon clocks (Patent No. 1886 taken out in 1903), but earlier patents by Kitson and Bulmer (Patent No. 3451 taken out in 1891) and S. Gibson (Patent No. 18996 taken out in 1892) have been noted. As most of the clocks were covered by patents taken out in the country of origin (mostly Germany or Switzerland) and as most pigeon fanciers are only interested in their clock's accuracy, little has been recorded regarding the early examples. It is, however, among these older clocks, now considered obsolete for pigeon racing purposes, that the collector should find items of interest. Many variations occur. Each inventor was attempting to improve upon the accuracy of the recording of the timepieces produced by his predecessor and at the same time to make his version less vulnerable to fraudulent use. The conditions under which these races were judged were extremely stringent and in the past each country had its own set of rules according to the governing body. The sport is now run on an international basis with the result that designs have emerged made to mutually acceptable specifications.

As with the night-watchman tell tale, there were basically two types of pigeon clocks — those that recorded the time by pricking a hole in a paper dial or tape and those that printed it. Two examples of the former are to be seen in the following illustrations.

Figure 264

View of the movement of a clock used to time racing pigeons, marketed and serviced in this country by The Automatic Timing Clock Co. Ltd. but manufactured to the Benzing Original patent (taken out in France). This particular example is in an oak case with a leather carrying handle, and was intended to be used to time twelve birds. The instructions for setting the clock appear on the lid.

£70+

Instructions

1. Wind Clock. Keyhole between 1 and 2.
2. Before Setting, move Brass Pin (as seen above 11) to the left, this allows the minutes to be completed when the Clock will stop.
3. Set Clock by the Minute Hand in front to time required and

re-start by releasing Pin as mentioned above, to original position.

4. To set Day, put Small Key on Square as seen between 3 and 4 and turn to No. 12 on day Wheel to line under 12 o'clock.
5. Dial Roll must be signed on the End, before connecting to Hook.
6. Place Ring-Plate on with No. 5 against Striking Piece.
7. The Small Glass MUST be signed on the INSIDE.
8. After Setting the Clock to the Master Timer, close the lid, draw the knob home to the LEFT. Place the Striking Key on the Square, then turn forward and Strike Time, this action moving the Puncture Hole and leaving the receptacle in position for the First Thimble.
9. To read variation at Locking, continue gentle forward action with Striking Key until Dial appears.
10. When Clock is Closed a puncture is made in Paper Roll, the Same occurs when Opening.
11. When fixing New Roll on, unscrew Adjusting Wheel covering the same.
12. Set Dolometer by turning the Pointer the way indicated on Dial.
13. Clock can be regulated by Screw as seen on side of movement.
14. To release Roll for reading, first put Key on Striking Arm and turn sufficient to bring Blank Part of Wheel as seen at base of same in contact with paper carrier, then release small finger click and draw paper from Roll.

When the bird returns to the loft the identifying ring is removed from its leg, placed in a small brass thimble which is then dropped in place through the lid of the clock into the ring dial, this is rotated by means of the large key at the back and the time of insertion is pricked onto the paper tape. This can then be noted through the small glazed window at the side of the case. The locked clock is taken to the Secretary of the local racing club when all the birds have returned to that loft and opened under surveillance and the times, etc. compared with those of the other competitors.

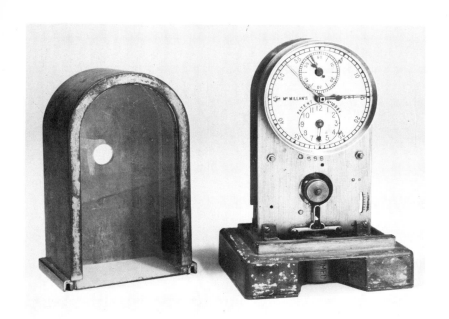

Figure 265

5in. high. An interesting example of a clock used to time racing pigeons patented in 1907 by W. McMillan and A.H. Osman which incorporated a lever escapement perfected and patented by W.G. Schoof in 1874. The outer case is brass with a glazed front, and the movement has a silvered dial. A paper disc would have been attached immediately below the dial, and as the thimble containing the appropriate pigeon ring was inserted through the aperture at the bottom of the case two pricks would be made in the edge of the disc.

Early, neat example £80+

Other Time Recorders

It was inevitable that both genuine and stimulated demand for timers for specific uses would be exploited by the manufacturers, and examples can be found intended for use in the photographer's dark room, in the kitchen, in laboratories or factories timing certain processes, or in the world of sport timing races, games, etc. This area does provide a veritable goldmine of collectors' items!

Figure 266

By the number of patents taken out at the time, it is known that clocks especially used for timing billiard games were extensively used in the 1890s. This example was being marketed immediately before the First World War. One invented by Thomas and Atkinson in 1897 was intended to have an arm or rod placed over the table to prevent play, the removal of which started a timing device. Others have been noted in which the insertion of a coin enabled the table to be used for a specified length of time, after which some form of obstruction made play impossible.

£100+

THE AUTO "COUSENS" BILLIARD TIME CHECKER.

No. T/38.

The present sensible system of charging for billiard games by time rather than by the obsolete way of so many " up," has created a demand for some accurate method of timing the games. This demand is fully covered by our Auto Billiard Checker, No. T/38.

Over and above the hundreds of licensed houses and billiard halls, this is being used by over 200 clubs in Lancashire and Yorkshire, and we have yet to hear one single word of complaint. Indeed, on the other hand, we are continually getting repeat orders.

The clock can be set for timing games of 15, 20 or 30 minutes duration. At the commencement of the game the cord is pulled which starts the timing hand. At the expiration of the allotted time, the ringing of the bell announces the end of the game. It is then immediately set for the next players.

These billiard checkers have many obvious advantages. They soon pay for themselves by saving the minutes usually lost between the games. They avoid the unpleasant disputes which are continually taking place between the player and the attendant when no mechanical check is used. They are an invaluable adjunct to all places where billiard tables are used, no matter whether games are charged for or not.

A very important point in connection with our billiard checker is that it is always possible to see at a glance how long the game has been in progress and how long there is still to play—a very great advantage to those entering the room during the game.

They are made in two styles :—No. 1. With hand for timing games only.
No. 2. With 3 hands, that is the ordinary hour and minutes as well as the timing hand.

These clocks are our own production and can be had only from us.

Orders must specify whether for 15, 20 or 30 minute games.

Figure 267

An amusing example of a rather elaborate eggtimer! By the case style (cheap brass case with steel alarm bell) it can be deduced that it was manufactured sometime prior to the Second World War. The movement is a conventional pin pallet.

£15

Figure 268

The metal case of the time stamp manufactured by the Stromberg Electric Company of Chicago is matt black, with a small one inch monitoring dial in the side. It operates off 110 volts and was used in conjunction with a master clock and secondary dial installations, by being included in the slave dial circuit. The stamping mechanism is housed in the spring loaded arm. The patent for this was taken out in November, 1909.

£65

Figure 269

Further example of a timer marketed for a specific purpose. Added interest to this particular example is the fact that it has its original box and instruction leaflet.

£15 – £20

Figure 270

"Assuming the apparatus is to be used in the reception of radio broadcast it will be placed in series with the filament circuit of the thermionic valves. If a listener desires only to hear a particular item or items of a previously published broadcast timetable, he or she will plug into a socket or sockets any desired number of said wander plugs appropriate to advertised time of rendition". This was the suggested use by the manufacturers of this timing device. Housed in a small mahogany case with a copper anodised surround to the enamel dial it is an attractive small piece. The dial carries the name 'Electrone' together with the Patent No. 250.001 (which was applied for in March, 1925) and the name Frederick J. Gordon & Co. Ltd., 92 Charlotte Street, London, W.1. This is the name of the manufacturer; the patentee was Graham Cotterell of Wanstead, London.

£40 − £50

Figures 271a and 271b

6in. high. The origins of the game of chess are lost in obscurity but in 1846 important publications and handbooks appearing in this country stimulated a revival here. Associations were formed and tournaments, both local and international, arranged. Rules and regulations had to be laid down in order to standardise competitions and one of the innovations was the limitation of the time allowed for each player to make his move. As the use of sand-glasses for measuring intervals of time whether for private devotions, lessons, auctions, or sermons was widespread at this time it was natural to extend their use to timing chess games. They were, however, soon superseded by clockwork timers. These took the form of double clocks which measured the total elapsed time each player took while playing. The example in this illustration is in an oak case with white enamel dials; the movement was manufactured by the Hamburg American Clock Company of Germany as confirmed by the presence of their trade mark (crossed arrows) on the dial. Note the small flags at the top of the dial which fall when the total time allowed has elapsed. Only one clock is operating at a given time. As a player makes his move he depresses the knob at the top of the case nearest him which, by means of a system of levers, etc., seen in Figure 271b, automatically raises the other knob thus releasing the balance wheel of his opponent's clock and stopping his own. When his opponent makes his move he presses the knob nearest to him and reverses the process. By looking at the two dials it is possible to see at a glance the length of time each player has consumed during the match.

£50+ depending upon quality of case

271a

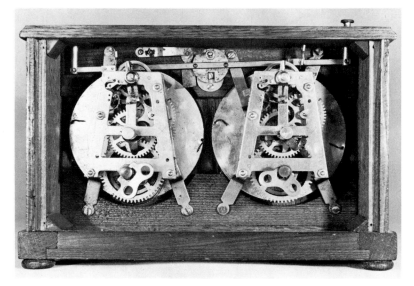

271b

Chapter XIV
GUIDE TO EVALUATION AND CURRENT PRICES NOTED DURING 1976

Although an attempt has been made by means of the preceding illustrations and text to demonstrate the factors that make one clock a superior collector's item to another (or for that matter of a higher value) this is not information which can be readily learned. It is only by using common-sense and constant observation backed up by textbook knowledge that this is acquired. The bibliography has been compiled with this in mind. Once a collector has decided in what field he wishes to specialise, his mind turns to cost of good examples. The horologist is no exception. The answer is not simple especially as there are always two aspects to consider — the aesthetic appeal and the mechanical interest. Some tentative guidelines have been given on the following pages, but it must be remembered that they are only guidelines and are not intended to be memorised and used blindly. If this is done there is a strong possibility of paying too high a price or missing a bargain. It is far more important to study the comparative prices and interpret the reasons behind them. Many factors govern price. Apart from the more obvious ones of condition, authenticity, rarity, etc., there is also a geographical element — some clocks fetch more money in various parts of the country but as these areas and types are constantly changing it is not possible to tabulate them! Even the time of year when purchasing or selling can contribute to a raised or lowered price. Continental and other foreign buyers tend to have set times for coming to this country to purchase and they obviously have a great influence on the current price. In 1976 problems were created by changing exchange rates, floods of tourists visiting the South Coast resorts and London, and the many Dutch who found travelling to the Midlands and North a simple matter. These factors have had some influence on price but it is difficult to gauge how much. Unfortunately the final decision must rest on the purchaser's own common-sense, perhaps tempered by the depth of his pocket and desire for a particular piece! There is always the consolation that, with the coming of the digital quartz crystal clocks, any mechanical timepiece will eventually become a novelty; even if it was not a tremendous bargain at the time of purchase the value must be caught up with one day. Not all pleasure can be calculated in pounds and pence and many of the examples covered in this book do not need hours of cogitation. The only consolation to any lack of concrete price guidance is that, without any standardisation of prices for many of the hitherto considered uncollectable items, bargains are still to be found. Possibly the following general comments will be of assistance.

Buying a damaged or non-working timepiece is a risky action by any but the well-equipped, reasonably skilled clockmaker. Naturally the cost of the item in question plays an extremely relevant part in this decision. It is one thing purchasing a marble-cased clock for a few pounds and enjoying the challenge of attempting to repair and clean the case and movement, but quite a different matter buying a skeleton clock or carriage clock for several hundreds of pounds and then deciding to dabble. Personal limitations must be acknowledged and also the fact that repairs carried out by a professional usually attract a higher charge than the customer expects. This is not because restorers overcharge but because amateurs frequently neither appreciate the time necessary to carry out some repairs satisfactorily, nor that in some extreme situations parts may have to be specially made. There is always the problem that arises when any mechanical object needs repair — more than one part may need attention but this is not always apparent until the movement is dismantled. Most restorers will be only too happy to give a customer an estimate and comment on the work that needs to be carried out if only to clarify the situation and avoid confrontation at the time of settling the bill.

Some concept of what is available must be gained in order to be able to judge whether a particular example is worth acquiring or whether to wait for something a little better to appear. So long as the finances are available there are many complicated carriage clocks to be had in preference to a simple timepiece, but you would search for ever for a Black Forest cuckoo clock in an ormolu case with porcelain panels. Quality must only be looked for where it can be found. Quality in this context can be explained as being the use of any material or process that increased the cost of producing the article in the first instance. This also includes additional time needed to embellish or finish cases or movements, as extra labour also increases the initial cost.

If a clock is extremely rare, or the chances of finding an undamaged example are negligible, it is feasible to contemplate purchasing one with a few minor defects. However, if the clock being offered is in the cheaper price bracket it needs to be virtually perfect to qualify as a collector's piece. Any prices mentioned on the following pages are intended to refer to perfect working examples.

Some attempt has been made in the following charts to give a basic price and then an estimation of the extra value placed on the various features. Although this is accepted as being the era of mass production it is remarkable to what extent the exceptions occur. Personal avarice also plays a great deal in deciding how much to pay for these!

Chapter I MARBLE-CASED CLOCKS

Plain black marble timepiece with plain white enamel dial		ADDED VALUE FOR FEATURES SHOWN						
		Good bronze/ brass mounts and/or coloured marble inlay	Porcelain dial or chapter ring	Visible escapement	Mercurial or Ellicott pendulum	Identifiable maker's name or trade mark on the movement	Strikes (on hours and half hours)	Side orna- ments
English movement with fusee	£120	£10+	+£5	—	—	£20+	+£10	£10+
French movement	£40	£10+	+£5	+£15	+£25	£10+	+£10	£10+
German movement	£15	£10+	+£5	+£10	+£20	£2+	+£10	£10+
American movement in black iron/wood marbleised case	£15	—	+£5	+£10	—	£5+	+£7	£10+

Remember 1. Extra large and heavy cases usually detract from the value.
2. Important bronze figures could be worth over £100 in own right.
3. Restoration of damaged porcelain dial   ) can be difficult to accomplish to achieve satisfactory results.
   Restoring depth of colour to 'grey' marble)

469

Chapter II SKELETON CLOCKS

Basic English skeleton timepiece on original base with original glass dome	ADDED VALUE FOR FEATURES SHOWN							
	Identifiable design, i.e. York Minster, Scott Memorial	Identifiable maker's name	One at the hour strike	Two train	Three train	Unusual escape-	Calendar work	Long duration
£450	£100+	£100+	+£50	£500+	£700+	£250+	£100+	£+++

Remember 1. The value for these clocks is greatly influenced by quality of work; i.e. high number of wheel crossings — no rounded internal angles; thick plates; well fretted plates with hand-finished edges and right-angles.

2. A three train skeleton clock with an unusual escapement made by an important maker *can* realise £4,000 to £5,000.

3. Domes — if obtainable — are expensive (£30+).

4. There are many modern reproductions on the market, which do not always upon examination compare favourably with the originals.

Chapter III TORSION CLOCKS

Basic 400-day torsion pendulum timepiece on original base with glass dome		ADDED VALUE FOR FEATURES SHOWN				
		Identifiable maker	Thirty-hour	Unusual escapement	Striking	Additional feature such as a method of overcoming problems created by changes in temperature
Victorian	£120	£10+	Rare	£20+	Rare	£10+
Edwardian	£70	£10+	—	£20+	Rare	£10+
Later	£40	£5+	—	£20+	Rare	£10+

Remember
1. Check suspension as this is the most likely point of damage.
2. Examples in ornate four-glass cases would need appropriate price of adjustment.
3. Dome replacements are not too difficult.

Chapter IV FRENCH CARRIAGE CLOCKS

Type	Basic price for 4½-5½ in. size	ADDED VALUE FOR FEATURES SHOWN							
		6½in. + size or maker's stamp	Alarm	'Gorge' case or Corinthian columns	Engraved case and masked dial	Oval case	Porcelain/ enamel panels	Early example	Calendar work
Miniatures approx. 3in.	£150	+£50	+£50	+£50	+£150	+£200	+£350	v. rare	+£280
Timepieces	£90	+£50	+£40	+£50	+£90	+£90	+£250	+£100	+£70
Hour Striking	£200	+£30	+£40	+£150	+£160	+£150	+£300	+£150	+£90
Hour Striking/ Repeating + alarm	£250	+(£50)	–	+£200	+£200-£400	+£200	+£300	+£150	+£110
Quarter Striking/ Repeating	£400	+£50	+£40	+£200	+£200-£300	£200	+£400	+£180	+£200
Grande Sonnerie	£800	+£100	+£50	+£200	+£200-£300	+£250	+£650	+£200	+£250
Minute Repeating	£1,600	+£250	+£100	+£200	+£200-£300	+£300	+£650	v. rare	+£500

Remember   1. Miniatures with repeating only £300+.   2. Beware of modern enamel panels made in Vienna.

3. English carriage clocks (with fusee and chain) are extremely sought after and a simple timepiece realises £600 with the price rising to £6,000+ for a complicated clock by a good maker.

4. Unusual escapements add further £200+.

Chapter V LONGCASE CLOCKS

| Conventional longcase clock after 1850 | Oak case | Mahogany case | Identifiable maker's name | ADDED VALUE FOR FEATURES SHOWN |||||
				White dial	Brass dial	Two train	Three train	Date and/or moon
Thirty-hour	£400	£100+	£100+	–	£50+	+£100	Unlikely!	£50+
Eight-day	£700	£100+	£100+	–	£50+	+£100	+£100	£50+

Remember 1. The range of quality of the cases for these clocks is infinite, as earlier styles were copied and/or adapted; skills of the maker also varied.

2. Similarly the quality and quantity of the decoration of the white painted dial varies enormously from small corner decoration to pictorial scenes in the dial arch.

3. Large, ill-proportioned cases stifle any other virtues a clock may have.

REGULATOR

A good mahogany-cased regulator with all the refinements of jewelled pallets, compensated pendulum, etc., that qualify it being called a 'Regulator', together with available evidence regarding its *maker* (not retailer), £1,000+.

Chapter V EDWARDIAN CHIMING LONGCASES

				ADDED VALUE FOR FEATURES SHOWN			
				Two train	Three train		
Large Edwardian longcase clock in plain oak or mahogany case		Ornately carved case. Glazed door	Date/ moon dial	striking hour on bell or coiled gong	Quarter chimes on bells or tubular gongs, hour strike on coiled gongs	Quarter chimes and hour strike on tubular gongs	Change of chimes
							Westminster Cambridge	Westminster Cambridge St. Michael
English timepiece with fusee	£750	£500+	+£100	£400	+£600	+£750	+£100	+£150
German timepiece with fusee	£300	£500+	+£100	£400	+£600	+£750	+£100	+£150

Remember 1. The overwhelming size of these clocks is ignored, with foreign buyers obviously enchanted by the multiple chimes.

2. Although the maker's name is immaterial at the moment, it is felt that eventually a documented example will have a higher value than a similar anonymous piece.

The post First World War movement, chiming on rods, which originated from numerous German factories, but were cased here, also appear as longcase clocks. Prices commence about £200 and rise according to whether the case is typical of that period, together with general quality and appearance of case and dial. Little interest is shown in the movement – only in the fact that it chimes.

Chapter VI LARGE BOARD ROOM OR DIRECTORS' CHIMING CLOCKS

Large Edwardian bracket clock		Ornately carved case or ebonised with good bronze/brass mounts	ADDED VALUE FOR FEATURES SHOWN				
			Two train striking hour on bell or coiled gong	Three train		Change of chimes	
				Quarter chimes on bells, hour strike on coiled gong	Quarter chimes and hour strike on coiled gongs	Plain chime	Westminster Cambridge
English movement with fusee	£300	£150+	+£50	+£90	+£80	+£100	+£150
German movement with fusee	£200	£150+	+£50	+£90	+£80	+£100	+£150
German movement without fusee	£100	£150+	+£50	+£50	+£30	+£90	+£120

Remember 1. Where size might be a deterrent, complicated chimes appear to redeem these clocks.

2. Maker's name plays little part in value; it will be interesting to note if this continues.

3. The post First World War German or English movement, chiming on rods, in Napoleon Hat style cases are beginning to creep up in price. Starting at £18–£28, examples in better cases with good clear dials realise a few pounds more. The narrow price range does not, at the moment, allow for emphasis to be placed on the different manufacturers or the slight variation in the quality of the movements. No doubt this will change in the future when these clocks come under the spot light and are the 'in thing'. It would be wise, therefore, to select examples with good cases and some identifying mark or name in order to capitalise at some future date.

475

Chapter VI CONVENTIONAL BRACKET CLOCKS

Timepiece in conventional styled case of an earlier design		ADDED VALUE FOR FEATURES SHOWN				
		Identifiable maker	Two train	Three train	Calendar work	Mahogany or ebonised case with good brass/bronze mounts
English movement with fusee	£350	£100+	+£50	+£100	£75+	£100+
German movement with fusee	£200	£100+	+£50	+£100	£75+	£100+
German movement without fusee	£150	£10+	+£50	+£100	£40+	£100+

Remember 1. Although *maker's* name is of prime importance, a known retailer's name does have some merit.

Chapter VI AMERICAN SHELF CLOCKS

Typical American spring-driven shelf timepiece with veneered soft wood case		ADDED VALUE FOR FEATURES SHOWN				
		Manufacturer's name	Strike	Alarm	Solid wood case	Eight-day movement
Small rectangular case under 8-9in. high. Thirty-hour movement	£15	£5+	+£5	+£5	—	—
Taller cases and shaped, i.e. Gothic. Thirty-hour movement	£25	£10+	+£5	+£5	£10+	+£15

Chapter VI GERMAN SHELF CLOCKS

Typical German spring-driven shelf timepiece with veneered soft wood case – in many instances replicas of American designs	ADDED VALUE FOR FEATURES SHOWN				
	Manufacturer's name	Strike	Alarm	Solid wood case	Eight-day movement
Tall Gothic, etc., cases. Thirty-hour movement £25	£5+	+£5	+£5	£10+	+£15

Remember
1. German made movements of this century are found in a large variety of cases – these are however Germany's first answer to the American mass production methods.
2. The Black Forest area also produced a unique clock – the cuckoo clock. Bracket cuckoo clocks are rare but examples can be found and these frequently make use of fusees. Their price range would commence at £400–£450.

Chapter VII SMALL CLOCKS

The variety is too great to enumerate them all here. The usual rules apply:—

1. Either select by quality or interesting mechanism — these do not always go hand-in-hand.
2. Trade marks, retailers' names, etc., all provide further material for research. Dealers rarely have time to chase up all the loose ends, whereas the private individual can greatly enhance the interest and value of his collection by doing so.
3. During 1976-1977 the following price trends were noted but these particular clocks have, with the exception of the Thomas Cole strut clocks, no established valuation.

| Small china cased clocks, usually with German movements — beware of modern Swiss replacements | Alone | £25 |
| | With side ornament | £45 |

British United Clock Company utilising patented movement.
The price will vary according to the quality of the case and knowledge seller has of the Company!

VAP movements in wooden drum cases	Alabaster case	Balance wheel	Pendulum	Alarm
Timepiece £75	+£10	+£8	+£5	+£10

Small Ansonia clocks with centre wind and large spring   £20+

Other small German, etc., clocks with interesting winding mechanisms, etc.   £20+

Chapter VIII ALARM CLOCKS

Again there are only established prices for a few clocks coming within this category. These are the exceptional examples that have frequently appeared in salesrooms, etc., and have been documented and appraised. Two examples are:

1. The French skeleton alarm by Pierret, which is extremely sought after and realises £500+.
2. The Gossage patent alarm — last noted example realising over one hundred pounds.

The remaining clocks fall into two main groups:

a) Those intended to serve a dual role of shelf clock by day and alarm clock by night. Many of the typical German and American shelf clocks fall into this category and it could be claimed that in these instances the alarm mechanism is incidental;

b) The drum alarm in its variation.

The latter provide a rich variety and can be found for a few pounds upwards. Be selective and make intelligent choices, while the market is untapped!

English dial clock ('schoolroom', 'kitchen', etc.). Circular mahogany surround		ADDED VALUE FOR FEATURES SHOWN					
		Unusual escapement	8in. dial	Strike	Drop dial	Identifiable maker	Fusee
Timepiece 1850-1900	£125	£20+	+£75	+£100	£50+	£75+	+£50
Timepiece after 1900	£50	–	+£75	+£60	£30+	£40+	+£50
American movement	£30	–	–	+£60	£30+	£20+	
German movement	£30	–	+£75	+£60	£30+	£10+	+£50

Remember

1. The American movements were frequently cased in England. In some instances the cases are attractively inlayed.

2. An identifiable retailer's name can often enhance the price, whereas other collectors desire examples bearing the monogram of one of the now defunct railway companies, e.g. G.W.R.

481

Chapter IX 'VIENNA REGULATORS'

Basic so-called 'Vienna regulator' in simple mahogany case and glazed door with spring driven movement		ADDED VALUE FOR FEATURES SHOWN			
		Heavily carved case, finials, crests, etc.	Strike	Weight driven	Additional features, i.e. seconds dial
German movement	£150	£100+	+£50	+£50	+£40
American movement	£100	£100+	+£50	+£50	+£40

Remember

1. A true Vienna regulator is rare and commands a price far higher than shown here.
2. At the other end of the scale the post First World War German movements, chiming on rods, were also housed in oak wall cases with glazed doors. Typical 1920/1930 examples with Westminster chiming movement are appearing on the market from £45.
3. Bear in mind that several firms are now manufacturing reproduction weight-driven movements similar to the original German examples.

Chapter IX AMERICAN WALL CLOCKS

Basic timepiece in ogee style veneered case, with glazed door. Weight-driven thirty-hour movement	ADDED VALUE FOR FEATURES SHOWN				
	Decorative tablet lower half of glazed door	Scroll and/or other extra features to case	Identifiable maker's name	Calendar work	Strike	Spring-driven
£75	£50	£50	£30+	£50+	+£30	Rare

Remember   1. Reproduction labels are printed at the present time in American, so beware!

Chapter IX GERMAN WALL CLOCKS
BLACK FOREST CLOCKS

	ADDED VALUE FOR FEATURES SHOWN		
Traditional cuckoo clock with weight-driven thirty-hour movement	Early example £300+	Late example £100+	Eight-day £50+

Remember 1. These clocks are still being manufactured today.
2. The 'Postman's Alarm' also had a substantial production run – prices for these start at £60+.

Chapter X MYSTERY and NOVELTY CLOCKS

Few precedents have been set as regards the value of these clocks. As each appears on the market it is appraised in many instances by its aesthetic appeal and gimmick value. Frequently the engineering ingenuity used to achieve the latter is not understood or appreciated. When expensive materials (onyx, ormolu, bronze) are used, examples realise several thousands of pounds. Salesroom prices have been given in the text where possible for the more exotic examples.

The following additional guide lines may help, but it is only possible to give starting prices:—

Rack clock £60+
Figures with rolling eyes £300+ (some reproductions on the market)
Davidson memorandum clock £300+
Ticket/plato clock £100

Chapter XI FOUR-GLASS CASE CLOCKS

Gilt four-glass timepiece		ADDED VALUE FOR FEATURES SHOWN				
		Visible escapement	Compensated pendulum	Ornate case	Side ornaments	Strike
French movement	£350	+£25	+£50	£100++	£50+	+£50
American movement	£200	+£15	+£50	£100++	£50+	+£50

Remember
1. No reference has been made to the larger precision four-glass mantel clocks, often with added complications of date, temperature indication, etc. These fetch several thousand pounds.
2. The quality and ornamentation of the case play a dominant role when evaluating these clocks.

		ADDED VALUE FOR FEATURES SHOWN
Eureka	*Basic Price* £300	The quality of the case and visibility of the movement are the major factors influencing the price of these clocks. Striking add several hundreds — extremely rare.
Bulle	*Basic Price* £80+	As well as quality of case and visibility of movement, date plays a part in valuing these clocks. Tall early movement add £150+ Striking add several Short — early movement add £50+ hundreds as extremely Short — late movement add £10 rare
Holden	*Basic Price* £300+	Add for case design. Add for type with oscillating coil.
Scott	*Basic Price* £600+	Add for early model.
Tiffany never wind	*Basic Price* £250+	Add for early model.
Reason	*Basic Price* £1,000+ —	Balance wheel type Pendulum type — impossible to value at the moment.
Electrically rewound skeleton	*Basic Price* £700+	Value would be halved for amateur contrived rewind mechanism.

Remember 1. This is a rapidly rising market with few dealers capable of assessing the truly rare examples, with the result that a high price is often placed on uninteresting and common pieces.

Chapter XII MASTER CLOCKS

Bentley electric clock	Synchronome			Gillett & Johnston	Brillie	Silent Electric	Lowne
	Early	Late	Experimental				
£1,500	£250+	£200+	£300	£200+	£250+	£200+	£350+

Remember 1. A master clock that was part of the production run of a factory will always realise a higher price than one made by an amateur.

2. Case style varies the price by very little – the only exception would be the clocks cased in a wide variety of cases, e.g. Bentley Electric Clock.

3. Slave dials are valued according to case style and are priced from £5.

4. Rarity is the key factor in assessing the price of these clocks.

5. Prices have not settled yet and non-specialist dealers tend to place swingeing values on their offerings and are playing on the fact that this is a rapidly rising market.

Chapter XIII TIME RECORDERS, NIGHT-WATCHMAN CLOCKS, ETC.

This is another area of horological collecting where precedents as regards monetary values have not been set as yet, the exceptions being early examples by such makers as Whitehurst of Derby which occasionally appear on the market for £200 or £300 depending upon condition, etc. Possibly the following comments will be helpful.

Night-watchman portable tell tales (examples without their set of keys command a lower price than those complete with keys and in original carrying case): £20+.

Pigeon clocks £50+

Time stamps £25+

Workmen's time recorders £25+

Chess Clock £30+

Timers for specific purposes – the price would depend upon case style and novelty as much as anything.

Do take care that access can be gained to any of the Workmen's or Night-watchman clocks. As they were made with the express intention of being tamper-proof, it can be exceedingly difficult to open an example that has been locked and then had the key mislaid.

Appendix

PAGES FROM A TRADE CATALOGUE OF WATCH AND CLOCK MATERIALS, circa 1916

For those who obtain part of their pleasure in 'doing up' some of the more robust examples it is hoped that the necessary details regarding parts and styles can be gleaned from the pages in this Appendix showing the materials offered to the clockmaker at the beginning of this century. It is still possible to obtain some of the more standard parts — springs, weights, spandrels, etc., from material dealers today. Many of these are willing to supply catalogues and conduct business through the post. List of addresses as well as display advertisements appear in current copies of the *Horological Journal* or the *Antiquarian Horological Journal*. Failing that, local trade directories at the local library can be consulted.

CLOCK MATERIAL SECTION.

ARBORS, &c.

No. 4301.   For **French** Clocks.   Per doz. 8/-   Each 10d.
No. 6202.   ,,   **Carriage**   ,,   ,,   7/-   ,,   8d.
No. 6203.   ,,   **Alarm**   ,,   ,,   5/-   ,,   6d.

No. 4302.   **Barrel Arbor Forgings** for English Timepieces.
Per doz. 2/6.   Each 3d.

No. 4304.   **Fusee Arbor Forgings**
for English Timepieces.
Per dozen 2/6.   Each 3d.

BELL HAMMERS.

1386

No. 1386.   For **French** Clocks.   Per doz. 4/-   Each 6d.

No. 1643.   For **English Case** Clocks.   Per dozen 20/-   Each 2/3.

BELL STANDS.

656

No. 656.   For **French** Clocks.   Per doz. 4/-   Each 6d.

No. 657.   For **English Case** Clocks.   Per dozen 8/-   Each 10d.

BIRDS AND BELLOWS FOR CUCKOO CLOCKS.

No. 6204.   **Birds** for Cuckoo Clocks.   Per dozen 3/8.   Each 5d.

No. 2060.   **Bellows** for Cuckoo Clocks.
Per dozen Pairs 13/2.   Per Pair 1/4.

BASEMENTS AND CAPITALS for Case Clock Pillars.

Sizes given are Diameters of Pillars and Inside Diameters of Basements and Capitals.

No. 1770.   1-inch.   Per doz. 21/-   Each 2/-

No. 1771.   ⅞-inch.   Per doz. 18/-   Each 1/9.

No. 1729.   ¾-inch.   Per doz. 14/-   Each 1/4.

No. 1772.   1-inch.   Per doz. 8/10.   Each 10d.

No. 1773.   ⅞-inch.   Per doz. 6/10.   Each 9d.

No. 1727.   ¾-inch.   Per doz. 5/2.   Each 6d.

Quarter dozen at dozen rate.

K 2

BELLS—Various.

No. 651. **Cast,** for English Case Clocks.　Per lb. 2/6.
　Any size of Chime-Clock Bell supplied to order

BUSH WIRE.

No. 650.　**French** Clock, Polished.
　Size 46 m/m.　Per dozen 2/8　each 4d.
　　,,　52 m/m.　　,,　2/11　,,　4d.
　　,,　60 m/m.　　,,　3/4　,,　5d.

No. 652.　**American** Clock, Blue.
　Size 7 c/m.　Per gross 16/- ;　per dozen 1/6 ;　each 3d.
　Size 8 c/m.　Per gross 20/- ;　per dozen 1/9 ;　each 3d.

No. 6318.　**German** Clock, Nickel-Plated.
Sizes	5	6	7	8 c/m
Per gross	11/-	14/-	22/-	54/-
Per dozen	1/2	1/6	2/-	4/9
Each	3d.	3d.	4d.	6d.

No. 658.ª　**BUSH WIRE.**　By separate sizes.

No. 658A.　Assortment of 3 doz.
　as illustrated.
Per doz. boxes 36/- ; per box 3/3.

No. 658B.
Per doz. boxes 9/- ; per box 1/-

No. 658.　Sizes 0, per gross 40/4 ; per dozen 3/6.
1—10	,,	19/6	,,	1/9.
11—20	,,	16/6	,,	1/6.
21—30	,,	14/6	,,	1/4.
31—40	,,	9/6	,,	1/-
41—50	,,	7/2	,,	9d.
51—60	,,	6/6	,,	8d.

BUSHES, for Dials.

Nʰo. 660—30-hour.　No. 660—8-day.　No. 661.　No. 6321.　No. 664　No. 6322.

No. 660.　**Brass,** for keyholes of dials, American or German, 8-day or 30-hour... ... ... per gross 1/6 ; per dozen 3d.
No. 661.　　,,　　for English case clock dials　... ... ... ,,　3/-　,,　4d.
No. 6321.　**Pipes,** for centre holes of French clock dials, solid brass　... ... per dozen 1/6　each 3d.
No. 664.　**Collets,** for French clock dials, solid brass　... ... ... ,,　1/-　,,　2d.
No. 6322.　**Bush Clavits** or Keys, for fixing keyhole bushes and pipes numbered 664 and 6321　per gross 9d.¹; per dozen 2d.

No. 6323.　**Bouchons,** for French and Vienna clocks,
　in boxes of 100, assorted.
　Per dozen boxes, 11/- ; per box 1/-

No. 6324¹　**Bouchons,** for American clocks, in boxes of
　100, assorted.
　Per dozen boxes 18/-; per box 1/8.

Quarter gross at gross rate ; quarter dozen at dozen rate.

BEZELS, Various.

No. 1384. **French Clock Front,** Hinged, complete, with glass.

Sizes	3½-in.	3¾-in.	4-in.	4¼-in.	4½-in.	5-in.	5½-in.
Per doz.	22/-	24/-	25/-	28/-	35/-	40/-	40/-
Each	2/-	2/3	2/3	2/6	3/3	3/6	3/6

State Size of Hole in Clock Case when ordering.

No. 1385. **French Clock Back,** Hinged, complete.

Sizes	3½-in.	3¾-in.	4-in.	4¼-in.	4½-in.	5-in.	5½-in.
Per doz.	16/-	17/-	18/-	19/-	25/-	25/-	30/-
Each	1/6	1/8	1/9	1/9	2/3	2/3	2/9

State Size of Hole in Clock Case when ordering.

No. 648. **American Clock,** 4½-in. to 14-in. diameter.

Sizes	4½-in.	6-in.	8-in.	10-in.	12-in.	13-in.	14-in.
Per doz.	10/-	14/4	15/6	16/6	17/8	39/8	46/2
Each	1/-	1/3	1/5	1/6	1/6	3/6	4/-

No. 4311. **Ansonia,** for Regulators, A. B. and Office, with Fittings, complete. Each 3/3.

No. 1117. **Weight Regulator.** Bezels only. Size 8-in.
Per dozen 8/4. Each 9d.

CLICKS AND CLICK SPRINGS.

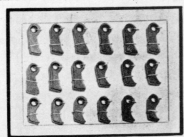

For **German** and **American** Clocks.

No. 4315. Assortment of 1½ dozen on Card.
Per dozen Cards 4/6. Per Card 6d.

No. 665. Assorted. Per gross 3/-. Per dozen 4d.

No. 2053. For Inside **English** Clock Fusees, Brass.
Per gross 18/-. Per dozen 1/9.
No. 668A. For **French** Clocks. Per gross 10/9. Per doz. 1/3. Each 2d.
No. 668B.   „   „   „   9/-   „   1/3. „ 2d.
No. 1107. „ **Weight Regulators.**
Per gross 10/6. Per doz. 1/3. Each 2d.
No. 667. **French** Clocks.   „   10/9.   „   1/3. „ 2d.
No. 668. „   „   „   with Spring combined.
Per gross 9/-. Per doz. 1/3. „ 2d.

No. 1725. For **English** Fusees
Per gross 7/6. Per doz. 9d.

No. 669. For **Bee** Clocks.
Per gross 2/-. Per doz. 4d.

Quarter gross at gross rate ; quarter dozen at dozen rate.

493

CLICKS AND CLICK SPRINGS Continued.

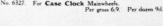

No. 6327.   For **Case Clock** Mainwheels.
Per gross 6.9.   Per dozen 9d.

No. 4326.   For **Case Clocks.** Circular with Spring combined. Per dozen 18 -   Each 1/9.

No. 6325.   **Assortment** of 1 dozen for **French** Clocks, on card as illustrated.   Per dozen cards 10/- Per card 1/-

No. 4325. For **Case Clock** Mainwheels.
Per dozen 4/-   Each 6d.
No. 1641. **Forgings** only. Per dozen 1 6.   Each 3d.

670A

741

No. 670A.   **Ratchet Clicks** for English Timepieces.
Per dozen 2/8.   Each 4d.
No. 741: **Ratchets** for English Timepieces.
Per dozen 3/2.   Each 4d.

1193.

No. 6326.   **Assortment** of 1 dozen for **German** Clocks, on card as illustrated. Per dozen cards 5/9. Per card 8d.

No. 1193. Circular for **Weight Regulators.**
Per gross 12/- Per dozen 1/6.   Each 3d.

Quarter gross at gross rate.   Quarter dozen at dozen rate.

BLOCKS FOR MOVEMENTS, BARRELS, &c.

No. 1975A.

No. 1975B.

No. 1975. Per gross 18/-   Per dozen 1/9.
Blocks. Hardwood, for Fixing American Movements in Cases.

No. 4518. **Barrel** and **Arbor** for English
Timepiece.   Per dozen 24/-   Each 2/3.

CASE CLOCK DRUM.

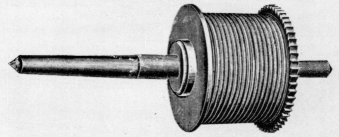

No. 4539. **Barrel** or **Drum,** mounted on Steel Arbor for Case Clock. Complete. Each 4/8.

COLLETS.

For **American** and **German** Clock Hands.
No. 4317. Assorted—Round, Square and Oblong Holes.
                    Per dozen Boxes 4/6.   Per Box 6d.
No. 4316. All Square Holes.   ,,   ,,   4/6.   ,,   6d.

For **French** and **German** Clocks, with Small Round Holes.
No. 6328. Polished Steel, Assorted.
                    Per dozen Boxes 16/6.   Per Box 1/6.
No. 663. Brass.   ,,   ,,   18/-   ,,   1/9.

Quarter gross at gross rate ; quarter dozen at dozen rate.

495

CLICK RIVETS, COLLETS, &c.

No. 666. **Click Rivets,** in Boxes of 1 Gross, Assorted. Per doz. boxes 9/- Per box 1/-

Collets for English Long Case and Spring Clocks. Solid Turned.
No. 4315. 1 Dozen Assorted on Card. Per doz. Cards 6/9. Per Card 8d
No. 662. For Spring Timepieces. Per gross 6/9. Per dozen 8d.
No. 6329. For Long Case—Round Holes. Per gross 6/9. Per doz. 8d.
No. 6473. ,, ,, ,, Square ,, ,, 6/9. ,, 8d.

No. 4791. Per dozen 6/- Each 8d.
Counterweights,
For 30-hour Case Clocks.

TURNED BRASS RIVETS.

1 Gross Assortment.

No. 1990. E/- per Box.

No. 1990. **Click Rivets.** Best Quality Turned. Assortment of 1 Gross as illustrated by 6 Separate Sizes. Per dozen boxes 13/6. Per box 1/6.

CHAINS.

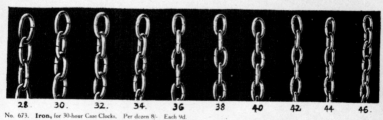

28. 30. 32. 34. 36 38 40 42 44 46.

No. 673. **Iron,** for 30-hour Case Clocks. Per dozen 8/- Each 9d.

Brass, for Cuckoo and similar Clocks.

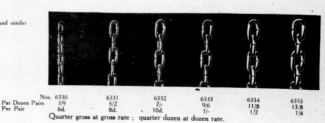

	Nos. 6330	6331	6332	6333	6334	6335
Per Dozen Pairs	3/9	5/2	7/-	9/6	11/8	13/8
Per Pair	6d.	8d.	10d.	1/-	1/2	1/4

Quarter gross at gross rate ; quarter dozen at dozen rate.

496

CHAINS, &c.

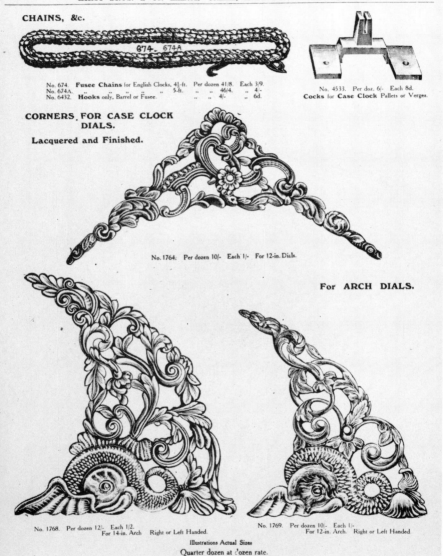

No. 674. **Fusee Chains** for English Clocks, 4½-ft. Per dozen 41/8. Each 3/9.
No. 674A. ,, ,, ,, ,, ,, 5-ft. ,, ,, 46/4. ,, 4/-
No. 6432. **Hooks** only, Barrel or Fusee. ,, ,, 4/- ,, 6d.

No. 4533. Per doz. 6/- Each 8d.
Cocks for **Case Clock** Pallets or Verges.

CORNERS FOR CASE CLOCK DIALS.

Lacquered and Finished.

No. 1764. Per dozen 10/- Each 1/- For 12-in. Dials.

For ARCH DIALS.

No. 1768. Per dozen 12/-. Each 1/2.
For 14-in. Arch Right or Left Handed.

No. 1769. Per dozen 10/-. Each 1/-
For 12-in. Arch. Right or Left Handed.

Illustrations Actual Sizes
Quarter dozen at dozen rate.

497

CORNERS FOR CASE CLOCK DIALS.

Lacquered and Finished.

Illustrations Actual Sizes.

No. 1765. Per dozen 12/- each 1/3. For 13-in. and 14-in. Dials.

No. 1766. Per dozen 10/- Each 1/-
For 12-in. Dials.

No. 1767. Per dozen 10/- Each 1/-
For 12-in. Dials.

Quarter dozen at dozen rate.

CORNERS, &c., FOR CASE CLOCK DIALS.   Illustrations Actual Sizes.

No. 4496.   Per dozen 36/-.   Each 3/6.   **Centre,** for top of Case Clock Arch Dial, Convex, Silvered, Engraved and Waxed.

No. 1763.   Per dozen 10/-.   Each 1/-.   For 10-in. Dials. Lacquered and Finished.

LOCKS for Case Clock Doors.

No. 6394.   Per dozen 10/-.   Each 1/-

FASTENERS and KNOBS,
For Clock Doors.

No. 6395. Per doz. 8d. Each 1d.   No. 6396. Per doz. 1/- Each 2d.

No. 6393.   Per dozen 36/-.   Each 3/6.   **Centre** for top of Case Clock Arch Dial, Convex, Silvered, Engraved and Waxed.

No. 6397. Per doz. 3/- Each 4d.   No. 6398. Per doz. 4/- Each 6d.

Quarter dozen at dozen rate.

499

DIALS.

For **Weight Regulators,** complete, with Brass Fittings.

No. 1114. White, 8-in. diameter. Each 3/6.
No. 1115. Ivory, 8-in. diameter.   „ 4/-

Enamel Dial Circles, for **Weight Regulators.**

No. 1116. White, 8-in. diameter. Each 2/3.
No. 6354. Ivory, 8-in. diameter.   „ 2/9.

Enamel Inner Centres, for **Weight Regulators.**

No. 6355. White. Per dozen 7/6. Each 9d.
No. 6356. Ivory.   „   9/-   „ 1/-

No. 676.   **Round,** Zinc, for American Clocks.
Sizes 4-4½-in. 5-6½-in. 7-7½-in. 8-8½-in. 9-10-in. 12-in. 13-in. 14-in.
Per dozen 4/-   5/-   6/-   9/-   9/6   10/- 16/- 20/-
Each, Bored
and Bushed 6d.   7d.   8d.   11d.   1/-   1/-   1/6   1/10
No. 676A.   **Square.**
Sizes ...   4-6-in. 6½-in.   7-in.   7½-in. 8-10-in. 11-in.
Per dozen ...   5/-   6/-   6/6   9/-   10/-   10/6
Each, Bored and Bushed 7d.   8d.   9d.   11d.   1/-   1/1
No. 676B.   **Gothic.**
Sizes ...   4-6in. 6½-in.   7-in.   7½-in. 8-10-in.
Per dozen ...   5/-   6/-   6/6   8/-   10/-
Each, Bored and Bushed 7d.   8d.   9d.   10d.   1/-

No. 6357. **Cardboard,** for French Cylinder Drum Clocks.
Per dozen 1/6. Each 2d.

No. 1434. **Dial Circles,** Ivory, for 8 or 14-day French or German
⅝⅜ Clocks.   Roman or Arabic Numerals.
Diameter Over All ...   10 c/m.   11 c/m.   12½ c/m.   13½ c/m.
„   of Centre Hole   64 m/m.   68 m/m.   70 m/m.   75 m/m.
Per dozen 15/-   18/-   22/6   30/-
Each 1/6   1/9   2/-   2/9
Special Sizes to Sample—**Extra.**

No. 3595. **Paper,** Gummed, for German and American Clocks.
Size of Minute ⎰
Circle ⎱ 3-in. to 3½-in. 3½-in. to 3¾-in. 4-in. to 4¼-in. 4½-in. to 4¾-in.
Per dozen ...   2/-   2/6   2/8   3/4
Each ...   3d.   3d.   3d.   4d.

Size of Minute ⎰
Circle ⎱ 5-in. to 5⅜-in. 5½-in. to 5⅞-in. 6-in. to 6½-in. 7-in. to 7½-in. 11-in.
Per dozen ...   4/2   4/8   5/-   6/2   9/8
Each ...   6d.   6d.   6d.   8d.   10d.
Quarter dozen at dozen rate.

No. 6362. Per dozen 1/6.   Each 2d.   **Cardboard,** for German
and American Lever Clocks, Assorted, Sizes 3½-in. to 4½-in. diameter.
When Special Size or Pattern is required, send Sample.

DIALS—Continued.

No. 1433. **Ivory,** for 8 and 14-day French or German Clocks,
Roman or Arabic Numerals, Without Keyholes.

Sizes...	To 10 c/m.	11 c/m.	12½ c/m.	13½ c/m.
Per dozen	13/6	16/6	22/6	27/-
Each ...	1/3	1/6	2/-	2/6

With Keyholes to sample 3d. per hole extra.

No. 6532. **White,** for 8 or 14-day French or German Clocks,
Roman or Arabic Numerals, Without Keyholes.

Sizes ...	To 10 c/m.	11 c/m.	12½ c/m.	13½ c/m.
Per dozen	10/6	13/6	19/6	24/-
Each ...	1/-	1/3	1/9	2/3

With Keyholes to sample 3d. per hole extra.

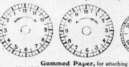

Gummed Paper, for attaching to Paper Dials.
No. 6533. Alarm Circles, Assorted. Per gross 1/- Per dozen 2d.
No. 6534. Seconds ,,   ,,   2/-   ,,   3d.

No. 6531. Per dozen 1 6. Each 2d.
Card, for 2-in. Lever Clocks.

Brass,
for **Grandfather** Clocks.

Roman Hour Circles,
Seconds and Date Circles
are engraved, waxed, silvered
and lacquered with transparent
lacquer. The rest of the
brass work is well finished
and lacquered with rich gold
lacquer.

No. 6535. Sizes 12-in.   13-in.   14-in. square.
    Each   30/-   32/6   35 -
Fitting to Movement ... from 5/- each extra.
Without Seconds Circle ...   2/6 less.
Without Date Circle ...   2 6 less.

No. 6537. **Roman Hour Circles** only, Engraved, Waxed and Silvered.
Diameters (Outside)   11-in.   12-in.   13-in.
    Each   9/9   10/6   11 3

No. 6538. **Seconds** or **Date Circles** only, Engraved, Waxed and
Silvered.
Outside Diameter 2½-in. to 3-in. Each 2/6.

No. 6536. Sizes 12-in. × 15½-in.   14-in. × 19½-in. sq.
    Each   37/6   43 9
Other Sizes at Proportionate Prices.
Without Calendar Circle ...   2/6 less.
Without Seconds Circle ...   2/6 less.
Without the "Tempus Fugit," but
  with Automatic Moon Plate .... 7/6 more.
Fitting to Movement ... from 5/6 each.

No. 6539. **Moon Wheel,** with Painted Landscape and
Seascape.
Sizes 7⅜-in.   8⅜-in.   9⅜-in. Each 7 -

Quarter gross at gross rate ; quarter dozen at dozen rate.

DIALS, ESCAPEMENTS AND ESCUTCHEONS.   Illustrations Actual Sizes.

Index Dials for Weight Regulators.
No. 989. White Enamel. Per gross 17/- Per doz. 2 - Each 3d.
No. 990. Ivory. Per gross 27/4. Per doz. 2/6. Each 4d.

No. 970. **Alarm Dials.**
Ivorine. For Backs of
Alarm Clocks.
Per gross 16 - Per doz. 1/6.
Each 3d.

No. 971. **Alarm Dials.**
Brass complete.
Per gross 29/6.
Per doz. 2 9. Each 4d.

ESCAPEMENTS.

No. 388. **Cylinder,** with Short Index. Per doz. 27/- Each 2/6.
No. 4237. **Cylinder,** with Long Index. Per doz. 27/- Each 2/6.

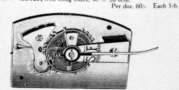

No. 4238. **Lever,** with Short Index, 40 × 26 m/m.
                                        Per doz. 60/- Each 5 6.
No. 4239. **Lever,** with Long Index, 40 × 26 m/m.
                                        Per doz. 60/- Each 5/6.

No. 4609. **Lever,** 52 × 26 m/m. Each 10/-.

No. 4757. **Lever,** Non-Magnetic, 40 m m × 50 m.m.
                                        Per doz. 66/- Each 6 -
No. 4240. **Short Indexes.** Per doz. 2/6. Each 4d.
No. 4241. **Long Indexes.** Per doz. 2 6. Each 4d.
No. 4242. **Index Centres.** Per doz. 2/- Each 3d.

ESCUTCHEONS for Case Clock Doors,
Lacquered & Finished.

No. 4537. Per doz. 8/-
                Each 9d.

No. 4536. Per doz. 8/-
                Each 9d.

No. 4538. Per doz. 8/-
                Each 9d.

Quarter gross at gross rate ; quarter dozen at dozen rate.

FEET, FIGURES, &c.

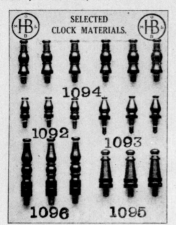

SELECTED CLOCK MATERIALS.

1094

1092

1093

1096   1095

For Nickel **Lever** Clocks.

No.	1094.	1092.	1093.	1096.	1095.
Per gross	6/-	3/6	6/-	6/10	14/6
Per doz.	8d.	6d.	8d.	9d.	1/4

No. 6336. Assortment of 1¼ dozen on Card as Illustrated.
Per dozen Cards 11/- Per Card 1/2.

1418A 1418B. 1418C.

No. 1418. For **French** Drum Clocks.
Per gross 7/4. Per doz. 9d.

4541.   4542.

No. 4541. For **Bracket** Clocks. Solid Brass Finished Per doz. 7/- Each 8d.
No. 4542. " " " " " " 7/- " 8d.

No. 4540. For **Case Clock** Dials.   No. 4527. For **Timepiece** Dials.
Per doz. 2/8. Each 4d.   Per doz. 1/9. Each 3d.

680A.

680B.

No. 680. For **Nickel Baby** Clocks.
Per gross 7/6. Per doz. 9d.

No. 1143. **Fly** and **Pinion** complete. For Weight Regulator. Finished.
Per doz. 4/6. Each 6d.

No. 4524. **Fusee Stop Studs,** for English Timepieces. Per doz. 2/6. Each 4d.

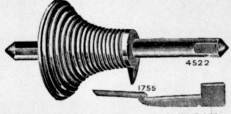

4522

1755

No. 4522. **Fusee,** with Arbor fitted, for Timepieces. Per doz. 25/-. Each 2/3.
No. 1755. **Fusee Stops.** Steel. Per doz. 1/6. Each 2d.

XII VII III

No. 1429. **Figures** for French Clocks, Gilt, Pierced.

	m/m. 7-8½	m/m. 9	m/m. 10-12	m/m. 13-15	m/m. 16	m/m. 17
Per Set	6/3	4/7	3/4	4/7	6/3	7/1
Each	8d.	6d.	5d.	6d.	8d.	9d.

GATHERING PALLETS.

715A.   715B.

712A.

		Per gross.	Per doz.	Each.
No. 715.	For **English Case** Clocks	28/-	2/6	4d.
No. 712A.	For **French** Clocks ...	9/8	1/-	2d.
No. 1130.	For **Weight Regulators**	12/-	1/6	2d.

XI XII II

No. 2061. **Figures** for Cuckoo Clocks.

Stock sizes	14,	16,	20 m/m.
Per dozen Sets	4/-	5/4	5/4
Per Set	6d.	8d.	8d.

Quarter gross at gross rate ; quarter dozen at dozen rate.

503

GONGS AND GONG BLOCKS.

No. 693. Round Wire for American Clocks.

Diameters	8	10	12 c/m.
Per dozen	1/4	1/8	2/5
Each	3d.	3d.	4d.

No. 918. Iron Blocks extra.
Per dozen 2/6. Each 4d.

No. 1121. For Weight or Spring **Regulators.**
Per dozen 3/3. Each 5d.

No. 694. For **French** or **German** Clocks.

Diameters	70	85	100	125	140 m/m.
Per dozen	9/-	9/-	9/9	11/6	13/9
Each	10d.	10d.	1/-	1/3	1/6

No. 6530. Per dozen 18/3.
Each 1/10.
For **Marble** Clocks, with
Pillar complete.
Diameter of Gong 100 m/m.

No. 942. Per dozen 14/- Each 1/3.
For Newhaven or other 8-day
Regulators and Ansonia
Mantle Clocks

No. 941. Per dozen 18/- Each 1/9.
For Ansonia **Regulators.**

For **Grandfather** Clocks, 6-in. Diam.
No. 5804. **Gongs** only, Flat Wire.
Per dozen 25/3. Each 2/6.
No. 6558. **Gongs, complete** with Iron
Block. Per doz. 51/- Each 4/6.

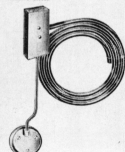

For **Grandfather** Clocks, 6-in. Diam.
No. 5804. **Gongs** only, Flat Wire.
Per dozen 25/3. Each 2/6.
No. 6559. **Gongs, complete** with Pillar
and Blocks. Per doz. 66/- Each 6/-

Quarter dozen at dozen rate.

No. 6560. Per dozen 14/-
Each 1/3
For Ansonia **Marble** Clocks.

GONGS—Continued.

WESTMINSTER GONG SETS.

No. 6471. Set of 5 Gongs, Large, for **Case Clock,** mounted on Pillar as illustrated. Per Set 18/-

No. 6472. Set of 5 Ditto, Small, for **Bracket Clock,** mounted on Pillar as illustrated, but Without Bottom Block. Per Set 12/9.

No. 5802. Set of 5 Gongs, Large, for **Case Clock** (Without Pillar). Per Set 9/8.

No. 5803. Set of Ditto, Small, for **Bracket Clock** (Without Pillar). Per Set 6/-

Nos. 6471 and 6472.

ROD GONGS for German Regulator and Bracket Clocks.

No. 5818. Sets of 5 **Westminster,** for Regulator. Longest Rod about 20-in. Per Set 5/4.
No. 5817. Sets of 5 **Ditto,** for Bracket. Longest Rod about 18-in. Per Set 4/-
No. 5816. Sets of 4 for Regulator. Longest Rod about 22½-in. Per Set 4/4.
No. 5815. Sets of 4 for Bracket. Longest Rod about 16-in. Per Set 3/3.
No. 5814. Sets of 3 for Regulator. Longest Rod about 22½-in. Per Set 3/3.
No. 5813. Sets of 3 for Bracket. Longest Rod about 16-in. Per Set 2/6.
No. 5812. Sets of 2 **Ting-Tang,** for Regulator. Longest Rod about 22½-in. Per Pair 2/3.
No. 5811. Sets of 2 **Ditto,** for Bracket. Longest Rod about 16-in. Per Pair 1/8.
No. 5820. **Hour** Rods only, for Regulator. Length 29-in. Per Dozen 13/- Each 1/6.
No. 5819. „ „ „ „ Bracket. Length 18-in. Per Dozen 8/- Each 1/-

Extra for Cast Rod Gong Blocks.

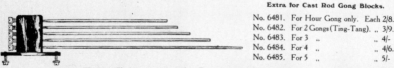

No. 6481. For Hour Gong only. Each 2/8.
No. 6482. For 2 Gongs (Ting-Tang). „ 3/9.
No. 6483. For 3 „ „ 4/-
No. 6484. For 4 „ „ 4/6.
No. 6485. For 5 „ „ 5/-

The same Block is correct for either REGULATOR or BRACKET CLOCK.
Quarter dozen at dozen rate.

505

GONGS (Tube).

No. 6400. **Hour Tube Gongs** only, for Grandfather Long-cased Clocks. Nickel-plated.

Diameter	Length	Each
1¾-in.	54-in.	14/-
1½-in.	50-in.	12/-
1¼-in.	46-in.	10/-
1¼-in.	42-in.	8/-

No. 6401. **Fixing only,** to suit any of above. Each 9/-

This Fixing is very practical and easily adapted to any ordinary Grandfather Clock, bell strike, by attaching the cord supplied to the bell hammer.

No. 6402. **Set of 5 Westminster Tube Gongs,** for Grandfather Long-cased Clock. Diameter of Gongs 1¼-in., Nickel-plated, with Fixing complete and Tube Hammers. Price per Set £6/19/-

No. 6403. Set of 5 Westminster **Gongs only.** Per Set £5/14/-

No. 6404. **Fixing only,** with Hammers for above. Per Set £1/5/-

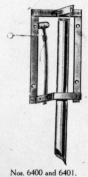

Nos. 6400 and 6401.

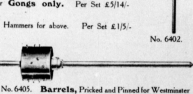

No. 6402.

No. 6407. **Hammer Work,** in Sets, for Westminster Gongs. Tails ¼-in. apart. Per Set 19/-

No. 6408. **Ditto,** for Sets of 8 Bells for Whittington, and to change to 4 Westminster. Tails ⅛-in. apart. Per Set 17/-

No. 6405. **Barrels,** Pricked and Pinned for Westminster 4-Bell or Gongs, to suit Hammer Work No. 6407. Each 4/-

No. 6406. **Ditto** for 8-Bell, to suit Hammer Work No. 6408. Each 5/-

Prices submitted for other Sizes of Tube Gongs either in Sets or separate.

Other Diameters and Lengths.

Sets of 8 or Sets of 4.

Gong Hammers for French or Vienna Regulator Clocks.

No. 1128. **Complete,** as illustrated.
　Per gross 52/3.　Per dozen 4/6.　Each 6d.
No. 1387. **Hammer Heads** only.
　Per gross 23/-　Per dozen 2/-　Each 3d.
No. 1388. **Hammer Rods** only.
　Per gross 29/3.　Per dozen 2/6.　Each 3d.

No. 1390. **Gong Stands,** for French Clocks.
Per dozen 8/6. Each 10d.

Quarter gross at gross rate ; quarter dozen at dozen rate.

GLASSES.

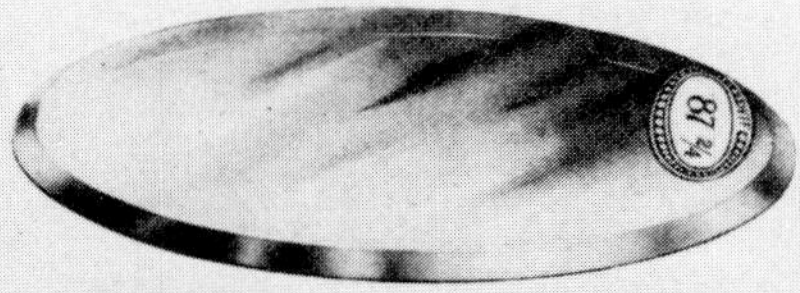

No. 833. **French, flat,** bevelled edges, by $\frac{1}{4}$ sizes in m m. Polished edges.

Sizes	61-65	66-70	71-75	76-85	86-95	96-100	101-105	106-110
Per 100	16/10	17/8	19/10	23/-	26/4	28/-	30/-	32/4
Per 10	1/10	1/10	2/3	2/6	2/9	3/-	3/3	3/6
Each	3d.	3d.	4d.	4d.	5d.	5d.	5d.	6d.

Sizes	111-115	116-120	121-125	126-130	131-135	136-140	141-145
Per 100	34/-	36/4	46/2	47/10	52/2	55/-	57/2
Per 10	3/8	3/10	4/9	5/-	5/4	5/8	6/-
Each	6d.	7d.	8d.	8d.	8d.	9d.	9d.

Sizes	146-150	151-155	156-160	161-165	166-170	171-175	176-180
Per 100	59/4	68/2	70/4	77/-	88/-	90/2	105/6
Per 10	6/3	7/-	7/3	7/10	9/-	9/3	10/9
Each	10d.	10d.	11d.	1/-	1/1	1/2	1/3

If fitted to Bezel, 3d. each extra.

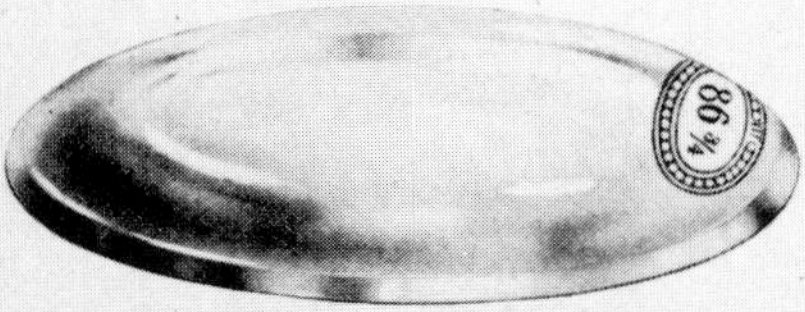

No. 825. **French, convex,** bevelled edges, by $\frac{1}{4}$ sizes in m/m. Polished edges.

Sizes	64-83	84-96	97-109	110-123	124-136	137-151
Per doz.	8/-	10/8	14/6	18/-	21/6	26/4
Each	10d.	1/-	1/4	1/9	2/-	2/6

If fitted to Bezel, 3d. each extra.

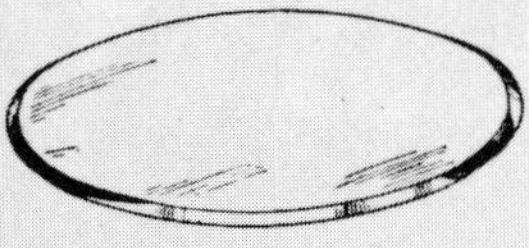

No. 4243. **Bevelled edge,** for German Lever Clocks. Assorted Sizes 2-in. to 4-in. Per doz. 4/- Each 6d.

Bevelled Glasses for Carriage Clocks, and Aneroid Glasses, with hole drilled, to order.

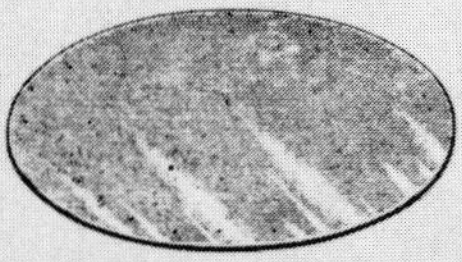

No. 832. **Plain,** for American and German Clocks.

Sizes	2-in. to 3-in.	$3\frac{1}{8}$-in. to 4-in.	$4\frac{1}{8}$-in. to 5-in.	$5\frac{1}{8}$-in. to 6-in.	$6\frac{1}{8}$in. to 7-in.
Per gross	6/8	8/10	11/-	13/2	18/8
Per doz.	8d.	1/-	1/2	1/3	1/9
Each	1d.	2d.	2d.	2d.	2d.

Sizes	$7\frac{1}{8}$-in. to 8-in.	$8\frac{1}{8}$-in. to 9-in.	$9\frac{1}{8}$-in. to 10-in.	$10\frac{1}{8}$-in. to 11-in.
Per gross	23/2	29/2	35/2	41/10
Per doz.	2/3	2/9	3/3	3/9
Each	3d.	4d.	4d.	5d.

Sizes	$11\frac{1}{8}$-in. to 12-in.	$12\frac{1}{8}$-in. to 13-in.	$13\frac{1}{8}$-in. to 14-in.	$14\frac{1}{8}$-in. to 15-in.
Per gross	46/2	57/2	68/2	77/-
Per doz.	4/-	5/-	6/-	6/9
Each	6d.	7d.	8d.	9d.

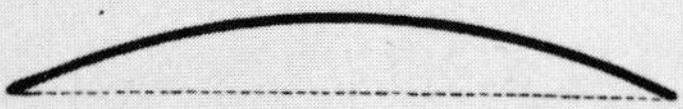

No. 2185. **Sheet, convex.**

Sizes	6-in.	8-in.	10-in.	12-in.	14-in.
Per doz.	3/8	4/9	7/2	11/4	14/-
Each	4d.	6d.	9d.	1/2	1/4

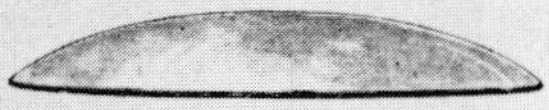

No. 6365. Per doz. 3/- Each 4d. **Convex,** thin, for Lever and other Drum Clocks. $2\frac{1}{4}$-in. to $4\frac{1}{2}$-in. diameter.

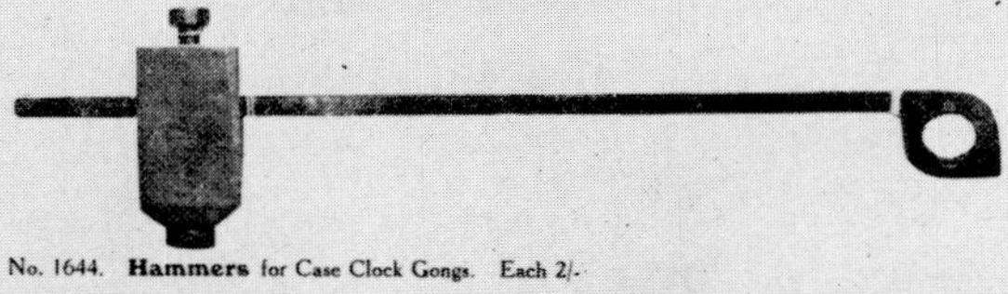

No. 1644. **Hammers** for Case Clock Gongs. Each 2/-

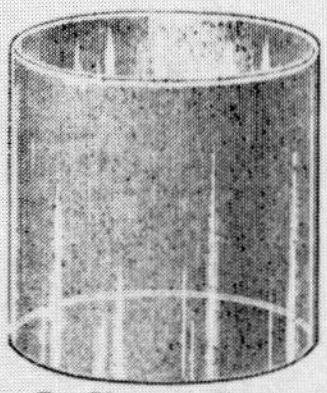

For **Chronos** Clocks.
No. 6366. Height $3\frac{1}{8}$-in. Each 1/-
No. 6366A. Height $3\frac{3}{8}$-in. Each 1/-

No. 1646. **Hammer Rod Forgings** for Case Clocks. Per doz. 3/- Each 4d.

Quarter gross at gross rate ; quarter dozen at dozen rate.

HOOKS AND HANGERS.

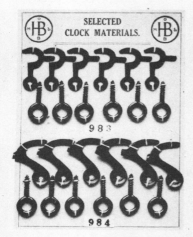

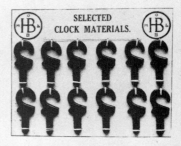

No. 1138. **Weight Hooks** for Regulators.
Per dozen Cards 7/6.   Per Card 9d.

No. 983. **Hooks with Eyes.** Per gross Pairs 8/9. Per doz. Pairs 9d.
No. 984.   „   „   „   „   „   „   12/-   „   „   „   1/3.
No. 984A. **Assortment** of 1 doz. Pairs as illustrated.
                                      Per doz. Cards 10 4.   Per Card 1/-

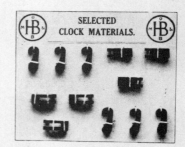

No. 725. **Pendulum Hooks** for French Clocks.
Per dozen Cards 10 -   Per Card 1/-

No. 1736. **Door Hooks**
or Bolts.
Per gross 3/3.   Per dozen 5d.

No. 1737. **Door Hooks** or Bolts.
Per gross 7/6.   Per doz. 9d.

No. 709. **Seatboard Hooks** with Nuts, Large or Small.
Per gross 18/-   Per dozen 1/9.   Each 2d.

HANGERS.

No. 976. Per gross 8/3. Per doz. 9d.

No. 975.   Per gross 13/9.
Per doz. 1/3.

No. 6339. Per gross 9/- Per doz. 10d.

No. 6340.   Per gross 7/6.
Per doz. 9d.

Quarter gross at gross rate ; quarter dozen at dozen rate.

HINGES.

 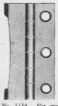

No. 1774. Per doz.
Pairs 2/-. Per Pair
3d. For **Long
Case** Clock Doors.

No. 1734. Per gross
10/-. Per doz. 1/-.
For **Bezels.**

No. 1735. Per doz. Pairs 12/-. Per Pair 1/3.
Cast, for **Long Case** Clocks.

SELECTED CLOCK MATERIALS.

No. 1731.
Per gross Pairs 3/8.
Per doz. Pairs 6d.

No. 1732.
Per gross Pairs 6/-.
Per doz. Pairs 8d.

No. 1733.
Per gross Pairs 6/10.
Per doz. Pairs 9d.

No. 981.
Per gross Pairs 19/8.
Per doz. Pairs 1/9.

No. 6353. **Assortment** of 1 dozen as Illustrated. Per dozen
Cards 9/-. Per Card 1/-.

HAIRSPRINGS.

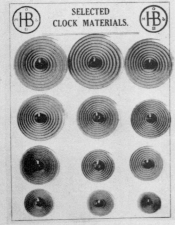

SELECTED CLOCK MATERIALS.

HANDSETTERS.

No. 6344. For **Lever Clocks.** 6 Dozen Assorted in Box
as Illustrated. Per Box 2/9.

No. 718. 1For **Lever Clocks** with Collets. Per gross 12/-.
Per dozen 1/6. Each 3d.
No. 718A. **Assortment** of 1 dozen as Illustrated.
Per dozen Cards 12/-. Per Card 1/6.
No. 6451. For **Ansonia** "Bee" Clocks. Genuine.
Per dozen 3/8. Each 4d.

Quarter gross at gross rate ; quarter dozen at dozen rate.

509

HANDSETTERS,
HAMMERSPRINGS AND
SECONDS HANDS.

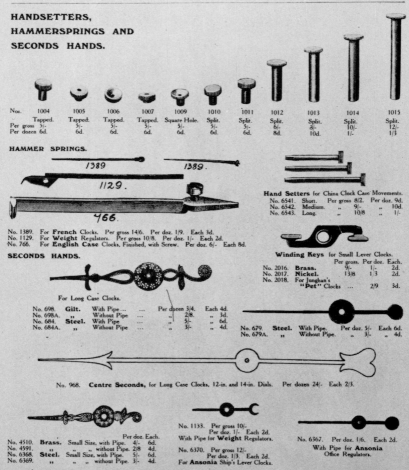

Nos.	1004	1005	1006	1007	1009	1010	1011	1012	1013	1014	1015
	Tapped.	Tapped.	Tapped.	Tapped.	Square Hole.	Split.	Split.	Split.	Split.	Split.	Split.
Per gross	5/-	5/-	5/-	5/-	5/-	5/-	5/-	6/-	8/-	10/-	12/-
Per dozen	6d.	6d.	6d.	6d.	6d.	6d.	6d.	8d.	10d.	1/-	1/3

HAMMER SPRINGS.

1389.   1389.

1129.

466.

No. 1389. For **French** Clocks. Per gross 14/6. Per doz. 1/9. Each 3d.
No. 1129. For **Weight** Regulators. Per gross 10/8. Per doz. 1/- Each 2d.
No. 766. For **English Case** Clocks, Finished, with Screw. Per doz. 6/- Each 8d.

Hand Setters for China Clock Case Movements.
No. 6541. Short.   Per gross 8/2. Per doz. 9d.
No. 6542. Medium.   „   9/-   „   10d.
No. 6543. Long.   „   10/8   „   1/-

SECONDS HANDS.

Winding Keys for Small Lever Clocks.
    Per doz. Per doz. Each.
No. 2016. **Brass.**   9/-   1/-   2d.
No. 2017. **Nickel.**   13/8   1/3   2d.
No. 2018. For Junghan's
    "**Pet**" Clocks ...   2/9   3d.

For **Long Case** Clocks.
No. 698. **Gilt.** With Pipe...   ...   Per dozen 3/4.   Each 4d.
No. 698A.   „   Without Pipe   ...   „   2/8   „   3d.
No. 684. **Steel.** With Pipe   ...   „   5/-   „   6d.
No. 684A.   „   Without Pipe   ...   „   3/-   „   4d.

No. 679. **Steel.** With Pipe.   Per doz. 5/- Each 6d.
No. 679A.   „   Without Pipe.   „   3/-   „   4d.

No. 968. **Centre Seconds**, for Long Case Clocks, 12-in. and 14-in. Dials.   Per dozen 24/- Each 2/3.

    Per doz. Each.
No. 4510. **Brass.** Small Size, with Pipe.   4/-   6d.
No. 4591.   „   „   „ without Pipe.   2/8   4d.
No. 6368. **Steel.** Small Size, with Pipe.   5/-   6d.
No. 6369.   „   „   „ without Pipe.   3/-   4d.

No. 1133.   Per gross 10/-
    Per doz. 1/- Each 2d.
With Pipe for **Weight** Regulators.

No. 6370.   Per gross 12/-
    Per doz. 1/3   Each 2d.
For **Ansonia** Ship's Lever Clocks.

No. 6367.   Per doz. 1/6.   Each 2d.
With Pipe for **Ansonia**
Office Regulators.

ANY KIND OF INDICATOR HANDS Supplied to Order or Quoted for.

Quarter gross at gross rate ; quarter dozen at dozen rate.

CLOCK HANDS—Various.

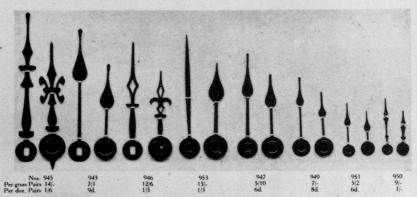

Nos. 945	943	946	953	947	949	951	950
Per gross Pairs 14/-	7/1	12/6	13/-	5/10	7/-	5/2	9/-
Per doz. Pairs 1/6	9d.	1/3	1/3	6d.	8d.	6d.	1/-

No. 6345.
For **Junghan's Mantle** Clocks.
Per dozen Pairs 5/-
Per Pair 6d.

No. 6346.
For **Junghan's Bracket** Clocks.
Per doz. Pairs 2/6.
Per Pair 4d.

No. 6347.
For Ansonia and Waterbury **Ship's Lever** Clocks.
Per doz. Pairs 1/3
Per Pair 2d.

No. 6348. Louis XV.
Pattern for **French** Clocks.
Sizes 3-3½-in. 5½-in. 6-in.
Doz. Pairs 2/11 5/10 11/8
Per Pair 4d. 6d. 1/-

No. 6349.
For **400-Day** Clocks. Any make supplied.
Doz. Pairs 5/-
Per Pair 6d.

No. 6350.
For H.A.C. **Lever** Clocks.
Per gross Pairs 11/- Per doz. Pairs 1/-

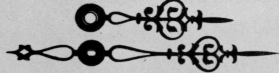

No. 965. For **Regulators.** Per gross Pairs 20/6. Per dozen Pairs 2/6. Per Pair 4d.
NOTE.—Size as Illustrated supplied, unless otherwise stated.
Quarter gross pairs at gross rate ; quarter dozen pairs at dozen rate.

511

HANDS.

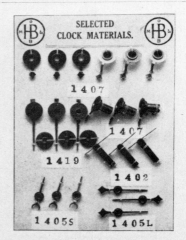

SELECTED CLOCK MATERIALS.

1407

1419   1407

1402

1405S   1405L

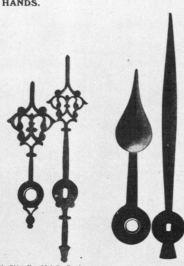

No. 966. For H.A.C. **Spring Regulators.**
Per gross pairs 13/4.
Per doz. pairs 1/6.   Per pair 3d.

No. 962. For H.A.C. **Regulators.**
Per gross pairs 34/-.
Per doz. pairs 3/6.   Per pair 4d.

Alarm and Seconds Hands for Lever Clocks.

No. 6351. **Assortment** of 1½ dozen as Illustrated.
Per dozen cards 10/9.   Per card 1/3.
No. 1407. **Alarm Hands** (Straight or Bent) for Backs of Lever
Clocks. Per gross 5/10. Per dozen 8d.
No. 1419. **Ditto,** for Junghan's Corona Clocks.
Per gross 13/-. Per doz. 1/3.
No. 1405S. **Ditto,** for Front of Lever Clocks ⎫
No. 1405L. **Ditto,** „ „ „ „ „ ⎬ „ 2/4 „ 4d.
No. 1402. **Seconds Hands,** for Front of
Lever Clocks „ 3/6. „ 6d.

No. 6352. For **Cuckoo** Clocks, Bone, Carved.
	3½ & 4-in.	4½-5½-in.	6-in. Dials.
Per doz. pairs	5/6	6/9	7/6
Per pair	8d.	9d.	10d.

No. 704. For **Cuckoo** Clocks, Bone, Plain.
	3½-in.	4-in.	4½-in.	5-in.	6-in. Dials.
Per doz. pairs	1/3	3/-	3/7	4/2	4/10
Per pair	2d.	4d.	4d.	6d.	6d.

No. 1113. Per dozen pairs 4/- Per pair 6d. For **Weight Regulators,** 7-in. or 8-in. Dials.
Quarter gross at gross rate ; quarter dozen at dozen rate.

HANDS FOR GRANDFATHER CLOCKS.

Fancy Patterns.

No. 697. **Brass
Gilt,** for 12-in. or
14-in. Dials.

Per dozen pairs 9/-
Per pair 10d.

No. 6372. **Blue Steel,** for 10-in.,
12-in., or 14-in. Dials.

Per dozen pairs 9/6.
Per pair 1/-

**Serpentine
Pattern.**

	Per doz. pairs.	Per pair.
No. 6373. **Brass Gilt.**		
For 10-in. and 12-in. Dials.	12/-	1/2
13-in. „	14/-	1/4
14-in. „	16 -	1/6
No. 6374. **Blue Steel.**		
For 10-in. and 12-in. Dials.	11/-	1/-
13-in. „	13/-	1/3
14-in. „	15 -	1/6

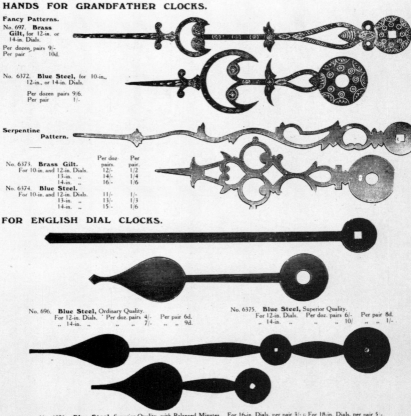

FOR ENGLISH DIAL CLOCKS.

No. 696. **Blue Steel,** Ordinary Quality.
For 12-in. Dials. Per doz. pairs 4/- Per pair 6d.
„ 14-in. „ „ „ 7/- „ „ 9d.

No. 6375. **Blue Steel,** Superior Quality.
For 12-in. Dials. Per doz. pairs 6/- Per pair 8d.
„ 14-in. „ „ „ 10/ „ „ 1/-

No. 6376. **Blue Steel,** Superior Quality, with Balanced Minutes. For 16-in. Dials, per pair 3/- 6 For 18-in. Dials, per pair 5/-
For 20-in. Dials, per pair 8/-

FOR AMERICAN DIAL CLOCKS.

No. 6377. **Blue Steel.** For 10-in. Dials. }
„ „ 12-in. „ } Per gross pairs 24 - Per doz. pairs 2/3. Per pair 4d.
Quarter dozen pairs at dozen rate.

513

HANDS FOR FRENCH CLOCKS.

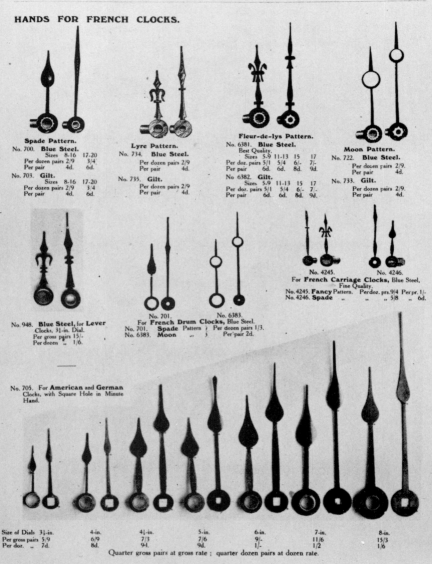

Spade Pattern.
No. 700. **Blue Steel.**

Sizes	8-16	17-20
Per dozen pairs	2/9	3/4
Per pair	4d.	6d.

No. 703. **Gilt.**

Sizes	8-16	17-20
Per dozen pairs	2/9	3/4
Per pair	4d.	6d.

Lyre Pattern.
No. 734. **Blue Steel.**
Per dozen pairs 2/9
Per pair   4d.

No. 735. **Gilt.**
Per dozen pairs 2/9
Per pair   4d.

Fleur-de-lys Pattern.
No. 6381. **Blue Steel.**
Best Quality.

Sizes	5-9	11-13	15	17
Per doz. pairs	5/1	5/4	6/-	7/-
Per pair	6d.	6d.	8d.	9d.

No 6382. **Gilt.**

Sizes	5-9	11-13	15	17
Per doz. pairs	5/1	5/4	6/-	7/-
Per pair	6d.	6d.	8d.	9d.

Moon Pattern.
No. 722. **Blue Steel.**
Per dozen pairs 2/9.
Per pair   4d.

No. 733. **Gilt.**
Per dozen pairs 2/9.
Per pair   4d.

No. 948. **Blue Steel,** for **Lever**
Clocks, 3½-in. Dial.
Per gross pairs 15/-
Per dozen „   1/6.

No. 701.
For French Drum Clocks, Blue Steel.
No. 701. **Spade** Pattern ⎫ Per dozen pairs 1/3.
No. 6383. **Moon** „   ⎭ Per pair 2d.

No. 4245.   No. 4246.
For French Carriage Clocks, Blue Steel,
Fine Quality.
No. 4245. **Fancy** Pattern. Per doz. prs. 9/4 Per pr. 1/-
No. 4246. **Spade** „   „   „   5/8 „   6d.

No. 705. For **American** and **German**
Clocks, with Square Hole in Minute
Hand.

Size of Dials	3½-in.	4-in.	4½-in.	5-in.	6-in.	7-in.	8-in.
Per gross pairs	5/9	6/9	7/3	7/6	9/-	11/6	15/3
Per doz. „	7d.	8d.	9¼.	9d.	1/-	1/2	1/6

Quarter gross pairs at gross rate ; quarter dozen pairs at dozen rate.

514

KEYS.

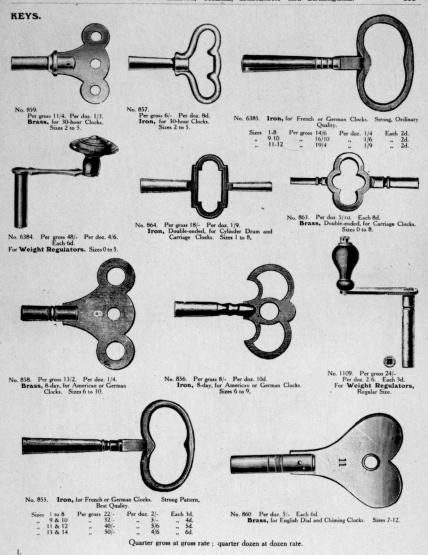

No. 859.
Per gross 11/4. Per doz. 1/3.
Brass, for 30-hour Clocks.
Sizes 2 to 5.

No. 857.
Per gross 6/- Per doz. 8d.
Iron, for 30-hour Clocks.
Sizes 2 to 5.

No. 6385. Iron, for French or German Clocks. Strong, Ordinary Quality.

Sizes	1-8	Per gross	14/6	Per doz.	1/4	Each	2d.
„	9-10	„	16/10	„	1/6	„	2d.
„	11-12	„	19/4	„	1/9	„	2d.

No. 6384. Per gross 48/- Per doz. 4/6.
Each 6d.
For **Weight Regulators.** Sizes 0 to 5.

No. 864. Per gross 18/- Per doz. 1/9.
Iron, Double-ended, for Cylinder Drum and Carriage Clocks. Sizes 1 to 8.

No. 863. Per doz. 5/10. Each 8d.
Brass, Double-ended, for Carriage Clocks.
Sizes 0 to 8.

No. 858. Per gross 13/2. Per doz. 1/4.
Brass, 8-day, for American or German
Clocks. Sizes 6 to 10.

No. 856. Per gross 8/- Per doz. 10d.
Iron, 8-day, for American or German Clocks.
Sizes 6 to 9.

No. 1109. Per gross 24/-
Per doz. 2 6. Each 5d.
For **Weight Regulators,**
Regular Size.

No. 855. Iron, for French or German Clocks. Strong Pattern,
Best Quality.

Sizes	1 to 8	Per gross	22/-	Per doz.	2/-	Each	3d.
„	9 & 10	„	32/-	„	3/-	„	4d.
„	11 & 12	„	40/-	„	3/6	„	5d.
„	13 & 14	„	50/-	„	4/6	„	6d.

No. 860 Per doz. 5/- Each 6d.
Brass, for English Dial and Chiming Clocks. Sizes 7-12.

Quarter gross at gross rate ; quarter dozen at dozen rate.

L.

KEYS—Continued.

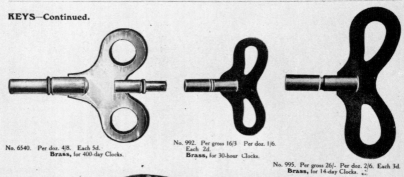

No. 6540. Per doz. 4/8. Each 5d.
Brass, for 400-day Clocks.

No. 992. Per gross 16/3 Per doz. 1/6.
Each 2d.
Brass, for 30-hour Clocks.

No. 995. Per gross 26/- Per doz. 2/6. Each 3d.
Brass, for 14-day Clocks.

No. 861. Per dozen 7/- Each 8d.
Crank, with Wooden Handles, Brass Pipes.
Sizes 9 to 15.

**For Long-Case Grandfather
Clocks.**

No. 1740. Per gross 10/-
Per dozen 1/-
Brass, for Fixing Main Wheels
on pieces of English Clocks.

No. 1741. Per gross 5/-
Per dozen 6d.
Brass, for Fixing Hour Hands
to Hour Wheel Pipes of English
Timepieces.

No. 868. Per dozen 2/- Each 3d.
For Musical Boxes.

No. 866.
Per gross 10/-
Per doz. 1/-
Iron, for American
O.O.G. Clocks.

Brass, with Four Pipes. Very
Useful for Clock Winders.
No. 6565. Sizes of Pipes 5, 7, 9, 11
No. 6566. „ 6, 8, 10, 12
No. 6567. „ 7, 9, 11, 13
No. 6568. „ 8, 10, 12, 14
Per dozen 14/- Each 1/3.

No. 6564. Per dozen 16/- Each 1/6.
Brass, with Three Pipes for Hexagon Nuts.
Very handy for the Clock Jobber.

Quarter gross at gross rate ; quarter dozen at dozen rate.

LINES, GUT, CORDS, &c.

Gut, for 8-day Case Clocks.

No. 685.   Good Reliable Quality.   Per doz. 7/6.   Each 9d.
No. 686.   Superior Quality.   „   9/6.   „   1/-

No. 683.   Per gross 64/-.   Per doz. 5/6.
Each 6d.

Gut, for 8-day English Spring Clocks,
Superior Quality.

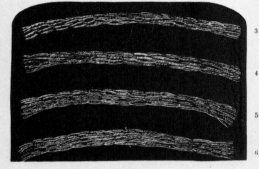

3

4

5

6

Rope, for 30-hour Case Clocks.

No. 691.	Sizes	3	4	5	6
Per Ball = 72 yards	... ...	6/9	7/6	9/-	10/3.
Per Length = 4 yards—Per doz.		4/6	5/-	6/-	7/-
	Each ...	6d.	6d.	7d.	8d.

No. 687.   Per gross 13/-.   Per doz. 1/3.
Gut, for Weight Regulators,
Best Quality.

Cords, for Square American Weight Clocks.
No. 690.   30-hour.   Per gross 5/-.   Per dozen 6d.
No. 690A. 8-day.   „   8/-.   „   10d.

Metallic Clock Cord (Galvanised) for Spring or Weight Clocks.
No. 692.   In 50 feet Coils—Per doz. Coils 27/-.   Per Coil 2/6.
No. 692A.   In 5 ft. Coils
for Spring Clocks—   „   „   3/-.   „   4d.
No. 692B.   In 7 yard Coils
for Grandfather Clocks—   „   „   11/6.   „   1/3.

Bronze Clock Cord.

No. 6386.   In 100 feet Coils—Per doz. Coils 98/-.   Per Coil 8/6.
No. 6387.   In 5 feet Coils for
8-day Spring Clocks—Per gross 65/-.   Per doz. 5/9.   Each 8d.

Quarter gross at gross rate ; quarter dozen at dozen rate.

LATHE GUT.

All Sizes.   ::   *To Order.*

Turret Clock Metallic Ropes.

To Order.

Prices on Application, on receipt of Size
and Length required.

517

MAINSPRINGS.

No. 759. Per gross 70/- Per dozen 6/- Each 8d.
For **American** 8-day Clocks.
Heights 5/8-in., 1 1/8-in. and 3/4-in. Diameter 1 7/8-in.

No. 2002. Per dozen 7/- Each 8d.
For **German** 14-day Clocks, to Hook in Barrel.
Height 11 m/m. Diameter 30 m/m.
Heights 16 to 22 and 25 m/m.
Diam. 45 m/m.

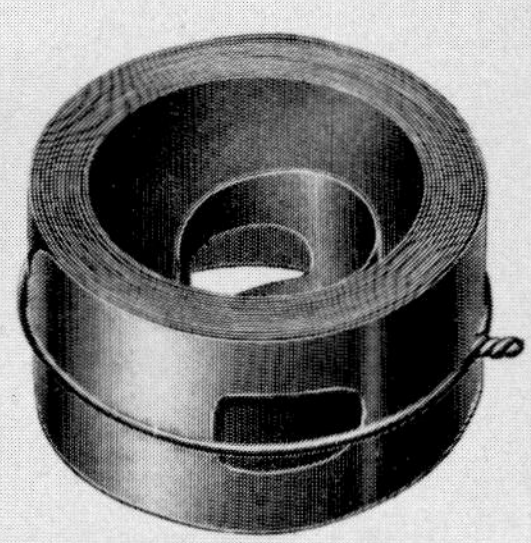

No. 758. Per dozen 11/- Each 1/-
For **English** Timepieces.
Stock Sizes.

Height.		Diameter.	Height.		Diameter.
1 5/16	×	2-in.	1 5/8	×	2-in.
1 1/2	×	2-in.	1 3/4	×	2-in.
1 3/8	×	2-in.	1 5/8	×	2 1/4-in.
1 1/4	×	2-in.			

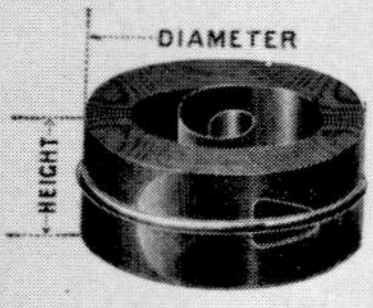

No. 1034. For **FRENCH CLOCKS.**

	Diameters 18 to 30.		32 to 36.		38 to 44 m/m.	
Heights	Per doz.	Each.	Per doz.	Each.	Per doz.	Each.
9 to 11 m/m	3/4	6d.	—	—	—	—
12 to 14 m/m	3/10	6d.	4/8	6d.	—	—
15 to 17 m/m	4/6	6d.	5/8	8d.	8/2	10d.
18 to 19 m/m	5/-	8d.	6/6	8d.	9/6	1/-
20 to 22 m/m	5/8	8d.	7/4	9d.	10/6	1/-
23 to 24 m/m	6/4	8d.	8/1	10d.	11/8	1/2

No. 754. Per dozen 10/8. Each 1/-
For **Ansonia** 8-day Ship's Lever Clocks.
Height 9/16-in. Diameter 1 7/8-in.

No. 761. Per gross 17/- Per dozen 1/6.
For **American** and **German** 30-hour Clocks. Heights 1/4-in., 5/16-in. and 3/8-in.

No. 6379. Per gross 17/- Per dozen 1/6.
For **Startler** and **Early-Riser** Alarms, going side. Height 9/32-in. Diameter 1 1/2-in.

No. 764. Per gross 22/- Per dozen 2/- Each 3d. For **Bee** Clocks. Height 1/4-in. Diameter 1 3/4-in.

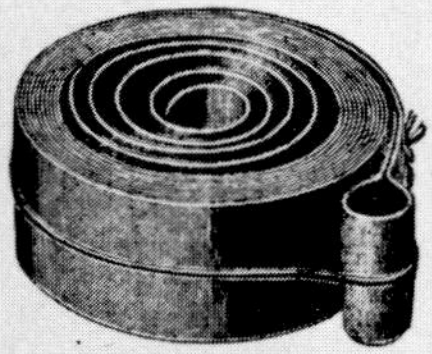

No. 757. Per dozen 10/2. Each 1/-
For **Ansonia Regulators.**
Height 3/4-in. Diameter 1 3/4-in.

No. 756. Per dozen 10/2. Each 1/-
For **Ansonia Marble** Clocks.
Height 5/8-in. Diameter 1 3/8-in.

No. 6380. Per gross 12/- Per doz. 1/3. For **2-in. Drum** Clocks, 30-hour, going side. Heights 5/16-in., 1/4-in., 3/16-in. and 3/8-in.

No. 6378. Per gross 18/4. Per doz. 1/9. For **H.A.C. Romeo** Clocks. Height 7 m/m. Diameter 22 m/m.

No. 4264. Per gross 21/- Per doz. 2/- Each 3d. For **Junghan's Pet** Clocks, to fit in Barrel. Height 9 m/m. Diameter 20 m/m.

No. 765. Per gross 12/- Per dozen 1/3. For **Alarms.** Heights 5/16-in., 1/4-in. and 3/16-in.

Quarter gross at gross rate ; quarter dozen at dozen rate.

MAINSPRINGS—Continued.

No. 6436. Per dozen 4/4. Each 6d.
Ansonia **Midge.**
Height ½-in. Diameter ⅔-in.

No. 6433. Per dozen 8/-. Each 9d.
Junghan's. 14-day.
Height 1¼-in. Diameter 1⁷⁄₁₀-in.

No. 6434. Per dozen 6/6. Each 8d.
U.S.C. 400-day.
Height ⅞-in. Diameter 1⁹⁄₁₂-in

No. 6435. Per dozen 8/-. Each 10d.
Waterbury **Spasmodic.**
Height ⅞-in. Diameter 1⅞-in.

No. 6440. Per dozen 4/4. Each 6d
Ansonia **Spark.**
Height ½-in. Diameter ¾-in.

No. 6437. Per dozen 4/4. Each 6d.
Ansonia **Peep o' day.**
Height ⅞-in. Diameter 1⅜-in.

No. 6438. Per dozen 4/4. Each 6d.
Ansonia **Pirate,** going side.
Height ⅞-in. Diameter 1¼-in.

No. 6439. Per doz. 3/4. Each 4d.
Ansonia **Pirate,** alarm side.
Height ½-in. Diameter ⅞-in.

No 2051. Per gross 2/- Per doz. 4d
Brass Springs for
Timepiece Minute Cannons.

ASSORTMENT OF MATERIALS
For Repairing Lever Clocks.

No. 6441. Per dozen 16/-. Each 1/6.
Newhaven or Ansonia
Ship's Lever.
Height ⅞-in. Diameter 1½-in.

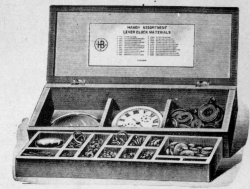

**To Manufacturers using Large
Quantities of Mainsprings:**

We are in a position to quote

**SPECIAL LOW PRICES for
CONTRACT ORDERS.**

No. 5169. Price, Complete 18/- Strong Wooden Box, containing :—

1 dozen Dials	1 dozen Pairs Hands.
1 „ Glasses.	1 „ Seconds Hands.
1 „ Going Mainsprings.	1 „ Alarm Hands.
1 „ Alarm Springs.	1 „ Pellets, complete.
1 „ Set Hand Knobs.	1 „ Feet.
1 „ Winding Keys.	½ „ Pendants.
1 „ Balance Screws.	1 „ Click Springs.
1 „ Balances, complete.	1 „ Hairsprings.
½ „ Bells.	1 „ Knobs for Setting Alarms.

Quarter gross at gross rate ; quarter dozen at dozen rate.

NUTS (BRASS) FOR CLOCK MOVEMENTS, &c.

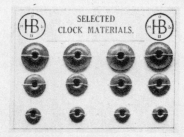

Round, for Pendulums.
No. 6409. **Assortment** of 1 dozen, as illustrated.
Per dozen Cards 5/10. Per Card 8d.
No. 6410. **Large** (not Carded). Per gross 7/2. Per dozen 9d.
No. 6411. **Medium** „ „ 5/8. „ 8d.
No. 6412. **Small** „ „ 4/10. „ 6d.

Round, for French Clock Pendulums and Bells.
No. 6417. **Assortment** of 1 dozen, as illustrated.
Per dozen Cards 7/4. Per Card 10d.
No. 6418. **Large** (not Carded). Per gross 9/- Per dozen 1/-
No. 6419. **Medium** „ „ 7/2. „ 9d.
No. 6420. **Small** „ „ 5/8. „ 8d.

Hexagon, for Lever Clocks.
No. 6421. **Assortment** of 1 dozen, as illustrated.
Per dozen Cards 1/9. Per Card 3d.
No. 6422. **Large** (not Carded). Per gross 2/2. Per dozen 4d.
No. 6423. **Small** „ „ 1/4. „ 2d.

Square, for Pendulums and Bells.
No. 6413. **Assortment** of 1 dozen, as illustrated.
Per dozen Cards 5/- Per Card 6d.
No. 6414. **Large** (not Carded). Per gross 5/- Per dozen 6d
No. 6415. **Medium** „ „ 5/- „ 6d.
No. 6416. **Small** „ „ 4/6 „ 6d.

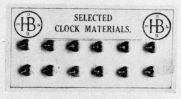

Round, for Fixing Hands of Ansonia Clocks, &c.
No. 6424. **Assortment** of 1 dozen, as illustrated.
Per dozen Cards 8/- Per Card 10d.
No. 6425. (Not Carded). Per gross 8/- Per dozen 10d.

Round, for Fixing Movements in China and other Cases.
No. 6426. **Assortment** of 1 dozen, as illustrated.
Per dozen Cards 4/6. Per Card 6d.
No. 6427. (Not Carded). Per gross 4/6. Per dozen 6d.

Quarter gross at gross rate ; quarter dozen at dozen rate.

ORNAMENTS FOR CLOCK CASES.

WOODEN KNOBS.

COMPOSITION.

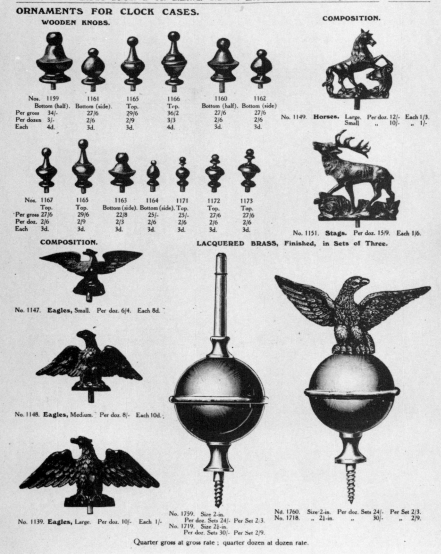

Nos.	1159	1161	1165	1166	1160	1162
	Bottom (half).	Bottom (side).	Top.	Top.	Bottom (half).	Bottom (side)
Per gross	34/-	27/6	29/6	36/2	27/6	27/6
Per dozen	3/-	2/6	2/9	3/3	2/6	2/6
Each	4d.	3d.	3d.	4d.	3d.	3d.

No. 1149. **Horses.** Large. Per doz. 12/- Each 1/3.
Small ,, 10/- ,, 1/-

Nos.	1167	1165	1163	1164	1171	1172	1173
	Top.	Top.	Bottom (side).	Bottom (side).	Top.	Top.	Top.
Per gross	27/6	29/6	22/8	25/-	25/-	27/6	27/6
Per doz.	2/6	2/9	2/3	2/6	2/6	2/6	2/6
Each	3d.	3d.	3d.	3d.	3d.	3d.	3d.

No. 1151. **Stags.** Per doz. 15/9. Each 1/6.

COMPOSITION.

LACQUERED BRASS, Finished, in Sets of Three.

No. 1147. **Eagles,** Small. Per doz. 6/4. Each 8d.

No. 1148. **Eagles,** Medium. Per doz. 8/- Each 10d.

No. 1139. **Eagles,** Large. Per doz. 10/- Each 1/-

No. 1759. Size 2-in.
Per doz. Sets 24/- Per Set 2/3.
No. 1719. Size 2½-in.
Per doz. Sets 30/- Per Set 2/9.

No. 1760. Size 2-in. Per doz. Sets 24/- Per Set 2/3.
No. 1718. ,, 2½-in. ,, 30/- ,, 2/9.

Quarter gross at gross rate ; quarter dozen at dozen rate.

ORNAMENTS FOR CLOCKS (Continued), &c.

30-hour.

8-day.

No. 719. **Pendulum Bob Wires.** Per gross 4/6. Per doz. 6d.

No. 2019. **Pegs,** for Anglo or English Cases. Per gross 5/6. Per doz. 7d.

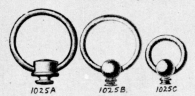

1025A.   1025B.   1025C.

No. 1025. **Pendants,** or Tops, for Lever Clocks.
Per gross 16/-. Per dozen 1/6. Each ½d.

No. 736. **Pinion Wire,** in 13-in. lengths.

Letter & Number Gauge Sizes.		Number of Leaves or Teeth.	In 13-in. Lengths, either Steel or Brass.	
			Per doz.	Each.
A to D			9/-	10d.
E „ M			12/-	1/2
N „ P		6, 7, 8, 10, or 12	18/-	1/9
Q „ T			24/-	2/3
U „ W			30/-	2/9
X „ Z			36/-	3/3
1 „ 11		6, 7, 8, 10, or 12	7/-	8d.
12 „ 30		6, 7, or 8	6/-	7d.
31 „ 59		6, 7, or 8	4/6	5d.
12 „ 60		10 or 12	6/-	7d.

No. 1758. Size 2½-in. Per Set 7/-.
Lacquered Brass, Finished, in Sets of Three.

PINS for Clock Movements.

1 Gross
CLOCK PINS
ASSORTED

No. 732. **Iron,** Assorted **Small.** Per doz. boxes 3/- ; per box 4d.
No. 6552. „ „ **Large.** „ 4/6 ; „ 6d.
No. 739. **Brass,** „ **Small.** „ 6/- ; „ 8d.
No. 6698. „ „ **Large.** „ 12 -; „ 1/2

No. 6517. Per dozen 3/-. Each 4d.
Minute Wheel Pinions, Brass, for 8-day
Grandfather Clocks.

Quarter gross at gross rate ; quarter dozen at dozen rate.

PINIONS.

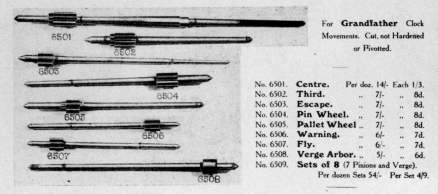

For **Grandfather** Clock Movements. Cut, not Hardened or Pivotted.

No. 6501.	**Centre.**	Per doz. 14/-	Each 1/3.
No. 6502.	**Third.**	,, 7/-	,, 8d.
No. 6503.	**Escape.**	,, 7/-	,, 8d.
No. 6504.	**Pin Wheel.**	,, 7/-	,, 8d.
No. 6505.	**Pallet Wheel**	,, 7/-	,, 8d.
No. 6506.	**Warning.**	,, 6/-	,, 7d.
No. 6507.	**Fly.**	,, 6/-	,, 7d.
No. 6508.	**Verge Arbor.**	,, 5/-	,, 6d.
No. 6509.	**Sets of 8** (7 Pinions and Verge).		
	Per dozen Sets 54/- Per Set 4/9.		

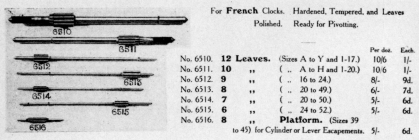

For **French** Clocks. Hardened, Tempered, and Leaves Polished. Ready for Pivotting.

			Per doz.	Each.
No. 6510.	**12 Leaves.**	(Sizes A to Y and 1-17.)	10/6	1/-
No. 6511.	**10** ,,	(,, A to H and 1-20.)	10/6	1/-
No. 6512.	**9** ,,	(,, 16 to 24.)	8/-	9d.
No. 6513.	**8** ,,	(,, 20 to 49.)	6/-	7d.
No. 6514.	**7** ,,	(,, 20 to 50.)	5/-	6d.
No. 6515.	**6** ,,	(,, 24 to 52.)	5/-	6d.
No. 6516.	**8** ,,	**Platform.** (Sizes 39 to 45) for Cylinder or Lever Escapements.	5/-	6d.

For **English Fusee** Clocks. Hardened, Tempered, and Leaves Polished. Ready for Pivotting.

			Per doz.	Each.
No. 6569.	**Centre.**	8 Leaves.	24/-	2/2
No. 6570.	**Third.**	7 ,,	12/-	1/1
No. 6571.	**Escape.**	7 ,,	12/-	1/1
No. 6572.	**Minute Pinion.**	6 ,,	9/-	10d.
No. 6573.	**Complete Sets** of 4 Pinions.			
	Per dozen Sets 54/- Per Set 5/-			

Quarter dozen at dozen rate.

L 2

PALLETS, PALLET CRUTCHES AND PULLEYS.

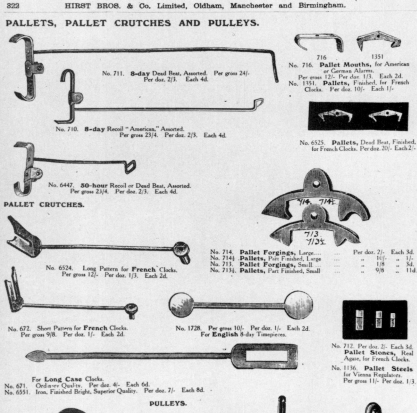

No. 711. **8-day** Dead Beat, Assorted. Per gross 24/-
Per doz. 2/3.   Each 4d.

No. 710. **8-day** Recoil "American." Assorted.
Per gross 23/4.   Per doz. 2/3.   Each 4d.

No. 6447. **30-hour** Recoil or Dead Beat, Assorted.
Per gross 23/4.   Per doz. 2/3.   Each 4d.

716   1351
No. 716. **Pallet Mouths,** for American
or German Alarms.
Per gross 12/- Per doz. 1/3.   Each 2d.
No. 1351. **Pallets,** Finished, for French
Clocks. Per doz. 10/-   Each 1/-

No. 6525. **Pallets,** Dead Beat, Finished,
for French Clocks. Per doz. 20/- Each 2/-

PALLET CRUTCHES.

No. 6524. Long Pattern for **French** Clocks.
Per gross 12/- Per doz. 1/3.   Each 2d.

No. 672. Short Pattern for **French** Clocks.
Per gross 9/8. Per doz. 1/-   Each 2d.

No. 1728. Per gross 10/-   Per doz. 1/-   Each 2d.
For **English** 8-day Timepieces.

No. 714. **Pallet Forgings,** Large....   ...   Per doz. 2/-   Each 3d.
No. 714½ **Pallets,** Part Finished, Large   ...   „ 10/-   „ 1/-
No. 713. **Pallet Forgings,** Small   ...   „ 1/8   „ 3d.
No. 713½ **Pallets,** Part Finished, Small   ...   „ 9/8   „ 11d.

For **Long Case** Clocks.
No. 671.   Ordinary Quality. Per doz. 4/-   Each 6d.
No. 6551. Iron, Finished Bright, Superior Quality. Per doz. 7/-   Each 8d.

No. 712. Per doz. 2/- Each 3d.
Pallet Stones, Real
Agate, for French Clocks.

No. 1136. **Pallet Steels**
for Vienna Regulators.
Per gross 11/- Per doz. 1/3.

PULLEYS.

No. 1640. Per doz. 12/-   Each 1/3. **Pallet
Forgings,** Dead Beat, for English Regulators.

No. 1112. Per doz. 3/-
Each 4d.
For **Weight Regulators.**

No. 738. For **30-hour, Rope.**
Per doz. 9/-   Each 10d.
No. 6448. For **30-hour, Chain.**
Per doz. 9/-   Each 10d.

No. 737. For **8-day** Grandfather,
Gut. Per doz. 6/6. Each 8d.

Quarter gross at gross rate ; quarter dozen at dozen rate.

524

PENDULUMS, &c.

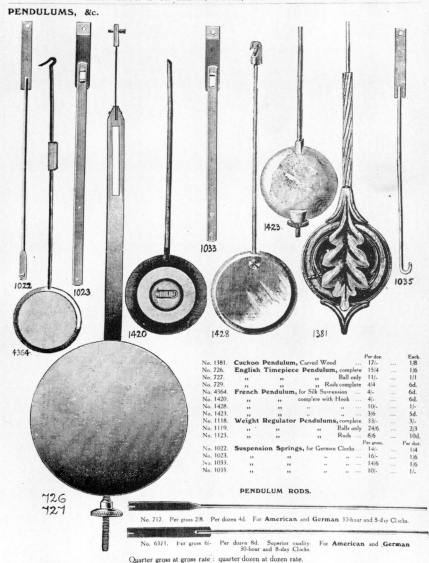

1022
1023
4364
726
727
1420
1428
1033
1423
1381
1035

			Per doz.		Each.
No. 1381.	**Cuckoo Pendulum,** Carved Wood	...	17/-	...	1/8
No. 726.	**English Timepiece Pendulum,** complete		15/4	...	1/6
No. 727.	,, ,, ,, Ball only		11/-	...	1/1
No. 729.	,, ,, ,, Rods complete		4/4	...	6d.
No. 4364.	**French Pendulum,** for Silk Suspension	...	4/-	...	6d.
No. 1420.	,, ,, complete with Hook	...	4/-	...	6d.
No. 1428.	,, ,, ,, ,,	...	10/-	...	1/-
No. 1423.	,, ,, ,, ,,	...	3/6	...	5d.
No. 1118.	**Weight Regulator Pendulums,** complete		33/-	...	3/-
No. 1119.	,, ,, ,, Balls only		24/6	...	2/3
No. 1123.	,, ,, ,, Rods ...		8/6	...	10d.
			Per gross.		Per doz.
No. 1022.	**Suspension Springs,** for German Clocks	...	14/-	...	1/4
No. 1023.	,, ,, ,, ,,		16/-	...	1/6
No. 1033.	,, ,, ,, ,,		14/6	...	1/6
No. 1035.	,, ,, ,, ,,		10/-	...	1/-

PENDULUM RODS.

No. 717. Per gross 2/8. Per dozen 4d. For **American** and **German** 30-hour and 8-day Clocks.

No. 6371. Per gross 6/-. Per dozen 8d. Superior quality. For **American** and **German** 30-hour and 8-day Clocks.

Quarter gross at gross rate : quarter dozen at dozen rate.

525

PENDULUMS, &c. —Continued.

No. 6442. Per doz. 10/- Each 1/- Complete, for
Dutch Clocks or **Postman's Alarms.**

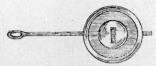

No. 1183. Per doz. 12/- Each 1/3. Complete, for
Ansonia Marble or Mantel Clocks.

No. 6443. Complete, for **Ansonia Regulators.**
Each 2/8.

No. 6444. **Wooden Rods** only for Ditto.
Per doz. 6/- Each 8d.

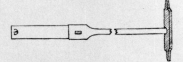

No. 1185. Per doz. 4/- Each 6d. **Pendulum Rods,**
for Ansonia Regulators, with Suspension.

No. 6445. Per gross 16/6. Per doz. 1/6. Each 2d.
Pendulum Tops, for U.S.C. Regulator Clocks.

Pendulum Bobs and Irons, for
Grandfather **Case** Clocks.
8-day or 30-hour.

No. 728. **Bobs** only. Per doz. 13/-
Each 1/3.

No. 6454. **Irons** only, with Nuts, Split or
Tapped. Per doz. 5/- Each 6d.

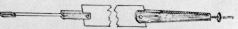

Pendulum Rods, for Grandfather **Case** Clocks,
with Flat or Round Rods.

No. 6455.	**Complete.**		Per doz. 14/- Each 1/3
No. 6454.	**Bob Irons** only.	-	,, 5/- ,, 6d.
No. 750.	**Suspensions** only, for Flat Rod.	,, 2/- ,, 3d.
No. 750½.	,, ,, ,, Round ,,	,, 2/- ,, 3d.
No. 749.	,, Single Ended. ,,	,, 1/3 ,, 2d.

No. 4368. Per doz. 9/10. Each 1/-
Complete for **Mirror-backed**
American Clocks, 8-day.

No. 720. 8-day. Per doz. 3/- Each 4d.
No. 721. 30-hour. ,, 2/8. ,, 4d.
Brass covered Pendulum Bobs, with Wires Complete.

Quarter gross at gross rate ; quarter dozen at dozen rate.

PENDULUMS (Continued) and SCREWS.

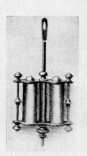

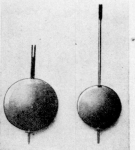

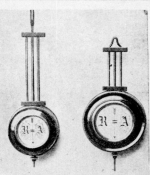

No. 724. Per doz. 15/9.
Each 1/6.
For **30-hour** Wood
Clocks.

No. 979. Per doz. 6/4.
Each 8d.
For **14-day** Mantel Clocks.

No. 978. Per doz. 11/-
Each 1/-
For **8-day** H.A.C.

No. 723. Per doz. 15/-
Each 1/6.
For **14-day** Spring
Regulators.

No. 1048. Per doz. 8/3.
Each 10d.
For **30-hour** Wood
Clocks.

SCREWS.

Iron.

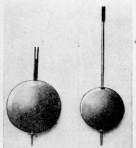

No. 1124. Per doz. 2/1. Each 3d.
Movement Screws,
for Weight Regulators.

Nos.	4276	4275	4274	4273	4272	4271	4270	4269	4268	4267	4266	4265
Diam. of Taps, m/m	5.0	4.5	4.0	3.5	3.0	2.6	2.3	2.0	1.7	1.4	1.2	1.0
Per gross	7/-	6/-	4/3	3/9	3/0	2/3	2/-	1/9	1/6	1/6	1/6	1/3
Per dozen	8d.	7d.	5d.	4d.	4d.	3d.	3d.	3d.	2d.	2d.	2d.	2d.

Special Quotations for Quantities and for Special Patterns, in Iron, Steel, or Brass,
with Metric, Whitworth, or B.A. Threads.

No. 6499. 1 gross Assorted. **Iron.**
Per doz. Boxes 9/- Per Box 10d.
No. 6500. 1 gross Assorted. **Brass.**
Per doz. Boxes 19/- Per Box 1/8.

No. 1126. Per doz. 2/3.
Each 3d.
Steadying Screws,
for Weight Regulators.

No. 743. Per dozen Boxes 27/- Per Box 2/6.
Useful Assortment of 1 gross in Box.

Nos.	6491	6492	6493	6494	6495	6496	6497	6498
Iron. Per gross	9d.	9d.	9d.	9d.	9d.	9d.	9d.	10d.
Brass. ..	1/6	1/6	1/7	1/6	1/7	1/6	1/7	1/10

These Screws are suitable for Clock Door Hinges and for fixing Clock
Movements in cases. The Round-headed Screws in Brass will be
found most useful for fixing Presentation Plates on Clocks, &c.

No. 1125. Per doz. 5/- Each 6d.
Steadying Plates, with Screws complete,
for Regulator Clocks.

Quarter gross at gross rate ; quarter dozen at dozen rate.

SCREWS (Continued), STRAPS, STUDS and WORMS.

No. 2116. Per gross 6/- Per dozen 8d.
Strap Screws, for French Clocks.

No. 6546. Per doz. Boxes 22/- Per Box 2/-
Brass Screws, Assorted, for Small Bee Clock Cases, &c. 6 doz. in each Box.

No. 1451. Per doz. Boxes 13/6. Per Box 1/3.
Screws for Lever Clock **Balance Pivots,** Assorted Sizes.
3 doz. in each Box.

No. 4292. Per gross 15/-
Per doz. 1/6.

Visible Escapement Screws, for French Clocks. Hardened and Finished.

742   2703   744

No. 742. **Screws** for French Clock **Minute Wheels.**
Per gross 3/- Per dozen 4d.
No. 2703. **Screws** for **English** Clocks.
Per gross 2/6. Per dozen 4d.
No. 744. **Click Screws,** Shouldered, Assorted.
Per gross 2/6. Per dozen 4d.

No. 745. Per gross 2/- Per dozen 3d.

Screws for Fixing **Platforms** of French **Clock Escapements.**

No. 6549. Per Assortment 9/6.
Useful Assortment of Screws, containing 3 gross, with Cheese Heads, for English, French, or German Clocks, or for Mechanics. Metric Threads.
For Refills see Nos. 4265 to 4276 on previous page.

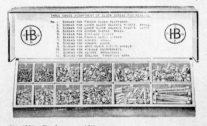

No. 6550. Per Assortment 12/6.
General Assortment, containing 3 gross of various Screws, as illustrated. Very practical for General Jobbing.

No. 1565. **Worms or Endless Screws** for Musical Boxes.

Sizes	13	17	35	40	45	55	70 m/m
Per dozen	2/8	2/8	4/8	5/-	5/6	6/6	7/-
Each	4d.	4d.	6d.	7d.	8d.	8d.	9d.

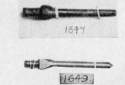

[Studs for Case Clock Movement Minute Wheels.
No. 1647. Forgings only. Per dozen 1/3. Each 2d.
No. 1649. Finished.   „ 2/- „ 3d.

No. 6547. **Straps,** with Screws, for French Clock Movements. Per dozen Pairs 2/10. Per Pair 4d.
Quarter gross at gross rate ; quarter dozen at dozen rate.

SUSPENSIONS (Various).

| 5 | 6 | 7 | 8 | 9 | 10 | 11 | 12 | 13 | 14 | 15 | 16 | 17 | 18 |

No. 3203. **Suspension Springs,** for English, French and German Clocks.

Patterns	5-6	7-9	10	11	12	13-14	15	16	17	18	19	20
Per gross	7/3	7/-	8/6	9/9	13/3	12/6	11/9	9/9	8/9	12/9	7/-	16/6
Per dozen	10d.	10d.	11d.	1/-	1/3	1/3	1/3	1/-	11d.	1/3	10d.	1/6

20

9

No. 6388. Per doz. 7/6. Each 9d.
Suspension Springs,
For Heavy Pendulums, Time
Recorders, &c.

No. 6389. **Complete,** as Illustrated. Per dozen 9/3. Each 1/-
No. 6428. **Wire** only. Per gross 10/8. „ 1/- „ 2d.
For **400-day** Clocks, U.S.C. Make (Other Makes also Supplied).

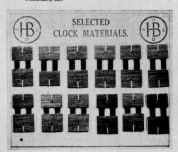

SELECTED CLOCK MATERIALS.

No. 6390. Per dozen Cards 7/3. Per Card 10d.
Regulator Suspensions, Assorted.

No. 755. **Suspension Steel,** in 1-oz. Ribbons.

Width ½-in.	Strengths 10/100 and 15/100 m/m.
	Per dozen 12/6 ... 11/3
	Each 1/3 ... 1/2

Special Prices for Quantities.
Other Sizes and Thicknesses to Order.

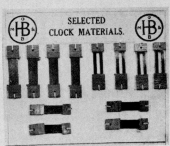

SELECTED CLOCK MATERIALS.

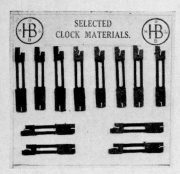

SELECTED CLOCK MATERIALS.

No. 6392. Per dozen Cards 12/9. Per Card 1/3.
French Brocot Suspensions, Assorted.

No. 6391. Per dozen Cards 10/- Per Card 1/-
French Suget Suspensions, Assorted.

Quarter gross at gross rate ; quarter dozen at dozen rate.

SUSPENSIONS—Continued.

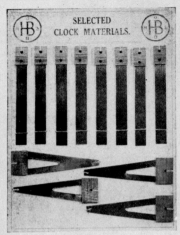

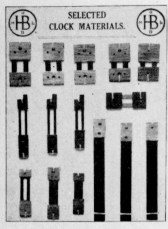

No. 6449. Per dozen Cards 10/3. Per Card 1/-
For **English Dial** Clocks, Assorted.

No. 6450. Per dozen Cards 11/3. Per Card 1/2.
Assorted Patterns.

749.

750

750½.

For **Grand ather Long Case C** cks.
No. 749. With Brass at one en i. Per gross 11/6. Per dozen 1/3. Each 2d.
No. 750. Split, for Flat Rod. Per d zen 2/- Each 3d.
No. 750½. Tapped, for Round Rod. „ 2/- „ 3d.

No. 1380. Per lb. 6d.
Iron, for **Cuckoo**
Clocks.

WEIGHTS.

No. 4791. Per dozen 6/- Each 8d.
Counterweights, for 30-hour
Case Clocks.

No. 1110. Per doz. 32/- Each 2/9.
Brass Lacquered, for **Weight
Regulators.**

No. 4366. Per Pair 4/.
Cast-iron, for **Grandfather
Long Case** Clocks.

Quarter gross at gross rate ; quarter dozen at dozen rate.

530

WHEELS and PINIONS, Finished, for 8-day Timepieces.

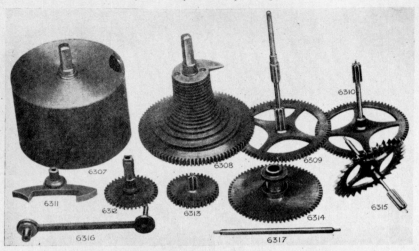

		Per doz.	Each.				Per doz.	Each.
No. 6307.	**Barrels,** with Arbors	28/10	2/6	No. 6313.	**Minute Wheels** and Pinions		4/6	6d.
No. 6308.	**Fusees,** Complete	89/-	7/9	No. 6314.	**Hour Wheels**		6/-	8d.
No. 6309.	**Centre Wheels** and Pinions	12/-	1/3	No. 6315.	**Escape Wheels** and Pinions		12/-	1/3
No. 6310.	**Intermediate Wheels** & Pinions	10/10	1/-	No. 6316.	**Crutches**		8/-	10d.
No. 6311.	**Pallets**	20/-	1/10	No. 6317.	**Pallet Arbors**		8/-	10d.
No. 6312.	**Minute Cannons**	4/-	6d.					

Only Stock Sizes and Counts supplied at above prices.

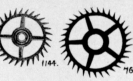

4514.
4515.

		Per doz.	Each.
No. 4285.	**Escape Wheels** for French Clocks	8/-	10d.
No. 1144.	" " " Regulators	5/3	6d.
No. 769.	" " " American and German Clocks, Nos. of Teeth 32, 35, 36, 40, 42, 45	3/6	4d.
No. 768.	**Pallet Alarm** Wheels	3/6	4d.
No. 4514.	**Escape Wheels** for Timepieces	5/-	6d.
No. 4515.	" " " Case Clocks	5/-	6d.

No. 1566. Per dozen 5/-; Each 6d. For **Dot** Clocks.

No. 1567. Per dozen 5/-; Each 6d. For **Gnat** Clocks.

No. 1568. Per dozen 3/8; Each 6d. For **Bee** Clocks.

No. 2047. **Brass Wheel Blanks.** Price on Application, stating Size, Thickness and Quantity.

Quarter dozen at dozen rate.

WHEELS, &c.—Continued.

No. 6519.   Per doz. 6/- ;
Each 7d.
Main Wheels for
Ansonia Bee Clocks.

No. 6521.   Per doz. 5/10 ; Each 7d.
Centre Wheels for Ansonia
Bee Clocks.

No. 6520.   Per doz. 7/- ; Each 8d.
Escape Wheels and Pinions
complete, for U.S.C. Weight
Regulators.

No. 5126.   Per Set 6/-
Sprocket Chain Wheels for 30-Hour
Grandfather Clocks. Set includes 2, or 1
pair Sprockets, with Click and Chain complete.

WINDERS FOR LEVER CLOCKS.

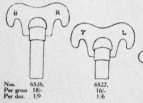

Nos. 6526/7.   Right or Left, and sizes 7, 8 & 9
Nos. 6528/9.   „   „   „   „   „   5 & 6
No. 1200.   For Pirate Alarms.

Nos.	6526.	6527.	6528.	6529.	1200.
Per gross	18/-	16/-	12/-	12/-	20/-
Per doz.	1/9	1/6	1/3	1/3	1/9

No. 1222.   Per dozen pairs 6/- ; per pair 7d.
Wings, Polished Hardwood, for Anglo Cases,
Light or Dark.

VARIOUS MATERIAL.

No. 1192.   **Balances,** Complete
Per dozen 3/8 ; Each 5d.
No. 1188.   **Balance Staffs**
Per gross 9/9 ; per doz. 1/-
No. 1194.   **Click Springs**
Per gross 8/- ; per doz. 9d.
No. 1195.   **Click Springs**
Per gross 8/- ; per doz. 9d.
No. 1196.   **Click Springs** for Main
Wheels.   Per gross 3/3 ; per doz. 6d.
No. 1189.   **Escape Wheels and
Pinions.**   Per doz. 2/- ; Each 3d.
No. 1186.   **Handsetters**
Per doz. 2/- ; Each 3d.
No. 1187.   **Handsetters**
Per doz. 1/6 ; Each 2d.
No. 1215.   **Pallets**
Per doz. 2/4 ; Each 3d.
No. 1200.   **Winders**
Per doz. 1/9 ; Each 2d.
No. 1190.   **Winding Wheels**
Per doz. 2/- ; Each 3d.
No. 1191.   **Winding Wheels**
Per doz. 1/6 ; Each 2d.

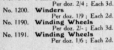

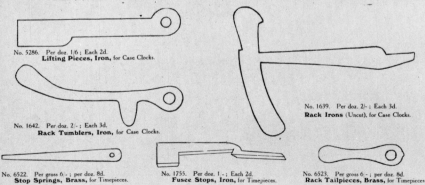

No. 5286.   Per doz. 1/6 ; Each 2d.
Lifting Pieces, Iron, for Case Clocks.

No. 1639.   Per doz. 2/- ; Each 3d.
Rack Irons (Uncut), for Case Clocks.

No. 1642.   Per doz. 2/- ; Each 3d.
Rack Tumblers, Iron, for Case Clocks.

No. 6522.   Per gross 6/- ; per doz. 8d.
Stop Springs, Brass, for Timepieces.

No. 1755.   Per doz. 1/- ; Each 2d.
Fusee Stops, Iron, for Timepieces.

No. 6523.   Per gross 6/- ; per doz. 8d.
Rack Tailpieces, Brass, for Timepieces.

Quarter gross at gross rate ; quarter dozen at dozen rate

Glossary

ARBOR –

axle or shaft upon which a wheel or pinion is mounted.

BALANCE –

oscillating wheel which controls the rate of the clock in conjunction with the escapement.

BARREL –

drum from which the clock receives its power, either by a spring coiled within the drum, or from a weight pulling gut or chain wound round the barrel externally.

BEAT –

'tick' of the clock.

BEZEL –

metal rim holding the glass covering the dial (or in some instances the glass door to the movement) in place.

BOB –

weight fixed to the bottom of the pendulum.

BREVET –

Patent (French).

CHAPTER RING –

ring on the dial marked with the hours and minutes.

COMPENSATED –

designed to reduce errors, i.e. temperature changes cause expansion and contraction of the pendulum rod and, unless this is compensated for, errors will occur in the timekeeping properties of the timepiece. See Gridiron and Mercurial Pendulums.

COMPLICATED WORK –

this usually refers to mechanisms not normally found in ordinary timepieces, e.g. repeating work, astronomical work, etc.

COUNT WHEEL –

early method of regulating striking mechanism, by means of a wheel with the appropriate number of notches cut around its perimeter.

CROSSINGS –

the arms or spokes of a wheel, the quality of the finish often determines the value of the clock.

CROSSING OUT –
   the making of the crossings by cutting them from the solid wheel
   and then, with the aid of files, shaping them.
CRUTCH –
   part connecting the pendulum to the movement.
D.R.G.M. –
   Deutsches Reichs-Gebrauchsmuster. This indicates that the article or
   clock is covered by a German Patent taken out pre-1918.
ESCAPEMENT –
   the part of the movement that 'measures' and controls the rate of
   power, among which may be numbered:–
   anchor, cylinder, coup perdu, dead beat, lever, Paul Garnier,
   platform, recoil, tic-tac, verge escapements.
FUSEE –
   method of obtaining an even pull from the mainspring by means of a
   spirally grooved, tapering barrel.
GONGS –
   these fall into two main categories:
   The type composed of a length of round, square or rectangular (in
      cross section) wire that is coiled into a volute.
   A series of straight lengths of round wire mounted in a block.
GRIDIRON PENDULUM –
   a type of compensated pendulum, with alternate steel and brass (or
   zinc) rods. This combination of alloys ensures that the effective
   length of the pendulum remains constant.
HELICAL SPRING –
   an upright spring with its coils one above the·other.
IMPULSE –
   the small amount of power applied to the pendulum or balance to
   maintain its swing.
INVAR –
   alloy of nickel and steel and named from the first five letters of
   'INVARiable', as its rate of expansion at varying temperatures is
   minimal.
LONGCASE CLOCK –
   usually floor standing and over six feet tall. Shorter examples are
   often coyly referred to as 'Grandmother' and 'Granddaughter'.
MAINSPRING –
   coiled spring for driving the clock.

534

MASTER CLOCK —
the main or central clock in an electrically-powered, multi-clock installation that controls slave dials, etc.

MERCURIAL PENDULUM —
a type of compensated pendulum, with jars of mercury as the means of ensuring that the effective length of the pendulum remains constant. Many of these are 'mock' mercury pendulums which are not manufactured to any scientific formula.

MODELE DEPOSE —
registered design of, in this instance, the case of the clock (French).

MOTION WORK —
the train of wheels and pinions between the minute and hour hands.

PALLET —
the part of an escapement that releases or locks the escape wheel.

PILLARS —
the distance pieces that hold the front and backplates of the movement together.

PERPETUAL CALENDAR —
a self-correcting calendar that automatically adjusts for long and short months and, usually, leap years.

PINION —
small, toothed gear (usually the driven wheel), which is commonly:

Lantern — a cylindrical pinion made up of small metal rods fitting into a solid circular endpiece. Usually found on cheaper mass produced clocks.

Solid — a cylindrical pinion with the leaves or teeth being cut or drawn from the solid.

RACK STRIKING —
the now universal method of counting the strike on a clock. Invented by Barlow in 1676, it utilises a toothed arm (the rack) which is allowed to fall only the requisite number of teeth by a snail on the same arbor as the hour hand. A small cam lifts the rack one tooth at a time as the striking proceeds.

S.G.D.G. —
Sans garantie du gouvernement. Indicates that the item is covered by a French Patent (usually accompanies the word 'Breveté').

SKELETON DIAL —
elaborately-pierced dial showing the movement behind.

SLAVE DIAL CLOCK —
a secondary clock operated by a master clock. These receive electro-mechanical impulses — normally at half-minute intervals. Pneumatically operated clocks have also been produced.

SUSPENSION —
the mounting of the pendulum. This is usually a flexible spring or silk cord, but may rarely be pivoted or knife edge.

TRAIN —
Series of engaging gears.

One train movement — Timekeeping only.

Two train movement — Timekeeping and striking on the hour and possibly on the half and quarter hours.

Three train — similar properties of a two train movement but with the additional train for chiming or musical complications.

TUBULAR CHIME —
chiming in a longcase clock on tuned lengths of tube.

Bibliography

In compiling the following list of suggested reading material for those who wish to extend their knowledge of horology with special reference to this period (1840-1940), consideration has been given to their availability. Where it is known that there has been a reprint the date of this has been given in preference to the earlier scarce edition. No specific edition has been given when this has been considered immaterial either through rarity or lack of significant variation of contents. As there are actually some four thousand titles on the subject in general, besides catalogue material and various references in periodicals, it is more than likely that someone's favourite source of information has been omitted. Many classical works on horology have been omitted as their content more closely reflects a study of an earlier period, and no doubt as interest grows most readers will seek this for themselves. Those who are sufficiently fortunate to live within reach of either the library of the Worshipful Company of Clockmakers or the library of the Antiquarian Horological Society (both housed and freely accessible in the Guildhall Library, Aldermanbury, London, E.C.2.) will have no difficulty in finding research material. It is frequently possible to borrow through the National Library Service, without too much delay, copies of books normally unavailable from the shelves of the local public library. Alternatively most specialist horological booksellers willingly keep a list of their customers' requirements, notifying them upon the book becoming available.

Allix, C. and Bonnert, P.,
Carriage Clocks, Their History and Development, 1974.
Bailey, C.,
Two Hundred Years of American Clocks and Watches, 1975.
Baillie, G.H.,
Watch and Clockmakers of the World, Volume I, 1974, latest edition, see Loomes.
Bain, A.,
Alexander Bain's Short History of the Electric Clock, 1852, edited by Hackmann and reprinted 1973.
Barraud, E.M.,
Barraud. The Story of a Family, 1968.
Beeson, Dr. C.F.C.,
Early Oxford Clockmakers, 1954.

Bellchambers, J.K.,
   Somerset Clockmakers, 1968; *Devonshire Clockmakers,* 1962.
Belmont, H.L.,
   La Bulle-Clock Horlogerie Electrique, 1975.
Britten, F.J.,
   The Watch and Clockmakers' Handbook, Dictionary and Guide.
   There have been no less than fifteen editions of this famous work.
   Possibly the best advice is to obtain a copy of the latest edition
   due out this year — the sixteenth — and also a copy of the 1976
   reprint of the 11th edition (1907). As the contents vary slightly
   many serious collectors attempt to own as many editions as
   possible.
Britten, F.W.,
   Horological Hints and Helps, 1977 reprint of the earlier edition.
Bruton, E.,
   Antique Clocks and Clock Collecting, 1974; *The Longcase Clock,*
   second edition, 1977.
Clutton, C., Baillie, G.H., Ilbert, C.A.,
   Britten's Old Clocks and Watches and Their Makers, 8th edition,
   1973. The earlier editions by F.J. Britten are of interest but
   frequently realise a high price through their antiquarian interest;
   however, a revised form of the third edition is now available.
Daniell, F.M.A.,
   Leicestershire Clockmakers, revised edition, 1975.
De Carle, D.,
   Teach Yourself Horology, 1965; *Practical Clock Repairing,* 1975
   reprint; *Clocks and Their Values,* 1975; *Watch and Clock
   Encyclopaedia,* 1976 reprint; *British Time,* 1947.
Dinsdale, N.V.,
   The Old Clockmakers of Yorkshire, 1946.
Distin, W.H., Bishop, R.,
   The American Clock, 1976.
Edey, W.,
   French Clocks, 1967.
Garrard, F.J.,
   Clock Repairing and Making, any edition.
Gazeley, W.J.,
   Clock and Watch Escapements, 1956; *Watch and Clock Making
   and Repairing,* 1975 reprint.
Goodrich, W.L.,
   The Modern Clock, any edition.
Gordon, G.F.C.,
   Clockmaking Past and Present, any edition.
Gunn, R.,
   Alexander Bain of Watten, 1976.
Haggar, A., Miller, L.F.,
   Suffolk Clocks and Clockmakers, 1974.

538

Hasluck, P.N.,
The Clock Jobber's Handbook, any edition.
Hawkins, J.B.,
Thomas Cole and Victorian Clockmaking, 1975.
Hope-Jones, F.,
Electrical Timekeeping, 1976 reprint; *Electric Clocks; Electric Clocks and Chimes,* 1976 reprint; *Electric Clocks and How to Make Them,* 1977 reprint.
Jagger, C.,
Paul Philip Barraud, 1968.
Langman, H.R., Ball, A.,
Electrical Horology, any edition.
Legg, E.,
The Clock and Watchmakers of Buckinghamshire, 1976.
Loomes, B.,
Westmorland Clocks and Clockmakers, 1974; *Country Clocks and Their London Origins,* 1976; *Yorkshire Clockmakers,* 1972; *The White Dial Clock,* 1974; *Lancashire Clocks and Clockmakers,* 1975; *Watchmakers and Clockmakers of the World, Volume II,* 1976.
Maitzner, F., Moreau, J.,
La Comtoise, La Morbier, La Morez. Histoire et Technique, 1976.
Miles Brown, H.,
Cornish Clocks and Clockmakers, 1970.
Miller, L., Haggar, A.,
Suffolk Clocks and Clockmakers, 1974.
Moore, N.,
Chester Clocks and Clockmakers, 1976.
Nicholls, A.,
Clocks in Colour, 1975.
Palmer, B.,
The Book of American Clocks, 1967; *A Treasury of American Clocks,* 1967.
Peate, I.C.,
Clock and Watchmakers of Wales, 1975.
Penfold, J.,
Clockmakers of Cumberland, 1977.
Philpot, S.,
Modern Electric Clocks, any edition.
Ponsford, C.N., Scott, J.G.M., Authers, W.P.,
Clocks and Clockmakers of Tiverton, 1977.
Roberts, K.D.,
The Contributions of Joseph Ives to Connecticut Clock Technology, 1810-1862, 1970.
Robinson, T.R.,
Modern Clocks – Their Design and Maintenance, any edition.

Royer-Collar, F.B.,
Skeleton Clocks, revised 1977 edition.
Smith, A.,
Clocks and Watches, any edition.
Smith, E.P.,
Repairing Antique Clocks, 1973; *Clocks, Their Working and Maintenance,* 1977.
Tardy,
La Pendule Française. A standard work in three volumes with the second part *(Du Louis XVI à Nos Jours)* having an English translation available; *Dictionnaire des Horlogers Français,* 1972.
Terwilliger, C.,
The Horolovar 400-day Clock Repair Guide, 1976; *The Horolovar Collection,* 1962.
Tyler, E.J.,
The Craft of the Clockmaker, 1973; *Clocks and Watches,* 1975; *European Clocks,* 1968; *Black Forest Clocks,* 1977.
Vaudry Mercer,
Edward John Dent and his Successors, 1977.
Wilding, J.,
How to make a Skeleton Clock, 1957; *How to make a Congreve Clock,* 1976.
Wise, S.,
Electric Clocks, any edition.

Magazines and Journals

Horological Journal (1858 to date):
Official journal of the   British Horological Institute,
Upton Hall,
Upton, Newark, Notts., NG23 5TE.
or obtainable from the publishers:
Brant Wright Associates Ltd.,
P.O. Box 22,
Ashford, Kent, TN23 1DN.
Watch and Clockmaker (1928 to 1939):
(*Practical Watch and Clockmaker* until August 1930).
Antiquarian Horology (1953 to date):
Journal of the Antiquarian Horological Society,
New House,
High Street,
Ticehurst, Wadhurst, Sussex, TN5 7AL.
Bulletin of the National Association of Watch and Clock Collectors Inc.
(1944 to date):
N.A.W.C.C. Building,
514 Poplar Street,
Columbia, Pa. 17512, USA.

OTHER BOOKS ON HOROLOGY
PUBLISHED BY THE ANTIQUE COLLECTORS' CLUB.

The Club's books on clocks and watches are well printed on high quality paper and the large number of high quality illustrations are particularly helpful. Classic reprints of books by the Brittens and Cescinsky and Webster are extremely popular with collectors.

Carriage Clocks, Their History and Development by *Charles Allix,* illus. by P. Bonnert. A mammoth volume covering the traditions, manufacture and multi-national nature of travelling clocks including hitherto undiscovered information on cases and descriptions of all known types. *484 pages. 500 b. & w. illus. 16 in col. ISBN 0 902028 25 1. £19.50.*

The Camerer Cuss Book of Antique Watches by *T.P. Camerer Cuss.* A completely revised new edition of this well-known standard work of reference. A newly added 250 page section provides an important illustrated chronology of the development of the watch. Most watches are shown over size so that details of decoration and mechanism are readily appreciated. *332 pages. 364 b. & w. illus. 8 in col. ISBN 0 902028 33 2. £17.50.*

Thomas Cole and Victorian Clockmaking by *J.B. Hawkins.* The names on most high grade Victorian clocks are those of the retailer. The quality and ingenuity of the work produced by Thomas Cole was of such a high order that his work was in demand by most of the leading retailers. *256 pages. 90 b. & w. illus. 3 in col. ISBN 0 9598503 0 9. £14.50.*

Watch and Clock Makers' Handbook, Dictionary and Guide by *F.J. Britten.* This is a reprint of the 11th edition, first published in 1907. It is in the form of a dictionary and contains much valuable information that was left out of later editions. *490 pages. Several hundred engravings. ISBN 0 902028 46 4. £12.00.*

The Antique Collectors' Club Edition of **Britten's Old Clocks and Watches and Their Makers – 3rd Edition.** Britten's great work which is arguably the best known clock book ever published. The 3rd Edition appeared in 1911 and has been out of print for many years despite the fact that it is considered to be one of the better revisions. To this great work have been added some 250 photographs, carefully chosen to supplement the text. *Some 520 pages. Approximately 1,000 b. & w. illus. ISBN 0 902028 69 3. £19.50.*

English Domestic Clocks by *Cescinsky & Webster.* The classic introduction has never been bettered by modern writers. *240 pages. Over 400 b. & w. illus. ISBN 0 902028 37 5. £15.00.*

Horological Hints & Helps by *F.W. Britten.* First published in the 1950s by the son of the world famous horological authority. This reprint with one or two necessary corrections will be widely welcomed. *375 pages. 157 line engravings. ISBN 0 902028 64 2. £6.95.*

English Dial Clocks by *Ronald Rose.* The first work to be devoted to this subject which covers cartel and "Act of Parliament" clocks but principally the wide variety of round faced large dial clocks, which were first introduced in the early part of the 18th century and came into wide use from the Industrial Revolution right up to the time when they were replaced by centrally controlled electric clocks. At one time there were some 400 dial clocks in the Bank of England alone. *Some 200 pages. Approximately 200 b. & w. illus., 16 col. pls. ISBN 0 902028 78 2. £15.00.*

FORTHCOMING
The Price Guide to Clocks 1650-1840
The Regency Bracket Clock.

For a fully up-to-date list, please write to:–
The Antique Collectors' Club, 5 Church Street, Woodbridge, Suffolk.